Software: Design, Impleme
and Support

£9-95+

THE COMPUTER STUDIES SERIES

Software: Design, Implementation and Support

David Leigh, David Hatter
and Roy Newton
Series Editor: David Hatter

Paradigm

Paradigm Publishing Limited
Avenue House
131–133 Holland Park Avenue
London W11 4UT

© David Leigh, David Hatter and Roy Newton 1987

First published 1987

British Library Cataloguing in Publication Data

Leigh, David
   Software : design, implementation
   and support.—(The Computer studies
   series).
   1. Computer programs
   I. Title   II. Hatter, David   III. Newton,
   Roy   IV. Series
   005.3   QA76.6

ISBN 0-948825-60-X

Typeset by Mathematical Composition Setters Ltd, Salisbury.
Printed in Great Britain by Hollen Street Press Limited, Slough, Berks.

Contents

Part III Software implementation

viii   Contents

Part V Summary

About the book

One of the aspects of the production of modern software systems is that of the professional approach. This is effectively a guarantee for the users of such systems that the work has been fully carried out in a proper fashion, and is thoroughly dependable. The foundations which need to be laid to attain this goal are described in this book.

Accordingly, the three main features upon which such an approach depends are described herein. They might, in somewhat old-fashioned terms, be regarded as the 'before, during and after' of the writing of programs. But it is more proper to regard them as the indispensable parts of any software production operation in its widest sense.

Part I of this book forms an introduction, allowing this approach to be explored and justified. This is followed in Part II by a discussion of design objectives and examples of design methodology. These are viewed not in their historical context alone, but with a view very much for the future. The holders of advanced qualifications in the field of Computing are naturally expected to be more aware than most of such aspects of the discipline.

The treatment of software implementation as such is dealt with more directly in Part III. The tools of the software engineer's trade are discussed and the importance of team work is particularly addressed. These topics are more and more characteristic of that approach to implementation where many programmers contribute to extensive complete systems. The position of more advanced imbedded systems is also introduced. It is the author's firm belief that knowledge of such systems forms an essential part of all professional practitioners' experience. Part IV deals extensively with the framework within which software maintenance takes place and with the widespread nature of its operation. The various components of a computer operating system, and the way in which they are organized, form that framework. The various forms of software maintenance, and other related matters, contribute to the final part. Part V then contains a summary of the whole.

About the series

This series of books is the first which presents an integrated approach to the complete range of topics needed by students of Computer Studies who are currently on the Higher National Certificate and Diploma courses or the first two years of a degree course.

Each volume has been so designed through its approach and treatment of a particular subject area to stand alone: at the same time the books in the series together give a comprehensive and integrated view of computing with special attention devoted to applications in business and industry.

The authors are experienced teachers and practitioners of computing and are responsible for the design of computing syllabuses and courses for the Business and Technician Education Council, the British Computer Society and the Council for National Academic Awards. In addition many of them are members of the appropriate boards of studies for the three organisations. Their combined experience in computing practice covers all aspects of the subject.

The series presents a uniform and clear treatment of the subject and will fit well into the syllabus of the great majority of undergraduate courses.

Acknowledgements

Thanks are due to the following sources of reference which are, perhaps, not as technically immediate as those given in the Bibliography. Nevertheless, they have proved useful as sources of inspiration, and thus remarkably valuable. Otherwise unattributed quotations have come from these sources, and the authors will be pleased to rack their memories for any enquirers who are frustrated in their search for such references.

The Bible (Authorised Version)
Reverend C. L. Dodgson
John Donne
Benjamin Franklin
Robert A. Heinlein
Douglas R. Hofstadter
Danny Kaye
Lord Kelvin
Tom Lehrer
Mad Magazine
Sir Isaac Newton (no *known* relation)
C. Northcote Parkinson
William Shakespeare
George Bernard Shaw
The United States Navy Department

More particularly, the authors would like to thank all those who have assisted in their efforts, especially in the latter and more time-consuming days of increasing excitement as other projects were placed on the 'back burner'. The assistance of Mike Curtis must not go unremarked. Thanks also from two of us to the Series Editor are essential: what the third member feels on the subject is a matter for conjecture.

Reference to SIMPLE is made with the kind permission of Prime Computers (UK) Ltd. SIMPLE is a trademark of Prime Computers Inc., Nalick,

Massachusetts, USA. The material in Chapter 6 is presented with the kind permission of the publishers of the Price Waterhouse IT review 1986/87.

One author wishes to place on record his continuing indebtedness to 'Little Red Hen' for every one of its operations, without which none of this could have happened.

PART I
Introduction

CHAPTER 1

Programming and software

1.1 Introduction

The steadily increasing involvement of the general-purpose digital computer in the lives of all of us has had an effect undreamed of by those pioneers who were the first computer programmers. The way in which this has come about is even evident from the way in which the English language has changed to reflect this. The word 'computer' identifies itself with the general-purpose nature of its computations, as accepted by nearly all of its users; and those who are as familiar with analogue operations as they are with digital ones form a very, very small group indeed.

The approach to analogue operations, though, is not within the scope of this text, and will not be elaborated upon. Digital operations will therefore be the topic addressed, but the generality of purpose will not be as transcendent as is often assumed. The dividing line between the special-purpose and the general-purpose will be made little of; the rules for each, however, are just the same for the production of efficient and accurate programs, and that will be the goal of the discussions.

It is notable that the term 'program' (with this spelling in England being acceptable from some time after 1960!) is of some antiquity—that is, as far as computing is concerned. The same cannot be said for 'software', as that is a somewhat later construction. But the idea that computing had two components (at least) is traceable into the decade starting 1940; at about the same time as computers really came to be. The distinguishing of those whose task it was to build the electronic circuitry from those whose job it was to invent the orders which it would obey may be difficult to establish. In the earlier times, these tended to be the same people, and it was not unknown for programmers who were having a particularly difficult time to modify the circuitry to fit, rather than going to the bother of correcting their programs.

Latterly, though, it has become reasonably easy to differentiate between those parts of the solution of any problem which can 'easily' be changed, and those which are fixed and immutable. This book will deal with those malleable components, and suggest ways which will make the building of them easier and safer. The goal here is the rapid and efficient production of reliable software components, using the ideas which are associated with engineering skills. The concept of software engineering is one which is becoming of steadily greater importance, and the time will soon be with us when no task of any importance whatsoever will be handled in any way other than as an engineering operation, with all that that entails.

1.2 The contents of this book

The stages through which any piece of software travels are reflected in the text of this book. First, the software must be designed: if this stage is omitted or is poorly carried out, the product will be similarly poor. In the same way that houses are not built on sand (if they are to continue standing for any reasonable length of time), so the foundations of any sensible piece of software, be it a single program or a large suite of them, must also be carefully and firmly laid.

After the design comes the implementation. It has always been of interest to the authors to follow the way in which implementors' habits change with increasing experience. The first impulses are to start writing software with the first line of the program—and the sooner the better! After a little reflection, and often a number of mistakes, the design phase becomes of some importance, and more care is lavished upon it. In some cases, it becomes the most important part. This is not recommended: design without implementation is at least as bad as implementation without design. This aspect

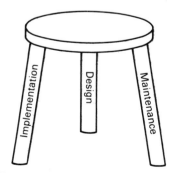

Figure 1.1 The most important leg

has been receiving more attention of late—not in itself, because it has also been present—but in the way in which it is carried out. The methods used and the tools which assist the operation are becoming of more and more concern to skilled implementors as aids to safe results, speedily produced.

Thirdly, that part of the full set of production operations which is far too often forgotten, or ignored, by novices in the business. The work which takes place after the customer has received the goods, or other similar after-sales service, was for a long time neglected as a formal part of the production. It received quite a lot of attention at the time, but the whole was not planned with it in mind. However, it is decidedly important, and any program or suite of programs which are not designed from the beginning with maintenance in mind can cause trouble out of all proportion to their worth.

This arrangement may remind us of the most important leg of the three-legged stool—the one that is missing (Figure 1.1). If any of the stages above is thought to be less important than the other two, the product will suffer accordingly.

Within each part, the chapters cover discrete parts of each topic. Three design methods have been selected for consideration, and are then compared with each other (Part II). Software implementation, in its turn, is given an engineering approach in Part III, and the increasingly important field of embedded software systems is also included in this part. Finally, in Part IV the support offered by systems at runtime is discussed, and the operations of software maintenance close the text.

Feedback operations are felt to be important in any engineering system: without them, there can be no control. Similarly, it is difficult for readers to ascertain whether they are making progress when reading a textbook unless there is some yardstick (or should that be metre-rule?) against which comprehension can be measured. For this reason, included after each chapter are some not-too-difficult discussion questions and topics which relate to the material of that chapter. They are usually well within the scope of the preceding text, although there are cases where wider reading will also prove rewarding. The authors feel that such pastimes are to be encouraged, because it is beyond belief that a single book could cover all of this fast-growing area in such a complete manner as that might otherwise suggest.

1.3 Exercise

1 Consider a piece of software which you have recently produced. How long was spent in its design; in its implementation; in its maintenance (i.e. correction)? Was this a reasonable way of dealing with the provision of this software? What suggestions would you make (to your earlier self) which would improve the efficiency of the operation (if any)?

CHAPTER 2

Validation and testing

2.1 The need for correctness

It seems a little peculiar that this topic should be addressed at any length. After all, what is the use of preparing a program if it is incorrect? Experience shows, however, that there are many programs which have been generally released even when they were not properly correct. Most odd: surely one would not expect (for instance) a house to have been built if it was unfit to live in?

But such things do happen. Houses have been sold when they weren't really fit to be lived in for some reason or another. It is not a desirable state of affairs, as far as the prospective house-owner is concerned. Of course, the same applies to the users of computer programs. The cost is not obviously as great, in general, but the principle surely remains the same.

It should not be assumed that the reason for this is dishonesty. It *may* be so, in some circumstances but, far more often (one hopes!), it is because of an oversight on the part of the supplier. A particular circumstance had arisen which, for some reason, had not been foreseen. Because of this (possibly extremely unlikely) happening, the program has not functioned as it should and an error has occurred. This may be of minor annoyance or it might have severe consequences. In any case, it would be better to avoid the problem. It is much better that any program released to its users should actually work in the way in which it was intended.

It is not always possible for the user of a program to go to its producer to enable it to be corrected, either. Many programs are written for general release, through retailers in several parts of the country, or the world. It is unlikely that a user in (say) Birmingham would travel to (say) Bristol to have a simple program put right. Also, programs are usually distributed in a form ready to run, rather than in a human-readable form. This means that it is seldom possible for a user to correct a program by following, for instance, telephoned instructions. Instead, a new version has to be supplied, perhaps on a magnetic tape or disc.

The economic consequences of such actions are important. The cost in time and money for corrections to be supplied might outweigh the original program cost. This applies both to the supplier and to the consumer. It follows, then, that it is to everyone's advantage for programs to be distributed only when they are correct. This applies no matter what the overall cost: even when the figures involved run into thousands or tens of thousands of pounds or dollars.

Finally, it does not follow necessarily that the lack of correctness might be confined to the program as supplied. Errors in documentation could be equally destructive. These might be in the descriptions of input or output formats and contents, or in the operating instructions. An example of the latter may be found during the television coverage of the general election held in 1958. At one point the computer in question needed to be told to proceed by pressing a particular key. The instructions were unclear, the wrong key was used, and the computer program promptly failed. Somewhat embarrassing at the time—the broadcast was live—but a good illustration of the dangers of imprecision!

2.2 How to achieve correct implementation

Of course, the solution is obvious: merely avoid mistakes; and there should be no need to say any more.

This viewpoint was reasonably widespread among the intelligentsia in the early days of computing. One needed then to have at least a research degree to be allowed near those expensive and advanced machines. It followed, therefore, that because the engineers and implementors were so clever, they would not make mistakes; and every program would work first time—as long, that is, as the machinery did what it was told.

Unfortunately, this did not seem to be the case. Intelligent as these people were (and they *were* clever), errors still had an unfortunate habit of creeping in. It became apparent, in fact, that there were other factors at work than intelligence as such. Despite everyone's best endeavours, it was still essential to check everything at every stage: and *still* mistakes were made. In time, of course, this became accepted as a fact of life. Programs were tested rigorously after they had been written, and the inevitable errors were removed by tedious attention to every detail.

Programming aids were produced to assist the implementors in their quest for accuracy. Methods of displaying the contents of the computer's store after a failure were used. Ways of reporting on the sequence of instructions being obeyed were invented and put into service. Extra routines were added to allow the program-testing staff to check the contents of parts of the store during execution (and to change them, if necessary). However, even with all of this extra assistance, some programs still went wrong.

The reasons were manifold. Even when the original programs were correctly written, errors still occurred during transcription into computer-acceptable form. Even before this, the ways in which programs were planned were overly complicated. This does not mean that they were too complex: the solutions to some problems are inherently complex. The complications in question generally arose when the solutions were approached in poorly structured ways.

The first computer languages in which the instructions were written were generally low-level ones. Such languages insist on more computational details being given to a program, with more scope for error. High-level languages did not appear until the 1950s and were not in widespread use until several years later. This is no longer a problem, however, and very few programs are now written in low-level languages. Because of this, it is possible for more powerful instructions to be used as the effective language levels become higher. Program generators allow complex problems to be solved in only a few statements. The fewer the statements, the less chance there is for errors to be added.

In summary, then, we have the following (Figure 2.1):

(1) It is important to plan the solutions carefully.
(2) A suitable language should be used to implement the solution.
(3) Solutions should be checked at all stages.

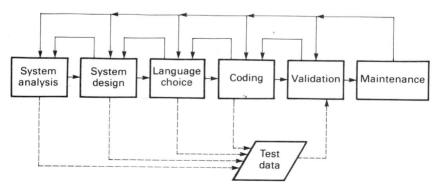

Figure 2.1 Software development cycle

(4) And appropriate software diagnostic tools should be available to make sure that any errors are easily trapped.

Is there any way to circumvent any of these stages? Not really: and as long as they are followed carefully, many of the difficulties with which implementors are only too familiar may be avoided.

2.3 The approach to validation

Various ways in which solutions may be planned are discussed in Chapters 3–7; some of the tools available are the subject of Chapters 8–11. Many texts have been written about programming languages, and it would be difficult to give a list of any length without committing some errors of omission or commission. The bibliography gives a very few which have appeared useful to the authors. This is a very personal approach, and should be treated with the caution it deserves.

However, the checking process described is of interest at this point. After all, how should one go about checking a solution to a problem? This is not the same as checking a program, because it occurs at least one stage earlier in the implementation process. This may well be illustrated by reference to a problem to be solved.

The solution to the quadratic equation $ax^2 + bx + c = 0$ is well known:

$$x = (-b + d)/2a \text{ or } x = (-b - d)/2a, \text{ where } d = \sqrt{b^2 - 4ac}$$

Suppose that this had just been derived by some means or another, completely fresh. Before committing this to a planning sequence, still less before coding it, it should be checked. How might this best be approached? By the use of simple values, but which are carefully chosen. There is no virtue whatsoever in throwing a large number of more or less random numbers at it in the hope that something useful will emerge.

Useful numbers always include zero and unity. Useful strings always include the null string (no characters) as well as space, letter A and digit 0. As this particular case is a numerical problem, the testing values should have a suitable mixture of zeros and ones. Straightaway, if $a = 0$, something peculiar happens. Division by zero is usually suspect, but when this occurs at the design stage—*not* the programming stage—it is merely cause for reflection, rather than panic. In this instance, it merely shows that $a = 0$ is a special case, where a different approach must be adopted to the solution.

A few more simple cases will probably result in an attempt to find the square root of a negative number. This is not necessarily wrong, but might give rise to a certain amount of difficulty if it hasn't previously been given any thought. Is it likely that this will have been produced accidentally? Under the restricted circumstances, using only zeros and ones, it will certainly occur. Such things should not be left entirely to chance, however.

At each stage of the solution, then, critical values should be noted. Two very familiar situations have been mentioned here: those of a zero divisor and of an imaginary square root. Other common cases might include very large numbers, if the data be numeric. In the case of other types of variable, lack of data on request might require attention. Strings being too long, or too short, or of the wrong type of contents might also happen.

With all of these in mind, the planning stage can confidently be approached. Any errors which have occurred in the solution have been corrected. A considerable amount of information has been gathered during this checking and correction process which will be most useful during the subsequent stages.

One final point here: there is no need for all solutions to be produced *ab initio*. There is no virtue in reinventing the wheel. If it is possible to look a solution up, that is better than spending one's time on working it out afresh. . . . 'Remember, always, to call it, please-Research.'

2.4 Planning and verifying programs

Because the abstract solution is now verified, the next stages concentrate on its accurate realisation. It is usually considered in two parts: that of system design and that of programming. Each of these has several subdivisions and each needs its own variety of care in execution.

System design takes the abstract solution and makes it ready for preparation for the computer system. (This assumes that the object is to do that. Not all problems should be processed by computers, but in this limited discussion, it has been assumed that this is the requirement.) During this operation, no new errors can be allowed to infiltrate the correct solution with which it commences. Hence, in each subdivision, checks must be activated to avoid such dangers.

Also, during the system design stage, various separate parts of the realisation of the solution will appear quite naturally. For instance, during the preparation of a telephone directory, it is likely that the input names are to be sorted into some given sequence. Two data structures will be associated with this—the list before sorting and the list after sorting. This 'natural' break can be made use of at a later stage, and note should be made of it during system design.

There are internal consistency checks which can be applied during the system design stage itself. The techniques involved with data flow analysis allow recognition of potential mistakes made with other methods and their subsequent correction. Unfortunately, it is as difficult to remove all mistakes during system design as it was during the original solution stage. Both of these are human dependent and therefore prone to error for that reason.

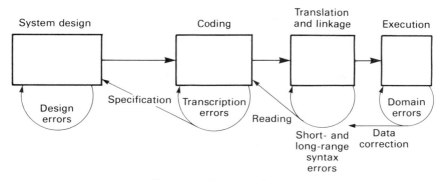

Figure 2.2 Sources of error

The next part of the operation has external checks built in. These are the familiar ones of error reports given by the computer system itself and can occur in several phases during the programming process. There are errors of structure, of interpretation and of domain. The structure errors relate to the micro- and macro-syntax of the program, found during its translation; they are often called lexical errors and syntax errors respectively. The interpretation errors refer to macro-syntax and are also found during translation. They may refer to the usage of variables—for instance, numeric values expected, but a string value given. The domain errors are similar, but are not found until the program in question is executed. A typical example, already given, is that of division by zero. Such errors are, in general, impossible for the system to diagnose until the program is being used. See Figure 2.2.

It is important that all of these sources of error are understood, because therein lies the potential for their correction. As during the solution stage, there will be obvious places where checks may be made. Critical conditions and corresponding values may be documented for later use. In this way, the customer for a given product may be satisfied that it is a correctly working version of what was required.

In all of these operations, *scrupulous* honesty is required. It is counterproductive to attempt even a minor deception to oneself. The excuse of 'it'll be all right on the night' leads to more work, not less, in the long run. The institution of a Devil's Advocate is useful here, if it can conveniently be arranged. One might not be attempting canonisation of one's programs: but a mechanism of such proven efficacy cannot lightly be ignored.

2.5 The assembly of test data

After the program has been produced, therefore, it must be checked. Following all these careful operations, it should work correctly first time.

As remarked upon previously, however, life isn't quite like that. It is necessary to verify that it does work in the way it should, and it is necessary to demonstrate that happy situation to the users of the program.

Where are the test data to come from? For the most part, they already exist, if the development path described above has been followed. They came into being in at least two places. One was at the critical points in the solution as it was being prepared, and the other occurred when the system design was taking place (see Figure 2.3). There are various critical points encountered during that stage also, where there are well-defined data structures with well-defined contents. If these may conveniently be inspected, they form ideal test areas. This is very likely to be the case with, for instance, the contents of external files.

There are other places where these data may conveniently be identified, apart from those positions logically associated with the solution and the subsequent system design. These may be found at natural break points in the program. Examples of these may occur after reading an input record, for it is at places of this nature that many errors may be trapped. It is fair to say that, in general, while a programmer has considerable control over the program under construction (after all, who else *could* have?), there is always the possibility of the input data being suspect.

When all of the test data from the various sources have been assembled, they should be matched up so as to avoid duplication. There is no use in checking the same area in the same way more than once, and there is little use, either, in calling for tests to be performed if there is nothing to check the output against.

Hence it also follows that for each test there must be appropriate expected results. The assembly of these should, of course, take place at the same time as the corresponding data, which is while the relevant informa-

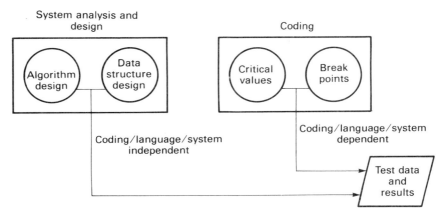

Figure 2.3 Test data generation

tion is still fresh in the mind of the solver, designer or programmer, as appropriate. There may well be a considerable volume of test data and results as a consequence of all this activity. It is therefore *essential* that the whole be carefully documented. The reasons for each test should be included, and the point during the program's execution where the results are to be found.

This latter point allows intermediate calculations to be checked. The production of incorrect results is less helpful if it does not allow the position of the relevant errors to be found. Hence the careful identification of each critical point is of importance here also.

From all of this, three things emerge:

(1) There is a set of test data, allowing the verification to take place.
(2) There is a set of corresponding test results. These may include suggestions concerning particular kinds of incorrect values which could occur under certain foreseen circumstances.
(3) And there is the corresponding documentation relating all of these items.

2.6 Automated testing

In all of the above, if we are not careful, there is a large amount of tedious repetitive work. Generate appropriate test data, feed it into the program, compare it with the expected results, and report on the outcome. If ever a computer system had a proper use, it was precisely to avoid this type of cycle of operations. It is so uncomplicated that it is ideal to give to even the simplest of computer systems.

Of course, it can be done in just that way. Among the software tools for program testing which have been mentioned above is that kind of framework, or testbed. It accepts the test data, arranges for them to be input into the program under test, and commences the test cycle. It then intercepts the results, both from specified intermediate points and from those which normally occur as the end products. It checks them for correspondence with what is expected. Instead of a task which is potentially boring, the 'pass' or 'fail' result appears automatically. This is much more satisfactory in human terms of productivity, of course.

Naturally, more information would be given in the case of failures identified during testing. Where possible, the nature of any mismatch between actual results and those expected would be reported. If an alternative output stream were available, it could be used to inform the testing team about the more likely kinds of error. Notification would then be automatic and easy. While hindsight may be a powerful tool in its own right, it is safer and better to predict probable outcomes for a number of reasons.

There is, unfortunately, sometimes the temptation to change test data to correspond to correctly working cases. Such activity is not to be recommended, but familiarly human. The fewer the misconceptions, also, the less likely it is that test cases will be omitted because 'they just can't happen'.

There are two further aspects of automated program testing to be covered. One is the generation of ranges of test data. Assume, for instance, that there are three parameters for a particular program which is to be tested. The first is an integer in the range 2 to 5 inclusive; the second is a real number in the range -1 to $+1$; and the third is a string of letters whose length is given by the first parameter. It is better to arrange for test data to be generated automatically in this format, if at all possible. Random number generators are sufficiently common and reliable to allow this to be done adequately. Such data sets are less liable to bias than if they had been produced by hand, and less human tedium is incurred.

The other aspect relates to the way in which the actual and expected results may be compared. Viewing these as two serial files—a reasonably valid approach—a simple record-by-record comparison is a little too straightforward to be useful in every situation. If a single record is missing from one file, all subsequent records would be out of step, with disproportionately unfortunate consequences. The comparison procedure should be able to compensate for this kind of error, among others. Single record errors, extra records or missing records would be among the most common of this nature. Within records, too many or too few spaces would be easy to recognise and report. The substitution of 'tab' characters for multiple spaces is also common, and should be accommodated.

Hence we should expect a greater degree of reliability in all implementations. The price to pay is that of more care in their preparation, but this must not be at the expense of a vast amount of extra tedium.

2.7 Program prototyping

There is a certain supposition in all of the above; namely, that the system meets the user's requirement. A considerable amount of work has been invested in solving, planning and programming, in test data, results and checking. But is this really what the user wanted?

What would be desirable in this instance is a quickly-produced working version for the user to see and use. Production may be carried out on any convenient system (although the real target system would be preferred) and the software should accept valid input and produce valid output while working on the actual system data.

Agreement on the form and content of input and output would allow confident development of the system. The user would be considerably happier under these circumstances, having been involved in the design. There is also the advantage to the software designer that the user has agreed to a particular format and it would be relatively easy to demonstrate any change of specification under these conditions, thereby strengthening the designer's position in this respect.

The overriding consideration in this process is the rapid production of the software and rapid implementation of agreed modifications. The use of the so-called very high-level (or fourth-generation) languages is indicated here and this aspect is amplified in Chapter 6.

2.8 Exercises

1 Investigate the facilities available to you which should help in producing correct programs. How many of them do you normally use? Are they the best tools for the job?
2 In section 2.3 a number of errors are described. With reference to a computer system with which you are familiar, describe the messages which arise when such circumstances are met. What improvements would you recommend be made to the reporting system to allow easier diagnosis of faults and their correction?
3 A number of semi-automatic testing systems are available for software production. What facilities would you expect such systems to provide? How are your expectations borne out?

PART II
Software Design

CHAPTER 3
The need for software design

3.1 The alternative to design

For many years, it was taken for granted that computer programs were to be written by the intelligentsia; and this was indeed substantially the case. It seemed to follow from this that because such people were so clever that they would understand what they were doing in all programming circumstances. This was not always so obviously true: mistakes were made, some of which were quite serious; but they were detected and corrected, and all was (mostly...) well.

In addition, as long as computers and computer systems were expensive and rare, the elite corps of programmers was more interested in getting whatever answers were required regardless of the cost in manpower, always provided that those expensive machines were kept busy. Parenthetically, it is probably significant that they were called programmers, although they would almost certainly now be titled 'programmer/analysts'. Analysis was what everybody did on pieces of scrap paper, and wrote down neatly later on when the answer was correct. So much so that the idea of systems analysis was described as 'what we've always done' when it first became widespread and was given its own title!

There is a very strong economic lesson to be learnt from the preceding message. If the cost of one of the components of a system is low and the cost of another is high, it is possible that the low-cost part will be misused. This was indeed the case for a number of years but, as everything changes in time, so did this situation. Programming departments (*sic*) grew and became quite large; management had to be found and used to get the best out of the personnel, and the cost ratio changed. At the same time, the size of the applications increased, and this led to further complexities in the organisation of the implementors, changing the cost ratio still further.

There have been two decision points discernible here. One relates to the relative costs. In the early days of computing, the hardware might well (and often did) account for some 80 per cent of the cost, with software provision and upkeep contributing the remaining 20 per cent. The ratio in present-day terms is probably still 80 : 20, but with the software aspect predominating. The other decision point may be given in terms of numbers, both of computers and of implementors. Instead of there being many more programmers than machines—the initial case—the situation is now reversed. The advent of the microcomputer system has tipped the balance.

The outcome was easy to foresee—or, more correctly, it is easy to look back and 'foretell' what happened next. It was noticed that the weak link in implementation was not in the programming operation, but in the design stages of solutions. Debugging was performed in reasonably efficient ways, but still needed to be done. This was most obvious in those tasks which were large: the difficulty with which they were implemented seemed to grow faster than their actual sizes. In this way, an implementation which was twice the size of another would be much more than twice as difficult to get working. The latter point was indeed the key. It was not the original ideas which were specifically harder to get right, but the actual realisation of them.

In the same way that a small building, such as a garden shed, can be erected straight on top of the ground without much preparation, so small programs can be written very rapidly without much planning. However, if one wants to build a skyscraper, a lot of effort has to be put into the foundations.

So it is with larger programs and collections of programs. As soon as this point was adequately appreciated, the quality of the product improved considerably. Of course, this was not an overnight happening. The design techniques which are in common use today took a considerable amount of work to implement and are the result of much carefully applied experience. However, the reasons for their use are plain for all to see and, while the history of computing is being retold, this aspect must not be forgotten.

There is one other point in which the analogy above can be of assistance. Even though a garden shed can be put up with a minimum of trouble and a skyscraper will require a large team for a long time, there is some paperwork to be considered in both cases. This is not used in a pejorative sense. Whether it is used as a storage medium or for information transmission between people, paperwork is a necessary part of any operation of this nature. However, changing the scale of the task can change that paperwork much more than other aspects. If any edifice is to be built without making plans first, it is likely to run into difficulties of one sort or another.

This may seem pretty obvious in the case of plans for buildings, but that is probably due to general familiarity with such matters. It must not shield the implementor from the similar 'obviousness' in planning solutions in computing terms. No job is too large, no job is too small. It does not matter whether the solution can be realised in a 10-line program or needs a multi-man-year operation—the correct undertaking of the design is an absolute requirement. The alternative is inefficiency in the best case, and chaos in the worst.

One final remark before the subject of paperwork in planning is left. In computing terms, the medium used may not actually be paper, although it often is. One of the developments assisted by computing technologies is the provision of planning facilities realised directly upon computer systems. The advent of word-processors and spreadsheet packages are only two of the most obvious aspects of this change. None of this alters the need for planning, although it will probably make the task itself easier. For modern professional computing, methodical design is an essential part of everyone's approach to implementation.

3.2 Features that designs should give

The reasons for the adoption of a methodical approach now lead to a discussion of the form which that approach should take. It is one thing to view the effects which the lack of such operations seem to lead, but tangible results are better in any demonstration. This is a relatively simple task to undertake, although its full benefit can only be judged by experience. Naturally, for best experiential results, one should attempt the development of a system without the advantages of proper design methods. After this, the true benefits would become much more readily apparent: but it would be unfair to subject anyone to those practices which are being called into question here.

First, the effect on individual implementors can be judged. Why should there be any benefit in the expenditure of effort over and above that required strictly for implementation? Because, quite simply, it forces the complete evaluation of systems which might otherwise contain suspect elements. These are typically characterised by 'Well, that should work', but without proof being given. This is often allied with a so-called gut-feeling that it looks all right, and that in the hands of an experienced implementor it will be correctly finished. There are also overtones of 'You know what I mean': and if anybody has a nodding acquaintance with computer systems, they shouldn't be fooled by that for any length of time at all.

Secondly, there is the effect on other implementors and members of any team organised to provide such a computerised system. The careful and complete plans which are necessarily the outcome of methodical design may be communicated much more successfully. They lead to much greater confidence in all their users, and therefore to increased efficiency and productivity.

One of the great hurdles which has to be jumped here is in the initial stages of implementation. There are no rapid returns. Instead of a program taking shape immediately, there must first be a great deal of formal planning work undertaken. This is at odds with 'traditional' practices, where programming starts very early in the implementation cycle. Any move in this direction must be firmly quashed—it is counter-productive in the long term (and very often in the short term as well).

This careful design leads to understanding, not only by other implementors, but by the author(s) as well. If there is any doubt, it should be faced honestly, squarely and immediately. Otherwise, the consequences will have to be suffered at some future time, when the understanding brought on by current awareness has long since faded. So one of the features given by careful design is that of understanding. It may seem trite, but it is by no means trivial. Without understanding, the whole process will be harder to complete and more liable to error, both immediately and also in the longer term.

A further advantage of careful design work is of benefit to both the implementation team and to the originators of the requirements. It is most likely that the system to be implemented has been requested by someone (otherwise, why bother?), and that there were suitable specifications attendant upon the request. Before any programming work has been undertaken as such, the designers may approach the originators and check that what is being done is actually what was originally wanted. There are too many cautionary tales of users being provided with excellent systems which, alas, had little relationship to their actual needs. (The difficulties arising in accurate communication between users and implementors are many, and there is no need to make an already difficult area any more strained.)

In present usage, it is quite to be expected that users cooperate with implementation teams to check the design at many stages. One of the advantages that accrues from standard methods being used is that they form a more universally understood language. The formal methods which can be adopted to prove to each team—both users and implementors—that the design matches the requirements are very widespread, to the advantage of all concerned. There are other methods which can be employed to arrange this kind of mutual satisfaction, but they have to be used somewhat later in the design phases: the design has to be undertaken initially under any circumstances. These aspects are further discussed in Chapter 10.

The immediate result of all of this labour is a system whose characteristics can be communicated to all. In case there is a feeling of much face-to-face communication here, it must be recalled that a significant amount of these data are held within computer systems. Because of this, the communication may take place over long distances, via computer networks, as easily as if it were in the adjacent room. The information may be in textual form, but with the increasing sophistication available in graphical processing, there is no need for complete restriction in its presentation to unadorned text.

There are many advantages which come from using a computerised approach to design which are not shared by manual methods. These take the form of software tools which may be invoked easily and, in some cases, automatically, during the realisation of a design. The checking for consistency which may take place has to be used to be appreciated to its full. The tedium of much that has hitherto been exclusively the responsibility of human beings can now, much more readily, be transferred to the computer systems themselves. This is becoming more and more widespread, and is no more than an extension of the proper use of any automatic process—to perform repetitive tasks without supervision.

The outcome of formal design methods will be a standard representation of the system or program to be implemented. This may be of such a nature that it can now be regarded as a very high-level language: related to COBOL, perhaps, as COBOL is itself related to an assembly code. In this way, not only may the design be checked for consistency, but may also be translated directly into a computer language. From this, of course, it may be translated once more for its actual realisation, and this facility is becoming increasingly available. Also, the provision of integrated systems, which perform this sequence of operations in an automatic way, is becoming more and more widespread.

Not only are these systems easier, in human terms, to produce, but they are much less prone to error. They go through fewer manually reliant stages and there is a lower likelihood of mistakes being introduced as this trend continues. The maintenance of such a system is an easier undertaking as a direct result of this, which makes it less costly in the long run for both of these reasons—as stated above, the human element is now a significantly greater factor in the costing of computerised systems than the hardware. In this sense, maintenance may also include change (as it does all too often, alas), and the problems associated with the ways in which users change their minds are also significantly reduced. Design methods which deal with considerations of this nature are treated further in Chapters 4, 5 and 6, while Chapter 17 discusses the nature of maintenance.

3.3 Reasons for the structured approach

Section 3.2 suggests that the design process is thus an essential one in the life-cycle of any software implementation exercise. This being the case, it should best be approached so as to make it as painless an operation as possible. It also follows that it should therefore be as automatic to carry out as can be arranged. This follows from observations made previously: if an implementation procedure can be effected more easily, its implementors are less likely to become fatigued and, therefore, less likely to make mistakes.

The systematic approach suggested in this section lends itself to the efficiencies sought after. It is characterised by the keyword 'structured' and divides naturally into three broad categories: implementation, testing and management.

3.3.1 Structured implementation

Approaching implementation in a structured fashion leads naturally to the question, 'How does one structure such an operation?' As with every such case, a set of (simple) rules is the most effective answer, as long as those rules fulfil the requirements of structuring. In this operation, they must lead in a reasonable way to the solution of any generalised problem. They must, therefore, be sufficiently flexible to accommodate a large number of alternatives without undue complication in and of themselves.

The software life-cycle (Figure 3.1) comes to our assistance at this point. The implementation of any process may be mapped out as a set of separate operations, each leading into the next. To ensure that the product which is the final result of the implementation is what was actually required at the outset, each stage must check that it has fulfilled the conditions which the previous stage placed upon it.

Structured implementation makes full use of software tools during its production to maximise efficiency. It can only do this, however, as long as the interface between the program produced and its environment is compatible with those tools. One of the essentials, then, is that appropriate standards are maintained. In this way, the procedure may be likened to the building of a house with standard units. The employment of bricks is not the most unusual sight in modern dwellings, but they were a tremendous innovation when they were introduced into England during the thirteenth

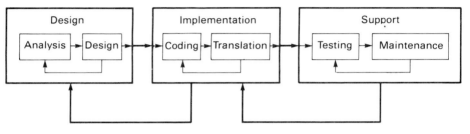

Figure 3.1 Software life-cycle

century. In the same way, the 'invention' of standard program building-blocks was a great help when it first came about. Because of this, it is now rather difficult to imagine the operation of modern computer systems before such an occurrence took place. Chapter 10, then, assumes familiarity with the modern situation and approach to implementation.

This is another of the situations which appear inevitable in retrospect, but which took considerable time and effort to evolve into the present situation. It implies a commitment to forward planning which cannot be avoided, and any attempt at structured implementation without it will be unsuccessful or, at least, remarkably inefficient.

3.3.2 Structured testing

The next stage cannot be divorced from this approach either. Before any testing can take place, its aims and objectives must have been carefully and completely specified. All test data should have been organised with the purpose of each testing procedure properly documented. This will avoid overlaps—there is no virtue in testing the same aspect of a system more than once unless it is inevitable. The expected result must also be available, otherwise it will have to be re-evaluated afresh at each testing run—again a duplication of effort which should not be allowed.

This does not rule out the repetition of those tests which are needed to establish an hierarchy of correctness. If one is implementing a compiler for a high-level language, it is probable that earlier tests will establish the correctness of (say) assignment statements. These may then be used to signal the correct implementation of (say) looping constructs; it is unlikely that any programs used for testing will subsequently avoid assignment statements thereafter. This aspect of software maintenance is discussed at greater length in Chapter 17.

The situation to be preferred is that of automated testing, which is achieved most readily in the context of a structured approach. It involves a carefully orchestrated plan, usually closely integrated with the operating system provisions of the target computer by careful use of the job-control language. This may then be invoked by a single command, which arranges the input of successive batches of test data to the program being tested, and receives the results of each in turn. These are then compared automatically against the results expected, and reports only in exceptional circumstances (i.e. in case of failure)! The message is the usual one—more planning in the initial stages, less work overall. Planning, done properly and in a structured fashion, only takes place once; but testing is a continuous operation, with each change in the requirements and environment of a computer system. If this appears to echo the sentiments of the previous chapter, this is hardly to be unexpected. It is sufficiently important to be a recurring refrain to the main theme; and the chorus is always the same!

3.3.3 **Structured management**

In modern terms, there is no profit in having highly structured operations for producing computer systems, be they hardware or software, without the management to take appropriate advantage of them. In this context, the implication is that of a structured approach. This aspect is developed to some depth in Chapter 10. Sufficient at this stage to draw attention to it, and recommend its adoption at the earliest stages of any strategic planning operations.

3.4 The user and software design

In any system, the user is the most important person. If this seems trivial, you must be one of the relatively few well-structured implementors among a large population of others. (Cheap shot, and unworthy, but there is a strong feeling in some quarters that there is a large helping of truth in there...) It is unfortunately too easy to lose sight of this most important aspect in the excitement of implementation. This is sometimes made more poignant by recollection that 'the customer is always right': after all, who pays for the work?

It is in each user's own interest to become involved in the process of design. Any interest shown, as long as it is not overbearing, is liable to infuse interest in the software providers. Once more: if the implementors are interested, they are not going to be bored; and if they are not bored, they are more likely to effect a better result. This does not imply that every user must become an expert in the field of computing design. It is reasonable, though, to anticipate a moderate and educated approach. Users are expected to have better things to do with their time than check on the actions of software writers, or at least they ought to have. If they are that interested, why aren't they doing it themselves? A moderate approach is always to be recommended.

The other side of the same coin concerns the software designers and providers. If the users can be interested in some of the more specific areas of the task, they can become more immediately involved in those parts which are going to be difficult to interpret, whatever they may be. It is not usually possible easily to predict which areas are going to cause difficulties: but a well-disposed user may make a considerable difference.

One has to be careful in these cases about too much involvement. It is all very well interfacing with an excited user, but there are times when all that one wants to do is to get on with the actual job in hand. Once again, the advantages of the moderate approach are to be recommended.

As any professional engineer will be pleased to tell you, one of the secrets of any well-controlled system is in its feedback. This may be obvious from the pathways shown in Figure 3.1, but that is not the whole story. The use to which feedback paths are put is of great importance; it is not sufficient merely to provide them.

The aspect which must be addressed is that of the type of feedback, because two kinds are recognised in engineering applications: positive and negative. In systems with any kind of feedback loop, small changes lead to corrections being applied further back in the system.

Under most circumstances, it is to be hoped that the effects are corrective in nature, so that the results will approach closer to those desired (in other words, the correct ones) with each change. Such feedback is termed negative, as the tendency is towards a steady state with all perturbations tending towards zero.

When the arrangements have not been made so carefully, though, things may get out of hand. Small corrections may be applied in exactly the wrong way and lead to further difficulties; and more corrections will be needed. These, too, cause their own brand of trouble, and it is only a short step to the whole getting thoroughly out of hand.

This is where a well-intentioned user may help—under suitable and careful 'supervision', of course. He or she is more interested in the result than in the method of solution and is less likely to be led astray than an implementor. This is a somewhat idealised representation, because everybody is liable to mistakes of one sort or another. The key here is in the diversity of viewpoints. To perceive a picture with proper depth, two eyes are necessary: and to appreciate a system properly, two differing approaches are better than one.

For the originators to be best used, they must be given reasonable help. For the most part, typical users do not appreciate or, in some cases, even understand their own problems once they have been translated into computing terms. They may then be requested to verify that their problems are indeed the ones which are being solved, and not merely some which have appeared in the minds of the software designers. The verification differs somewhat from that applied within a computerised system. It has to be done in terms of the original problem, rather than in respect only of the solution.

To achieve this, a number of approaches may be used, one of the more obvious of which is the employment of prototyping. A prototype, as is widely appreciated, is a sort of dummy for the final system. It is employed in many engineering situations and forms the basis for further studies. It is built to correspond to the known requirements of the system, but is not normally made particularly pretty! If a prototype car is constructed, it may well not be painted. It may have the correct engine in it, or merely an approximation. It will have four wheels (one assumes), but some of its aspects will be unlikely to appear in the final version. However, it is readily and quickly available for testing purposes, even if it is sent to the scrapyard immediately testing is complete.

The same approach can also be used in software design terms. Using appropriate tools and languages, an approximation may be assembled quickly for the benefit of the users, for their comments. As long as neither side expects this to be the final product, there is unlikely to be any problem. Both sides should be ready to make allowances for the experimental nature of the system under discussion, in the interests of rapid advances. More is said on the subject of prototyping in Chapter 6; and about tools in general in Chapter 9.

Once the user's terms have been agreed, at least in outline and quite often in more definite terms, the real implementation can proceed. The results can be checked at each stage against those achieved from the prototype system and any mistakes put right. There is then less need to put the originators to any trouble by persistent requests for verification. This is liable to instill confidence in them, which must be desirable. There is likewise less time used in consulting the prototype than in questioning the users: a similar saving.

The testing of such well-designed systems is also made easier, for a number of reasons. The users have confidence in the product and feel fully involved in the situation. The test data, and their corresponding results, have been available from the earliest stages of the implementation. They will feel able to be involved in the testing of the system if necessary; but will have confidence in the implementors following their close involvement throughout. The pervading structure of the whole edifice binds the implementation together into a strongly unified result.

3.5 Conclusions

The keystone of the whole, then—the one which binds and compresses the arch together—is planning (Figure 3.2). This encompasses design, and implies forethought. It also assumes proper knowledge, not only of the system being constructed, but also of the tools and methods being used in the construction. To attempt the implementation of any software, of any size whatsoever, without proper preparation, is to undertake more work than is strictly necessary—in the long run. Nobody can really be in favour of that.

The other message is that implementation is a team activity. This still applies even when it is not so apparent. Chapter 10 gives some ideas which relate to this and demonstrates that computer systems, and their operating systems as well, are all the result of much cooperative effort. Even if the implementor feels somewhat alone and not involved with others (as, for instance, in the completion of a set scholastic exercise), it is best to assume that the software under construction will require upkeep. This will involve the same implementor at a later stage, or other implementors, and that

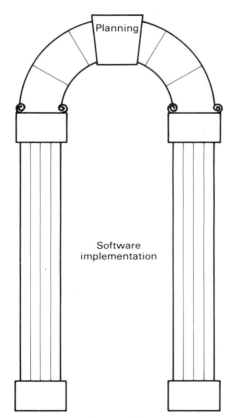

Figure 3.2 The keystone

invokes the teamwork aspect straightaway. It is a good habit to get into. The more automatic the operation can become and the less conscious thought that it needs, the easier it grows, especially in the long term: foresight and planning are part of the approach of the true professional.

3.6 Exercises

1 Read a copy of Brooks' *The Mythical Man-Month* (see the bibliography). Why do large parts of it seem (painfully) familiar?
2 Critically investigate your own design operations or, even better, get someone else to do it for you (you can do the same for them!). Where do they fall short of what might reasonably be expected, and consequently lead (ultimately) to significantly increased work overall?
3 Compare your implementation operations with the software life-cycle described in Figure 3.1. How does your work compare with the 'ideal' described there?

CHAPTER 4

Stepwise refinement

4.1 The need for structure

The design of software must be approached in an organised and ordered manner. There is often, among newcomers to the art, a temptation to jump straight into writing code without having given due consideration to what code is required. Coding, as a phase of software design, should be almost an incidental process. If a piece of software is designed properly, the transition from the last phase of the description of the algorithm to the program code will be almost imperceptible. To demonstrate this we will now look at two very similar methods of describing a piece of software. These methods, known as *structured English* and *pseudocode*, will each be used in a process called stepwise refinement to convert an imprecise description of a piece of software into a finished product. It must be remembered that the reasons for structure are readability and maintainability; a software product that is well structured will be easy to understand and will consequently be robust and easy to maintain and modify.

Stepwise refinement, which is also described as top–down decomposition, is a means of breaking a process into successively more detailed steps until the detail of the steps allows them to be expressed in a programming language. It will be obvious that the level of detail required will depend upon the type of language used; for example, assembler language requires more detail than a high-level language such as COBOL or Pascal, and these in turn require more detail than the very high-level or fourth-generation languages described in Chapter 6. For our purposes here we will assume that the software is to be written in a high-level structured language such as Pascal, C or COBOL.

Before looking at the use of structured English and pseudocode for designing software, consider an example of stepwise refinement applied to describing a problem which has nothing to do with software.

We will describe the process of driving to work as:

Get the car out.
Drive into the road.
Follow the route to work.

This is the top-level description and is necessarily rather vague, making, as it does, assumptions about the reader's perceptions. For instance, we understand the first statement to mean that we open the garage doors, get into the car, start the engine, back out and so on. So refine the statement to include this—but, before doing so, suppose that you got home late the night before so that the car is already in the road. Include this in the description. While you are tidying things give the description a name and indicate where it finishes:

driving-to-work

```
IF the-car-is-in-the-garage THEN DO
    open-the-garage-doors
    get-into-the-car
    start-the-engine
    drive-into-the-road
ENDIF
follow-route-to-work
END driving-to-work
```

(Note the use of hyphens to concentrate each statement into a single action.)

So, we now have some detail in the first part of the process; but what about the second part? It is obvious that a lot more detail is required here. Just think about driving away from the kerb:

drive-away-from-kerb

```
look-in-mirror
WHILE traffic-approaching DO
    keep-looking-in-mirror
ENDWHILE
signal
pull-out
REPEAT
    change-up-gear
```

UNTIL car-in-top-gear OR road-speed = 30 mph
END drive-away-from-kerb

The rest of the drive to work again needs more detail. A first refinement of this might be:

follow-rest-of-route

WHILE NOT at-work DO
    take-all-appropriate-turns
ENDWHILE
END follow-rest-of-route

Now it is obvious that there is still insufficient detail to consider the problem fully defined. For instance, suppose that roadworks cause a diversion or you have to stop for petrol; all of these would need to be built in if the problem were to be fully described. However, for the purpose of this explanation, such detail is unnecessary. What is more important is to note that we can remove all of the detailed instructions into another self-contained piece of text thus preserving the simple form of the first level; and in this is the basis of the process of stepwise refinement: to keep each successive step as clear and simple as possible until eventually the transition into source code can be carried out.

Driving-to-work

IF the-car-is-in-the-garage THEN DO
    hit-the-road
ENDIF
drive-away-from-the-kerb
follow-rest-of-route
END driving-to-work

PROCEDURE hit-the-road

open-the-garage-doors
get-into-the-car
start-the-engine
drive-into-the-road
END hit-the-road

PROCEDURE drive-away-from-kerb

look-in-mirror
WHILE traffic-approaching DO
    keep-looking-in-mirror
ENDWHILE
signal
pull-out

REPEAT
    change-up-gear
UNTIL car-in-top-gear OR road-speed = 30 mph
END drive-away-from-kerb

PROCEDURE follow-rest-of-route

WHILE NOT at-work DO
    take-all-appropriate-turns
ENDWHILE

END follow-rest-of-route

Describing a process even so mundane as going to work can become a long activity. It might come as some relief that we are not going any further with this particular problem but will now extract from it the constructs which are used in structured English.

4.2 Constructs used in structured English

In the example above, a number of fundamental constructs and concepts have been used. In the descriptions below, the constructs are described in a formal way using what is known as Backus Naur Form (BNF). In this form, items (that is, words or symbols) not enclosed in ⟨ ⟩ are used as written while items enclosed in ⟨ ⟩ are used according to their description:

(a) ⟨condition⟩
    A condition is controlled by either a boolean variable (e.g. car-in-top-gear) or a boolean expression (e.g. road-speed = 30 mph) which can take either of the values TRUE or FALSE.
(b) ⟨statement⟩
    In order to display the logic of the software as succinctly as possible, the main algorithm is kept short by means of PROCEDUREs, such as drive-away-from-kerb and follow-rest-of-route. A statement may therefore be a procedure, in which case it refers to a self-contained block of further statements, or it may be a simple statement requiring no further refinement. For example, if we decide that start-the-engine requires further refining, we could make it into a procedure containing such statements as 'insert-key', 'If automatic-choke THEN . . .', 'WHILE engine-not-firing . . .' and so on.

The actual word PROCEDURE is not always used in structured English and its use here is considered optional. Readability is assisted by the judicious use of indentation of text and of upper case for keywords.

The constructs are as follows:

(1) Sequence:

DO   ⟨statements⟩

(2) Selection:

IF ⟨condition⟩ THEN DO
    ⟨statements⟩
ENDIF

This can be extended to include the use of ELSE as follows:

IF ⟨condition⟩ THEN DO
    ⟨statements⟩
ELSE DO
    ⟨statements⟩
ENDIF

The IF construct can be nested as many times as required, to give a series of optional actions:

IF ⟨condition1⟩ THEN DO
    ⟨statements1⟩
ELSE IF ⟨condition2⟩ THEN DO
      ⟨statements2⟩
      ELSE IF ⟨condition3⟩THEN DO
              ⟨statements3⟩
ENDIF

This method soon becomes untidy and difficult to follow. A tidier construct is the CASE:

CASE ⟨Variable⟩ OF
⟨value1⟩ : ⟨statements1⟩
⟨value2⟩ : ⟨statements2⟩
⟨value3⟩ : ⟨statements3⟩
ENDCASE

Examples will be given below.

(3) Iteration:
First, a construct controlled by a condition tested at the beginning of the loop:

WHILE ⟨condition⟩ DO
    ⟨statements⟩
ENDWHILE

Alternatively, the condition can be tested at the end of the loop:

REPEAT
    ⟨statements⟩

UNTIL ⟨condition⟩

We will now look at a problem in software design using this method of program definition.

4.3 Application—insertion into a linked list

A common method of sorting is by means of a linked list. The data structure is as follows:

Each item links to the next in the sequence. The logical order is independent of the physical order. This is demonstrated by adding Azharunian to the physical end of the list and inserting links to preserve the logical sequence.

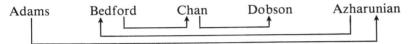

Deletion is achieved by simply removing the pointer to the deleted item. Note that the item still exists in the file. For example, to delete Chan:

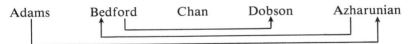

We can now examine the algorithm for insertion into the linked list. Note the following points:

(1) The names are held in an array or a file in sequentially ordered locations starting from location 1.
(2) There is a pointer to the first item in the logical sequence (start-pointer). When the list is empty, start-pointer holds a value of zero.
(3) The links are held in a second array or in another field of the file record.
(4) If an inserted item is lower in the collating sequence than the item which is currently first, then the value of start-pointer is changed. Otherwise the appropriate links are altered to preserve the logical sequence.
(5) A link value of zero indicates the end of the list.

The structure as shown above would appear as shown in Figure 4.1.
    The first outline of the insert routine may be stated as:

insert-into-list

set next-node to 1
WHILE NOT end-of-input
    read-new-value-into-next-node

```
    IF new-value < name[start-pointer] THEN DO
        insert-at-beginning
    ELSE DO
        searchlist
    ENDIF
    set next-node up by 1
ENDWHILE
END insert-into-list
```

start-pointer: 1

Node no.	Name	Link	
1	Adams	5	
2	Bedford	4	Note that this value is here
3	Chan	4 ◄───────────	from before Chan was deleted.
4	Dobson	0	Chan is no longer accessible.
5	Azharunian	2	

Figure 4.1 Linked list data structure

There are three statements in the algorithm, namely: read-new-value-into-next-node, insert-at-beginning and searchlist. Of these, the first needs no further refining since it will map directly on to the syntax of most high-level languages; the other two need refining.

First, note some more points:

(6) Each insertion takes place in the next available node. For instance, in Figure 4.1 the next insertion would be into location 6. The next available node will be called next-node.

(7) As the refinement becomes more detailed, we will use a number of key-words such as save, get, add, divide etc. If the technique is used properly, the context will explain the meaning of the key-words.

(8) The variable, temp, is used to hold the value of the pointer while inserting items into the list.

(9) While searching the list we need a marker which may take different values (and which we will call pointer); and we also require a boolean variable to indicate when the position for the node has been found. This will be called position-found.

PROCEDURE insert-at-beginning

```
save start-pointer in temp
set start-pointer to next-node
set link[next-node] to temp
END insert-at-beginning
```

PROCEDURE searchlist

```
set pointer to start-pointer
```

```
set position-found to FALSE
WHILE NOT position-found DO
    IF   name[pointer] < new-value THEN DO
            set temp to pointer
            set pointer to link[pointer]
    ELSE DO
            set position-found to TRUE
    ENDIF
ENDWHILE
set link[temp] to next-node
set link[next-node] to pointer
END searchlist
```

If this algorithm is desk-checked it will be found to work as long as there is already at least one node in the list *and* we do not try to insert an item beyond the current end of the list. In other words, the design is incomplete in that we have not considered these end conditions. However, the structure allows the enhancement of the algorithm to include the missing parts.

First, to accommodate the empty list, we modify the first level:

insert-into-list

```
set next-node to 1
WHILE NOT end-of-input
    read-new-value-into-next-node
    IF empty-list THEN DO
            start-new-list
    ELSE IF new-value < name[start-pointer] THEN DO
                insert-at-beginning
            ELSE DO
                searchlist
            ENDIF
            set next-node up by 1
    ENDIF
ENDWHILE
END insert-into-list
```

This now leads to another procedure, start-new-list:

PROCEDURE start-new-list

```
set link[1] to zero
set start-pointer to 1
set next-node to 2
END start-new-list
```

This deals with the empty list. To allow an item to be inserted at the end of the list, we have to modify searchlist. Remember that a zero link value indicates the current end of the list.

PROCEDURE searchlist

```
set pointer to start-pointer
set position-found to FALSE
WHILE NOT position-found DO
      IF   name[pointer] < new-value THEN DO
           set temp to pointer
           set pointer to link[pointer]
      ELSE DO
           set position-found to TRUE
      ENDIF
      IF pointer = 0 THEN DO                    *
           set position-found to TRUE           *
      ENDIF                                     *
ENDWHILE
set link[temp] to next-node
set link[next-node] to pointer
END searchlist
```

The lines of text marked * deal with insertion at the end of the sequence. The insertion algorithm is now complete and can be coded into any suitable structured language.

Before dealing with another example, we will compare structured English with an alternative method of describing an algorithm, known as pseudocode.

4.4 Pseudocode

This method is broadly similar to the use of structured English. The process of stepwise refinement is identical and the same constructs are used. The main difference is that where structured English uses key-words, pseudocode uses a notation that is similar to a high-level programming language to describe the data manipulation. There is a profit and a loss involved in this; the profit is that the transition to the implementation language is easier while the loss is that there is probably less readability.

Also, the details of the pseudocode can be influenced by the programming language which has been designated for the implementation because there are idiosyncracies of, say, COBOL which are less easily coded in, say, Pascal and vice versa.

The method is now applied by rewriting the insert routine in pseudocode.

insert-into-list

```
next-node = 1
WHILE NOT end-of-input
    read new-value
    IF start-pointer = 0 THEN DO
        start-new-list
    ELSE IF new-value < name[start-pointer] THEN DO
                    insert-at-beginning
    ELSE DO
                searchlist
    ENDIF
    next-node = next-node + 1
    ENDIF
ENDWHILE
END insert-into-list

PROCEDURE start-new-list

link[1] = 0
start-pointer = 1
next-node = 2
END start-new-list

PROCEDURE insert-at-beginning

temp = start-pointer
start-pointer = next-node
link[next-node] = temp
END insert-at-beginning

PROCEDURE searchlist

pointer = start-pointer
position-found = FALSE
WHILE NOT position-found DO
    IF   name[pointer] < new-value THEN DO
        temp = pointer
        pointer = link[pointer]
    ELSE DO
        position-found = TRUE
    ENDIF
    IF pointer = 0 THEN DO
        position-found = TRUE
    ENDIF
ENDWHILE
link[temp] = next-node
link[next-node] = pointer
END searchlist
```

It is clear that the transition to high-level language code is very simple. If, for example, this code were to be translated into Pascal, it would need only the insertion of data declarations and parameter lists and the replacing of endifs and endwhiles by begin-end markers for the code to be complete. To translate it into COBOL it needs only removal of the endifs and endwhiles and appropriate use of paragraphs and perform and move statements.

Both the techniques of structured English and pseudocode allow the software designer to develop the design in an ordered manner. The algorithm can be dry run before it is finally coded into the implementation language and can be extensively tested at this stage. Use of structured techniques has proved to provide more robust and reliable software.

4.5 Further application—administration of car racing

The following case is taken from the authors' experience in software design. The actual product was a fairly large piece of software but because of limitations of space in this book, the description here is a simplified one. All of the system requirements described here were implemented; the main differences between that system and the one described here is the omission of much of the detail of such things as the file design and intricacies of classification of the cars.

Also, within each of the modules the fine detail has been omitted since its inclusion would require levels of refinement of the program description which would add little to the reader's understanding.

4.5.1 Description of the problem

A motor racing club holds race meetings at which speed trials take place. A race consists of up to 20 cars taking part in a speed trial in which two cars at a time race along a quarter-mile track at the end of which their speeds are measured over a distance of 25 metres. The elapsed times (ETs) for the competitors are placed in ascending order and the winner is the driver whose ET for the quarter-mile is the shortest. Ties on ET are decided on the terminal speed (TS) over the last 25 metres.

The cars are divided into classes depending on their power, engine size and so on. Thus at a meeting there will be up to 15 different races taking place, one for each class. However, due to the unpredictable delays in preparing cars for the races, not all of the competitors in any class will arrive for their runs together. Consequently, although any two cars on the track will be from the same race, successive pairs might be from different races, the only necessity being that every competitor gets two runs down the track during the meeting, the better run being the one which decides the results.

While the runs are in progress, there is a race commentary which tells the spectators details of the two cars currently on the track as well as the current race position. In order to do this, the commentator has a screen display which contains details of the two competitors in action in the top half and the current race position in the bottom half. The outline of the screen layout which was agreed by the designer with the user is shown in Figure 4.2.

The last line on the screen is the option menu which is discussed in section 4.5.5 below.

The areas marked NO, ET and TS allow the input of a car number and its time and speed on its latest run. It will be seen that there is a large amount of cursor control required for this part of the software.

When any two competitors from any race are on the track, the data in the lower half of the display must, of course, be the current position associated with that race. Consequently, there has to be a facility to change the display as necessary.

The commentator has to be able to choose from the options of displaying competitor details in either the left or right lanes, entering ETs and TSs, changing the display for the situation in another race or, and this is very important, correcting an error in an earlier entry of ET or TS. This last item is crucial because it is a characteristic of real-time processing—and especially

L. H. LANE				R.H. LANE			
No. S26 Car Name THE MILE END RAT				No. S55 Car Name NORTH STAFFS FLYER			
Name JOHN WILLIAMSON				Name SID MASTERS			
Eng: JAGUAR 4.2				Eng: ROLLS ROYCE V8			
Index				Index			
Sponsor BARKING BREAKERS				Sponsor NEWTON'S SCRAPYARD			
ET:Best 9.90 Today 9.95				ET:Best 10.11 Today 10.15			
TS:Best 195.3 Today 189.4				TS:Best 183.7 Today 181.6			

NO	DRIVER	ET	MPH	NO	DRIVER	ET	MPH
1	PATTERSON	8.87	204.8	9			
2	BURROUGHS	8.93	203.8	10			
3	MARLEY	9.05	199.6	11			
4	WILLIAMSON	9.95	189.4	12			
5	DOBSON	9.95	188.9	13			
6	MASTERS	10.15	181.6	14			
7				15			
8				16			

NO	E.T.	T.S.	Race: 12

L(eft lane)	R(ight lane)	T(ime)	A(mend)	C(hange file)	(e)X(it)

Figure 4.2 The screen

under unfriendly conditions of noise, exhaust fumes, unreliable power supply and so on—that not surprisingly errors of data entry do occur. So an easy method of correction is an essential aspect of the software.

4.5.2 First stages of the design

It is not feasible in this book to deal with the complete design process for this product and so a few assumptions will be made.

(1) There exists a main file with all of the driver and car details. The details include the driver's best ET and TS to date; and this file must be updated at the end of every race meeting. The system requires facilities to add to, amend and delete from this file.

(2) When a race meeting is held, a separate file is set up for each race. (These will be called racefiles.) A racefile holds for each car the car's race number, the driver's name and the current value of ET and TS for the meeting. Initially, all ETs are set to 1000 and all TSs to 0. (This means that any competitor who has not yet had a run will automatically be sorted to the bottom of the file; it is unlikely that a time of 1000 seconds for a quarter-mile would win any prizes.) A racefile layout is shown in Figure 4.3.

(3) The whole system will be menu-driven. A menu is a list of options presented to the user on the screen. Any option is selected by its number and will invoke either another menu (which can then invoke another to any depth necessary) or it will initiate a particular action by the program. Obviously, a menu maps very simply on to the CASE statement in the program description.

Race number: 12

Record	Number	Name	E.T.	T.S.
1	S41	PATTERSON	8.87	204.8
2	S66	BURROUGHS	8.93	203.8
3	S77	MARLEY	9.05	199.8
4	S26	WILLIAMSON	9.95	189.4
5	S45	DOBSON	9.95	188.9
6	S55	MASTERS	10.15	181.6
7	S59	MULLIGAN	1000.00	0.0
8	J77	ROBINSON	1000.00	0.0

Figure 4.3 Racefile

The first level of the program description can now be stated:

race-administration

finished = FALSE
WHILE NOT finished DO

offer-main-menu
ENDWHILE
END race-administration

The main menu will contain all the first-level options described above. First-level means that in most cases they will invoke further menus. Let us look at the procedure offer-main-menu, since it is necessary to take care that all of the requirements are included. It should be observed that the technique allows forgotten (or, for those who want to save face, additional) options to be inserted later with a minimum of trouble. The next step is to refine the procedure offer-main-menu.

PROCEDURE offer-main-menu

clear screen
display header
display 'Choose an option'
display '1 Add to mainfile'
display '2 Amend mainfile record'
display '3 Delete mainfile record'
display '4 Create racefile'
display '5 Commentary'
display '6 Update mainfile from racefiles'
display '7 Exit from system'
get option
CASE option OF
1: add-to-mainfile
2: amend-mainfile
3: delete-from-mainfile
4: create-and-process-racefile
5: commentary
6: update
7: finished = TRUE
ENDCASE
END display-main-menu

Note that in this program description it is not necessary to include details of screen layout since they can be considered to be part of the display statement and can be written in detail at the coding stage. Note also the use of the CASE and that in the seven values listed, six invoke further procedures while the last simply sets the boolean, finished, to TRUE.

As was mentioned earlier, to go through the whole of the design of this piece of software would not be appropriate for this book, so we will concentrate on two of the procedures, namely: create-and-process-racefile and commentary.

The first of these requires that we can set up and name a new file, add, amend and delete records—remember, this is a temporary file which exists for one race meeting—and list the file to either the screen or the printer. Obviously, this will require a second level of menu which in turn will invoke further procedures.

4.5.3 Create-and-process-racefile

PROCEDURE create-and-process-racefile

```
clear screen
display header
finished = FALSE
WHILE NOT finished DO
     display 'Choose an option'
     display '1 Set up a new file'
     display '2 Add new record(s)'
     display '3 Amend record(s)'
     display '4 Delete record(s)'
     display '5 List file'
     display '6 Return to main menu'
     get option
     CASE option OF
     1: set-up-file
     2: add-records
     3: amend-records
     4: delete-records
     5: listfile
     6: finished = TRUE
     ENDCASE
END create-and-process-racefile
```

It is evident that this type of structure will be common to all of the menu programs in the system. Note that the name of the boolean variable, finished, is shown as the same in all the procedures. If the implementation language is Pascal, for example, finished would be declared locally in each procedure. If, on the other hand, COBOL were to be chosen, such duplication would not be permitted.

4.5.4 Further refinements

Let us now turn to the next level of procedures. Again, we will not attempt to cover all of them but will choose as examples the first two: set-up-file and add-records. This latter procedure enables the user to select from the main-file the data concerning the competitors in a particular race. It is assumed that the mainfile has been created earlier. Also, we will not worry about the details of retrieval from the mainfile. (In practice, it is a hash-addressed file with an index held in main memory but all we need to know for the purpose of this procedure is that the instruction 'get-driver' will access the file and report either that the driver is found or that the required record does not exist. The hashing is carried out on the driver's name.)

There also exists an index which contains the numbers of all of the racefiles already created. The procedure check-index checks whether the new number already exists and can be called from any of the first five options. If check-index is called from the procedure set-up-file it returns the value FALSE in the boolean valid; otherwise the returned value is TRUE and the new file name is added to the index.

If check-index is called from any of the other options, it returns valid as TRUE. (This, of course, is because setting up a file requires that it does not already exist; while processing, it requires that it does.)

PROCEDURE set-up-file

```
valid = FALSE
WHILE NOT valid DO
      display 'File number'
      get file number
      check-index
      IF NOT valid THEN DO
            display 'This file already exists. Please respecify.'
      ENDIF
      no-of-records = 0
      write-header-rec
      close-file
ENDWHILE
define file (using the appropriate facilities)
END set-up-file
```

PROCEDURE add-records

```
valid = FALSE
WHILE NOT valid DO
      display 'File number?'
      check-index
      IF NOT valid THEN DO
            display 'This file does not exist. Please respecify'
      ENDIF
ENDWHILE
more-entries = TRUE
open-file
read-header-rec
```

```
WHILE more-entries DO
     display 'Next entrant name in the form X.X.XXXXXXX'
     hash-address
     check-main-file
     IF not-in-main-file THEN DO
          display 'This entrant is not in the main file'
     ELSE DO
          read-main-file
          write-to-racefile
          no-of-records = no-of-records + 1
     ENDIF
     display 'Any more?'
     get answer
     IF answer = 'N' THEN DO
          more-entries = FALSE
     ENDIF
ENDWHILE
write-header-rec
close-file
END add-records
```

A number of points emerge from inspection of this procedure. First, it is longer than the others but it retains readability. However, were it to become much longer there would be a danger that it would become difficult to follow; and so some of the text (for instance, that enclosed by the second WHILE-ENDWHILE) would need specifying as a procedure itself. Again, this depends on the judgement of the designer.

Note the use of the header record in the racefile. Since records may be added at any time, it is necessary to know where the last one was written and so a count of records is kept in the first record of the file. This is set to zero when the file is created and is incremented every time a record is added.

Another matter is the fact that in the first WHILE-ENDWHILE there is no way out of the program if the user is unable to find a valid file number. The code needs modifying to allow this path. It is achievable in a number of ways; they are left as an exercise.

Note also that this piece of text will be required in all of the options which require the file number to be verified and so will be put into a procedure, verify-number.

Aspects such as this last one should be discovered by examining the paths through the program. Testing all of the possible combinations of data is an essential feature of design and a methodical approach is essential to ensure that such occurrences, however unlikely, can be corrected without leaving the user stranded.

4.5.5 Commentary

This procedure is a fairly complicated one since it requires screen-handling as well as fast file access. In the user's specification, it states that the system must be proved against power failure. In other words, if the power supply is accidentally lost, the loss of data should be no more than the last ET and TS entered. This means that every time the race position on the screen is updated, the data must be written back to the racefile *which must then be closed and reopened* immediately. This is because on the installation on which the system is implemented, a file write statement does not cause an actual transfer of data to the disc until either the file buffer is full or the file is closed. Since you cannot be sure that the buffer is full, it is necessary to close and open the file to force a disc write to occur.

This is an example of the interdependence of design and implementation. If, for example, the software were intended for a system in which a file write operation did exactly what it said, then the facility would be unnecessary. The moral is that the more data you can obtain early in the design the better.

Figure 4.2 also shows how the menu is provided for the commentary program. At the end of section 4.5.1 we enumerated the options required and it is obvious that there is no room to list them vertically. Also, to clear the screen in order to display the menu is not permissible because it would take too long to redraw it. The solution is to put the menu along the bottom of the screen.

Instead of numbering the menu options, the operations offered are listed with a key letter in bold upper case and the user selects the option required by means of this letter. Again, the CASE can be used.

Options L and R allow display of car and driver details in either the left- or right-hand lane. If the user returns one of these options, the cursor will move to NO and the user will type the car number. This will access both the racefile (to find the current times for today's meeting) and also the main-file (to display the details of the car and driver).

Option T means that a car has just completed a run, in which case the cursor will again move to NO and then to ET and TS for the input of the time and speed. After a T entry is made, the racefile is sorted (using a linked-list sort) and the updated race position is shown on the lower half of the screen. Next the data is written back to the racefile and the file is closed and reopened as described above.

Option A allows amendment to previously entered data. It will be obvious that if a driver's second run is slower than his first was, then it will not appear in the list since it does not improve his position. Or, put another way, option T does not allow input of a worse time. Consequently, if an erroneous fast time were entered it could not be overwritten using the T option, so the A option allows such an overwrite.

Option C allows a change of racefile. When it is used, the screen is cleared for the user to supply the new race number after which the screen is repainted.

Option X exits to the main menu.

PROCEDURE commentary

```
paint screen
valid = FALSE
WHILE NOT valid DO
    verify-number
ENDWHILE
processing = TRUE
WHILE processing DO
    get option
    IF option = 'L' OR option = 'R' THEN DO
        display-racer
    ELSE IF option = 'A' THEN DO
            amend-timings
        ELSE IF option = 'T' THEN DO
                enter-timings
            ELSE IF option = 'C' THEN DO
                    change-files
                ELSE IF option = 'X' THEN DO
                        processing = FALSE
                    ENDIF
                ENDIF
            ENDIF
        ENDIF
    ENDIF
ENDWHILE
END commentary
```

This structure has too many nested IFs. It would obviously be better to use a CASE construct. This is left as an exercise.

This is as far as we will go with this study. There is enough description of the problem for the reader to take the refinements further and deal with, for example, check-index, enter-timings and so on.

4.5.6 Summary

Using structured English and pseudocode allows a design to be developed from the top downwards in a methodical and ordered manner. The techniques allow the software to be built from small sections of code, the logic of each one being easy to follow. If the stepwise refinement is carried out properly, the final transition into an implementation language is relatively easy and results in source text which is also easy to read, understand and maintain.

4.6 Exercises

1 Refine the driving-to-work algorithm to include stopping for petrol, having to follow a diversion and any other procedures you might think appropriate. At which level does this example cease to be of use and why?
2 Code the linked-list insert algorithm firstly in Pascal and then in COBOL. What effects do the language characteristics have on the ease of transition from the pseudocode?
3 For the car racing case, carry out the tasks below. Make any reasonable assumptions necessary.

(a) Modify the procedure add-records to allow the user a way out if he does not remember any valid file number.
(b) Rewrite the procedure commentary using the CASE statement.
(c) Continue the refinement to the level of check-index and enter-timings.
(d) Implement the Amend option. Remember that you have very little spare room on the screen and you do not want to erase the display. The option must allow you to overwrite an ET, a TS or both for a competitor.

CHAPTER 5

Structured programming

5.1 The relationship between program structure and data structure

The techniques introduced in Chapter 4 were based upon the premise of methodical design of software starting from the top—a top–down strategy. The software produced from such an approach consists of components which go together in a tree structure which shows the whole of the system and the relationships within it.

The process of stepwise refinement allows the construction of the software in manageable pieces and assists the designer in devising and carrying out meaningful testing on the finished product.

The examples chosen in Chapter 4 were ones with relatively little data. Although the main file in the car racing example could conceivably contain several thousand records, the program design needed to pay little attention to the existing structure of the data since there was no restriction on how that data might be stored. Data structuring was not a restriction on the design of the software since the form of both the input and the output could be modified as required.

In this chapter we will briefly summarise a technique which bases the program structure on the data structure. The technique is named after its originator and is known as Jackson Structured Programming or, more familiarly, as JSP.

5.2 Jackson Structured Programming

A detailed treatment of this topic will be found in Naylor (for which, see the bibliography). In this chapter we examine the technique and compare it with the methods discussed in Chapter 4.

The stages of JSP are as follows:

(1) Construct input and output data structure diagrams. Depending upon the nature of the software which is being produced, this stage might allow the designer complete freedom of choice or, if, say, some new processing is required for an existing system, there might be considerable restriction on the possible courses of action.
(2) Superimpose the input and output data structures and examine the points of correspondence between them to produce the program structure.
(3) Allocate meaningful names to the components of the structure and specify the processing conditions. For example, 'at end of file' or 'until no more departments'.
(4) List all of the detailed actions in the program and allocate them to the appropriate program components.
(5) Convert the program to schematic logic. This is an idiosyncratic technique which is used in JSP. It will be seen to be similar to structured English or pseudocode except for the use of particular keywords. This step is not essential, in that it is possible to convert from stage (4) directly to the implementation language. However, with the increasing use of so-called JSP pre-processors (see Chapter 6) it is possible to use the schematic logic itself as the source and have the program automatically generated. So, in the interests of completeness, the schematic logic phase will be described below.
(6) Implement the program and test it. As stated above, the conversion to the implementation language may be either a manual or an automatic process.

We will see as the chapter develops that there are characteristics of the technique which resemble those discussed earlier. For example, the tree structure will appear; as we break down the system into its components, the level of detail increases; the implementation of components lends itself to the use of procedures. The conclusion is that there are some fundamentals in a methodical approach to software which are common to all methods.

5.3 Phase 1—data structure diagrams

Data structures, no matter how complex, can be represented graphically by means of the same three basic constructs as were discussed earlier, namely: sequence, selection and iteration. The three are illustrated in Figures 5.1, 5.2 and 5.3.

5.3.1 Sequence

Figure 5.1 means that A consists of B followed by C followed by D. Using COBOL as an example, the DATA DIVISION entry might be:

```
01 A.
    05 B PIC XX.
    05 C PIC 9(5).
    05 D PIC X(8).
```

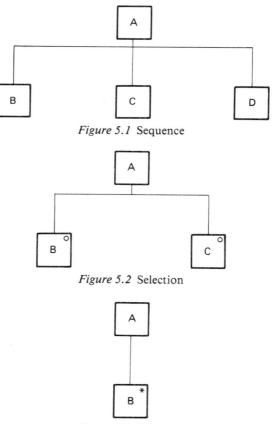

Figure 5.1 Sequence

Figure 5.2 Selection

Figure 5.3 Iteration

5.3.2 Selection

This means that A consists of either B or C. The COBOL DATA DIVISION entry to illustrate this might be:

01 A.
    05 B PIC XX.
    05 C REDEFINES B PIC 99.

5.3.3 Iteration

This means that A consists of a number (as yet unspecified) of Bs. It can be demonstrated in COBOL with the entry:

01 A.
    05 B PIC XX OCCURS 10.

These three structures are all that are required to specify any data structure. Figure 5.4 shows the structure of a serial file containing records of sales for a company. The company is made up of a number of departments and the file is organised in sequence of department.

Consider now how these data might be processed. Suppose that the requirement is for a program which produces a listing of all the sales records

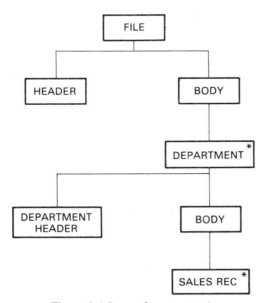

Figure 5.4 Input data structure

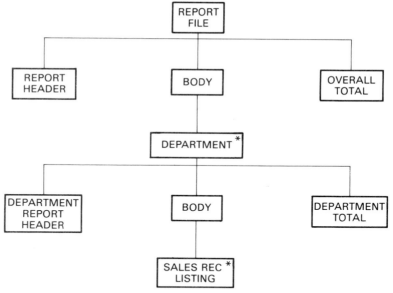

Figure 5.5 Output data structure

together with departmental totals and a total for the whole company. The data structure for this is shown in Figure 5.5.

We will return to this later. The next matter to consider is the constructs used in specifying program structure.

5.4 Program structure diagrams

The ideas introduced by Figures 5.1, 5.2 and 5.3 still apply. Their similar use for specifying program structure is shown by demonstrating the equivalent COBOL text for each one.

5.4.1 Sequence

A-PARA.
    PERFORM B-PARA.
    PERFORM C-PARA.
    PERFORM D-PARA.

The statements within A-PARA need not be PERFORM statements; they may be any executable COBOL statements. The implication of the PER-FORMs is that the nesting may continue to any depth required.

5.4.2 Selection

A-PARA.
    IF CONDITION1 THEN PERFORM B-PARA
    ELSE PERFORM C-PARA.

Note that this construct can also be nested. As stated in Chapter 4, nesting of IF constructs should be used sparingly because the eventual code used at the implementation stage might otherwise become difficult to follow. For example:

A-PARA.
    IF CONDITION1 THEN PERFORM B-PARA
    ELSE IF CONDITION2 THEN PERFORM C-PARA
        ELSE IF CONDITION3 THEN PERFORM D-PARA.

Complexity of this level of nesting is possibly acceptable but further indulgence should be resisted.

5.4.3 Iteration

A-PARA.
    PERFORM B-PARA VARYING VARIABLE1 FROM 1 BY 1
    UNTIL VARIABLE1 IS GREATER THAN VARIABLE2.

We can now examine how the input and output data structures are combined to produce the program structure.

5.5 Phase 2—superimposing the data structures

This process is carried out by locating corresponding items in the two diagrams. The diagrams are placed side by side and each component in the input diagram is compared with the output diagram. Correspondences are marked on the composite diagram. For a correspondence to be valid, program components must contain the same number of data components and the sequences in the two diagrams must correspond as well.

It should be noted that any component in each diagram may correspond to either one component or none in the other diagram. A corollary of this is that when the program structure diagram is drawn it must be possible to extract from it two configurations of components each of which maps exactly on to one of the two data structures. The combining of Figures 5.4 and 5.5 is shown in Figure 5.6 and the resulting program structure is seen in Fig. 5.7 which shows each component with its input and output.

Inspection of Figure 5.6 shows that there are five places where there is correspondence. Where the correspondence is between two components

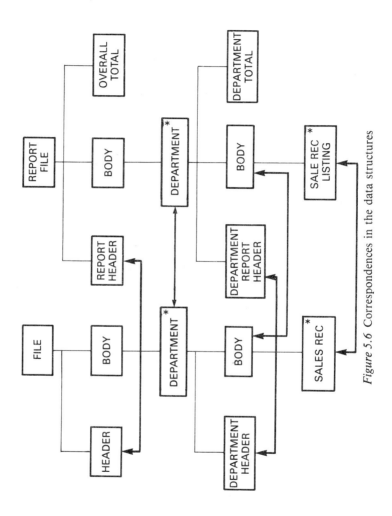

Figure 5.6 Correspondences in the data structures

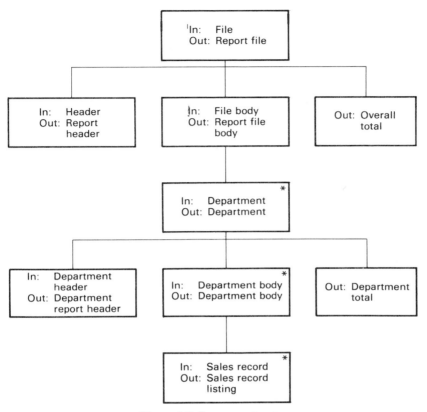

Figure 5.7 Program structure

which are iterative, it will be seen that the number of occurrences of the data item in question is the same in the two corresponding components. It will also be seen that by taking the appropriate subsets of the components of Fig. 5.7, the structure of the two original data structures can be reproduced.

5.6 Phase 3—allocating component names

The program structure can now be derived and we can redraw the diagram allocating names to the components. At the same time, the conditions which control the iterations can be inserted. The resulting structure is shown in Figure 5.8.

Assuming that the implementation language is to be COBOL, the names given to the components in this diagram can be the basis of the paragraph or section names in the source code. The names will also be used later in the schematic logic specification.

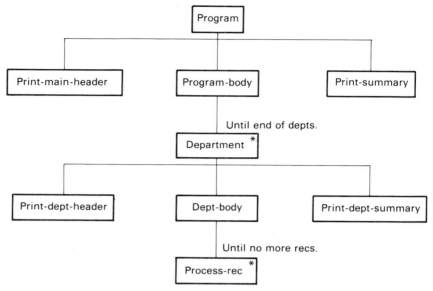

Figure 5.8 Program structure

Note that the order of these processes is central to the operation. The program structure must be derived from the data structures. Any temptation to reverse the order must be resisted.

5.7 Phase 4—listing the program actions

The action list or function list is a numbered list of all of the detail processes needed to carry out the processing as specified in the program structure diagram. In preparing such a list it is not important that we place the items in any particular order; the only important matter is that we omit nothing from the list.

The actions required for the program structure described in Figure 5.8 are as follows:

(1) Open files
(2) Close files
(3) Read a record
(4) Write a departmental header record
(5) Write the overall header record
(6) Write a sales record
(7) Write the overall total
(8) Write the departmental total
(9) Initialise departmental total

(10) Initialise overall total
(11) Increment overall total
(12) Increment departmental total
(13) Stop program

The next step is to allocate these actions to the components of the program. A number of points should be noted.

(1) The actions of opening and closing files and of stopping the program do not strictly belong in any of the components because they do not map on to any part of the data structure. In Figure 5.9, these actions are accommodated in the new components, initialise and terminate.
(2) In any processing of serial files it is normal practice to start the reading of the file outside the main body of the loop. It will be seen that action 3 appears both in the innermost loop and in the initialising component. This is the 'read-ahead' phenomenon; it is amplified in section 5.9 below.

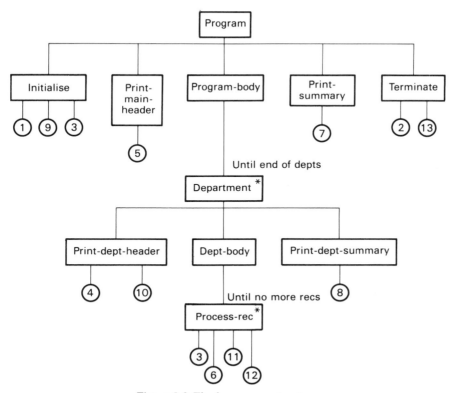

Figure 5.9 Final program structure

5.8 Phase 5—schematic logic

This phase can be described simply as an alternative form of the structured English discussed in Chapter 4. It uses a specialised notation but apart from this its only difference from structured English is that it does not have the CASE construct. The three basic constructs again are sequence, selection and iteration. Note that the component name always appears more than once within its section of text. The notation is as follows.

5.8.1 Sequence

component-name seq

:

  ⟨statements⟩

:

component-name end

5.8.2 Selection

component-name sel if condition1

:

  ⟨statements⟩

:

component-name or if condition2

:

  ⟨statements⟩

:

component-name end

5.8.3 Iteration

component-name iter while condition

:

  ⟨statements⟩

:

component-name end

5.8.4 General notes

(1)   The underlined words are the keywords in the technique.
(2)   The 'while condition' may be replaced with 'until condition'.
(3)   Many people feel that it is less pleasant to read than structured English. This is, of course, a matter of taste. There appears no reason why structured English could not be used for this phase of the design.

The next step is to represent Figure 5.9 in schematic logic. This is shown below:

```
PROGRAM seq
    Open files
    Read a record from the input file
    Initialise overall total
    Write the main header
    PROGRAM-BODY iter until no more departments
        Initialise departmental total
        Write the departmental header
        DEPT-BODY iter until no more sales records
            Write a record to the report
            Increment departmental total
            Increment overall total
            Read a record from the input file
        DEPT-BODY end
        Write departmental total
    PROGRAM-BODY end
    Write overall total
    Close files
    Stop program
PROGRAM end
```

This structure is well-suited to translation into COBOL; and in fact most, if not all, JSP pre-processors produce actual COBOL code which is then presented to the COBOL compiler. As was the case when we were considering structured English, this method leads directly to the use of procedures—or subroutines—when the amount of text within a program block starts to become difficult to follow.

5.9 Read ahead

This aspect of processing was mentioned earlier in this chapter and was also implicit in the linked-list sort treated in Chapter 4. It is concerned with the condition of a program on entry to a loop.

Using COBOL as a vehicle for explanation, the COBOL construct 'READ file AT END ...' means that the end of file condition is automatically trapped. As a consequence, if the program is running with a null data set (that is, when the program starts, the input file is empty), the action to be taken by the program is probably (if not invariably) different from that which is required when the end of a normal data set is reached. Putting a read ahead into the program allows this to be trapped.

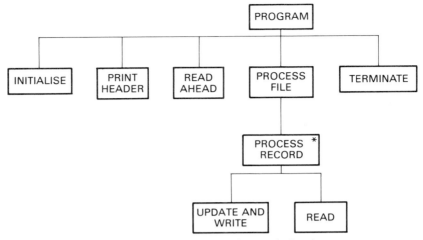

Figure 5.10 Program using read ahead

If there is not a null data set, the loop is entered with the first record already available. Therefore the loop will contain the processing first, and the last action within the loop will be the next read operation. Figure 5.10 shows a simple example. The schematic logic for this is as follows:

PROGRAM seq
    Initialise
    Write header
    Read input file
    PROCESS-FILE iter until OF
        PROCESS-REC seq
            Update and write record
            Read input file
        PROCESS-REC end
    PROCESS-FILE end
    Close files
    Stop program
PROGRAM end

It will be seen that this is the method which appears in the schematic logic for Figure 5.9. Coding the read ahead into COBOL might produce the statement:

READ INPUT-FILE AT END
    DISPLAY 'EMPTY FILE'
    STOP RUN.

5.10 Limitations of JSP; problems of structure clash

JSP is based on the structure of the data. It follows, therefore, that if the input and output data structures are not naturally in a form that provides the correspondences needed to derive the program structure, there will be difficulty in arriving at the form needed to produce the program.

The phenomenon which gives rise to the problem is called structure clash.

5.10.1 Forms of structure clash

When we introduced the idea of correspondence between input and output data structures, it was stated that it is essential that there be both the same sequence and the same number of occurrences of data component between corresponding items. If either of these conditions is not met, then it is defined as a structure clash; if the sequence is at fault, it is called an order clash; and if the number of occurrences of the data item is at fault, it is called a boundary clash. These two cases will now be examined.

5.10.2 Order clash

Figure 5.11 shows the input and output data structures for a system. The input is from a serial file which contains records which may be of either type A or type B; they are filed in random order. The output required is a listing of type A records followed by type B records.

Although there are the same number of records in the input and output files, the order is different; and a correspondence cannot be drawn between the type A records or the type B records in the two structures.

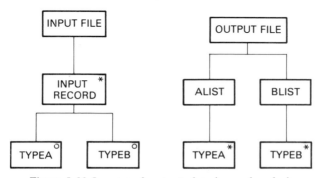

Figure 5.11 Input and output showing order clash

A number of options are presented:

(1) The input file can be processed twice, the first run producing the type A records for output and the second producing the type B.
(2) The input file can be sorted using the record type as the primary key. It can then be processed once to produce the required listing.
(3) The whole input file can be read into RAM and accessed directly.

Option 3 can be rejected on the grounds of memory size (although this is changing as time passes and RAM sizes increase). We are left therefore with the first two options.

There are arguments in favour of both alternatives. Option (1) is probably quicker since it requires only the two runs through the data set. Sorting the file, as required by option (2), will almost certainly take more time than would be required by the second pass through the file.

However, which of the options is chosen is, in fact, of secondary relevance to this discussion. What is important is that the problem of order clash can be resolved without too much difficulty. Assuming that the option of sorting the file is chosen, Figure 5.12 shows the procedure for resolving the order clash. This method of approach is often used in systems which find sorting particularly easy because it is done by a prewritten utility program (as in MSDOS) or is part of the implementation (as in COBOL).

Figure 5.12 Resolution of order clash

5.10.3 Boundary clash

To illustrate the problem of boundary clash, consider the following system.

A company holds a file of orders, each of which may contain a number of items, which may range from one or two up to several hundred.

Orders are held in a serial file. Each order consists of a record containing customer details followed by a second record holding up to 75 ordered pairs of item codes and quantities ordered, as below:

Bytesmith, 52,High St,Ilford
0123,24,0432,4,9874,45,8234,6,0654,27...

A report is required which lists the orders in detail; that is, lists of all the items on all of the orders in an expanded form giving the item description, unit cost and item cost. (The description and unit cost are looked up in a direct access file.) A typical section of the report would look as follows:

Bytesmith 52 High St Ilford

0123	Floppy disk	24	1.25	30.00
0432	PC Clone 1 mb RAM	4	299.50	1198.00
9874	Syllablestar	45	99.99	4499.55
8234	Printer ribbon	6	15.00	90.00

Since there are several hundred orders to be processed at any time and since many of them are short, it is decided not to print them one to a page but to fill each page, giving the customer total at the end of each order and the running total at the end of each page. The report will also have a header giving the date of the run and a summary giving the total number of orders processed, the total number of items and the total value. The input and output data structures are shown in Figure 5.13.

This problem requires some careful attention.

The next action is to look for correspondences between the input and output data structures. Well, we have the repeated component, item, in both structures and, obviously, there will be the same number of items in the input as in the output.

But the rules for correspondence in section 5.5 say that the number of occurrences of a sub-component within a component must be the same throughout the structure; and here we come to a difficulty.

The difficulty arises from the fact that in the input structure the component, item, occurs within the item record while in the output structure it occurs within line. Since item body can contain any number of item records, we are faced with the fact that we have different numbers of occurrences in the two structures. This is known as a boundary clash.

There is no possibility of altering the data structures because there is no fixed ratio of orders per page or pages per order. That is, there may be several orders on a page or an order may occupy several pages.

The solution to the clash is similar to that used for the order clash; similar, that is, in the use of an intermediate file. It is necessary to provide an intermediate structure which will correspond to both the input and output data structures.

To decide how to go about this, it is necessary to choose which component of the data is the one for which the correspondence should be sought. A convenient item to pick is the line of output which corresponds to either

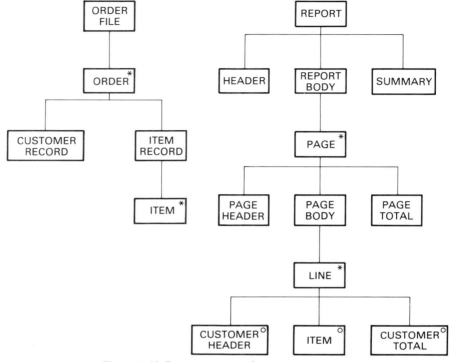

Figure 5.13 Data structures for report program

an order header or an item in the input. The intermediate file will therefore consist of records which are either order headers or order items.

Once the intermediate file has been constructed, it can be used in two programs, one to convert data from the input structure to the intermediate structure and the other to convert from the intermediate to the output. It follows that the structure of the intermediate file will appear different to the two programs. This is illustrated in Figure 5.14.

This file gives correspondence between both the input and output data structures, and the boundary clash is thus resolved. The correspondences are shown in Figures 5.15 and 5.16.

It should be noted once again that an alternative solution to the boundary clash problem is to read the whole of the input file into main memory and then to process it as a simple text file. We are still assuming that such a process is not feasible, the file size prohibiting the loading of it all at once. However, as mentioned earlier, the rapid and continuing growth of memory sizes available on modern systems is such that a solution which reads a whole file becomes less and less unreasonable. As the size of RAM moves inexorably into the multi-megabyte range—already common on the so-

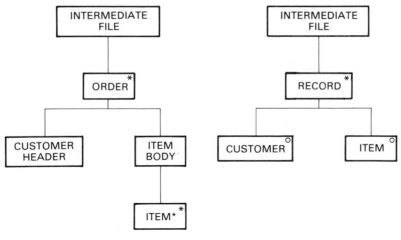

(a) As viewed by input program   (b) As viewed by output program

Figure 5.14 Intermediate file

called super-minis, let alone the mainframe systems—so the size which can be accommodated will increase. It is unlikely that we will see for a long time, if ever, the largest files being accommodated in this way but, as a solution to the problems involving medium-sized files, it begins to approach feasibility.

Now that the correspondences for the two pairs of data structures can be

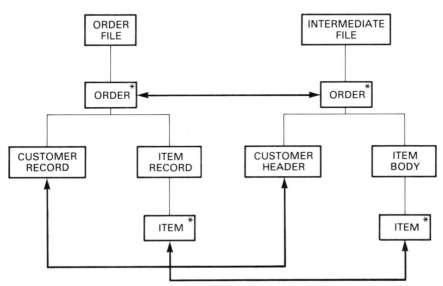

Figure 5.15 Correspondence between input and intermediate files

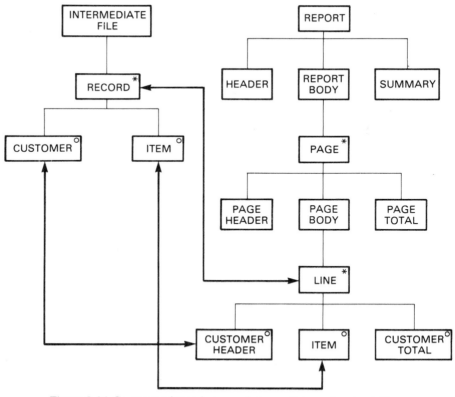

Figure 5.16 Correspondence between intermediate and output files

drawn (that is, between the input and the intermediate data structures and between the intermediate and output data structures), the problem is solved.

We may now draw two program structures by combining the pairs of data structures and can complete the process with the action lists and the schematic logic.

These activities are left as an exercise. The important aspect of this part of the treatment of the topic is to indicate that the apparent obstacles to the application of the method can be overcome.

In fact, it is unnecessary to implement the two programs as separate processes and they can be combined by means of a technique called program inversion which is omitted here for reasons of space. For further explanation, see Naylor (listed in the bibliography).

5.11 JSP compared with stepwise refinement

Designing any general-purpose facility is always difficult and not only within the area of computer programming. A mechanic's toolbox contains spanners, pliers, screwdrivers, files, saws and so on because to combine all of these functions into a single multi-purpose gadget would be to produce a device which would be of nightmare complexity and low efficiency at all of the tasks it was built to perform. To carry the allegory further, the reason for carrying a large set of spanners rather than using a single adjustable one is that a spanner made to fit one size of nut works more efficiently.

So it is with programming tools. There are some classes of problem better served by some methods than others. JSP is particularly well suited to processing large files, almost invariably in batch mode, and is less well suited to the type of example which we discussed in Chapter 4. Indeed, JSP originated and was really designed to deal with the large-throughput programs such as payrolls, invoicing, stock control, accounting and so on.

In comparing JSP with the method of stepwise refinement discussed in Chapter 4, a number of points should be noted.

(1)   Stepwise refinement is clearly a method of top–down design. In the example in Chapter 4, the design was developed by setting out the top-level menu and successively introducing more and more detail at the lower levels. A significant advantage of such a process is that to a large extent it mirrors the process of systems analysis in which the user's requirements are elicited in increasing detail. The process allows the use of prototyping (see Chapter 6) to demonstrate intermediate levels of the final program and also easy division of the design of components of the software among a number of people.

(2)   JSP is not simply a top–down approach. The fact that it is—in the words of its originator—data-driven means that the solution does not evolve only from the top. The action list is compiled from the most detailed actions within the program and this part, at least, of the design is bottom–up.

(3)   A point often made in favour of JSP is that it removes the 'inspirational requirement' from program design. The implication is that in using stepwise refinement the designer is required to see the way to the solution intuitively while the user of JSP is provided with a more mechanistic method of achieving the solution.

A counter-argument is that JSP is more difficult to use. This is, of course, a contentious statement but it is founded upon the fact that undoubtedly there is a rigour in its application which many people find daunting. There is often the cry that 'Before I heard of JSP I could have written this program in ten minutes and now I don't know where to start'. The example in section 5.10 is perhaps a good example of this phenomenon. The answer to this last criticism is found in the fact that, when properly applied, JSP produces good software which stands up to intense scrutiny. Further, it is found that there is more consistency among the solutions offered by different people to a particular problem; that is, the technique leads to a standardisation of solutions and thence to greater ease of understanding and portability of the software. As in many instances, nothing is achieved without sacrifice.

5.12 Conclusion

Chapters 4 and 5 have briefly outlined some methods of program design. The characteristics common to both chapters have been that the designer requires a methodical approach and an implementation language in which to code the program. A feature of JSP, however, which moves us on is its use as a basis for automatic code generation and this, in turn, leads to a general discussion of very high-level—or fourth-generation—languages in Chapter 6.

5.13 Exercises

1 For the example in section 5.10.3:

    (a) Draw the program structure for writing from the input to the intermediate file.

    (b) Draw the program structure for producing the report from the intermediate file.

    (c) Draw up the action lists and the schematic logic for both programs.

2 Investigate the process of program inversion and rework the problem. How much of the processing carried out in exercise 1 remains applicable?

CHAPTER 6

Fourth-generation languages

6.1 Definitions □ 6.2 Background and characteristics □ 6.3 Query languages □ 6.4 Prototyping □ 6.5 Other types of 4GL and other uses of the term □ 6.6 Summary □ 6.7 Exercises

6.1 Definitions

The term 'fourth-generation language' entered common—or, at least, occasional—use in about 1980. It had, in fact, been in use before then but it is really since that date that the expression and its contraction, 4GL, has gained popularity. Unfortunately it has been probably the most abused in all of computing terminology (with the possible exception of another vague expression, 'information technology').

The term 4GL has been used with immense licence. It has been used to enhance the credibility of idiosyncratic languages, the sales of enfeebled textbooks and the attendance at colloquia of dubious utility. In short, it has become a buzzword of an heroic stature.

In order to approach the subject in a logical and ordered manner, a working definition of a 4GL is proposed as follows:

A 4GL is a member of the next generation of programming languages which will make communication with the machine easier, will allow quicker production of reliable software and will generally improve the way in which computers serve people.

Although idiosyncratic, this definition has the advantage of providing objectives for the design of a 4GL and also of eliminating the use of the term to describe such current products as Unix, C and MSDOS. All of these are examples of excellent third-generation software but none of them comes into our definition of a 4GL.

A further advantage of such a definition is that, as we will see later, it does not force us into a situation where all 4GLs have to be similar in the applications for which they are written. We will examine a number of types of 4GL which differ considerably in appearance and operation but still meet the definition given above.

6.2 Background and characteristics

6.2.1 Specification of a 4GL

Having provided a definition, we need to see what the product will look like and how it will work. This is effectively a design problem and we therefore need a specification in more detail. In order to arrive at this, it is necessary to look at the development of programming languages during the time from the advent of the digital computer to the present day.

6.2.2 The first three generations

The instructions which drive a digital computer must, at the lowest level, be a series of signals which operate the circuits forming the processor. Consequently, the first programming languages consisted of numeric codes which represented the operations to be carried out and also indicated the addresses of the operands. For example, to add the contents of address 345 to the contents of 346 and to put the result in 347 you might have code as follows:

```
23 345
26 346
32 347
```

These instructions each consist of an operation and an address. So the codes 23, 26 and 32 might respectively mean 'load the accumulator', 'add to the accumulator' and 'store from the accumulator'. Such a language represents a typical first-generation programming language.

The next step was to make the language easier for the programmer to remember. Mnemonic assembly languages were devised and in these the operations and the addresses were replaced by mnemonics and operand names respectively. The code for the instructions above would then be something like:

```
LD A
A  B
ST C
```

In this second-generation language (2GL), the mnemonics LD, A and ST represent load, add and store and the operands are A, B and C.

Second-generation languages are, of course, still used in the form of modern assemblers. This class of languages includes variations such as two- and three-address instructions.

The third-generation languages (3GL) comprise the class collectively known as high-level languages and include COBOL, FORTRAN, BASIC, Pascal, C and so on. The code shown above becomes a single instruction in a high-level language; for instance, in Pascal:

A : = B + C;

An important characteristic of a third-generation language is that the translator used to turn it into machine instructions—the compiler, that is— has to analyse the syntax of each statement in order to break it down into instructions elementary enough to produce code which is executable by the processor. It is the increasing complexity of the translation processes which separate the generations; from the machine code, which needs no trans- lation to speak of, to the mnemonic assembly language which needs an assembler to translate the mnemonics; from the assembler to the high- level language compiler which has to examine the syntax and extract the semantics from often lengthy statements. These are the mileposts along the road towards the fourth generation.

6.2.3 Characteristics of 4GLs

4GLs are also sometimes referred to as very high-level languages (VHLLs). This follows from the progression described above and indicates that we expect such a language to possess characteristics which distinguish it from a 3GL in a manner similar to the way in which a 3GL differs from a 2GL.

Before looking at the specific characteristics of a 4GL, therefore, there are some fundamentals which extrapolation suggests must be inherited from the third generation.

We will begin the specification with these points.

(1) The language must be well structured.
(2) It must be easily understood by other users and allow easy modification.
(3) It must be easy to debug.
(4) It must be self-documenting.

Next, consider the succinctness of the code. In the example in section 6.2.1 above, the difference between the assembly language and the Pascal is not very great; but the Pascal certainly is shorter. Look now at the following Pascal code and imagine it rewritten in an assembly language; clearly, the difference in length of code would be much greater.

```
WHILE not eof(master-file) DO
BEGIN
    read(master-file,master-record);
    IF (age > 30) AND (grade > 4) THEN
        writeln(name, address)
END;
```

We can now use further extrapolation to deduce some other characteristics of what we might expect to see in a 4GL:

(5) The code must generally be significantly more compact than that needed in a high-level language.
(6) The code must be easier to understand than a high-level language. (This follows from the observation that high-level language code is easier to understand than assembly language code.)

As a result of even this brief list of requirements, we can suggest how the 4GL code equivalent to the Pascal above might appear:

List names and addresses of all employees over 30
with grades greater than 4.

Or, perhaps:

Find all employees who are over 30 and have grades
over 4. List their names and addresses.

This might be ambitious; it requires the translator to have the ability to make decisions, to deal with varied syntax and to make assumptions about how the user wants the data presented. We will not worry about whether or not the requirements are ambitious. Add them to the list.

(7) The language must be as close to a natural language as possible.
(8) It must be able to decide about output formatting without being told any more than the user chooses to tell it.

Some other points might be inferred simply from thinking about how easy we would like programming to be.

(9) It should be usable by non-specialists.

This is an interesting assertion. There is no doubt that as the spread of computers to non-specialists increases it will not be feasible (nor, perhaps, desirable) that only specialists design software. The analogy has been drawn with car driving: in that in the early days of motoring the driving of a car required a specialist; but as the technology spread, everybody started doing it. (Admittedly, not everybody does it well, but analogies are there to learn from.)

It is not always remembered that one of the original intentions of the designers of COBOL was that the language was to be used by the non-specialist; that is, the manager of a business would sit in her office and interrogate the database by writing COBOL code—in detail—and so obtain the data she required. This was too ambitious for the language; it was too complex and insufficiently user-friendly.

However, the state of the art has progressed to the extent that 4GLs can go a long way towards achieving this requirement so perceptively stated at a relatively early stage in the development of the industry.

We will add to the list:

(10) It must be user-friendly.

This ten-part specification will do for a start. It is not meant to be exhaustive nor is it implied that all the points must be apparent in any one 4GL. We will be flexible enough to accept as a 4GL one which contains a significant number of these points as long as it meets the definition given earlier. Above all, it must be remembered that we are concerned here with how the language suits the people using it. There is no consideration of the machine in the definition or in the specification.

Indeed, it is likely that code produced by a 4GL will be less efficient than that produced by a 3GL (as is usual when the 3GL is compared to a 2GL). The problem of efficiency of the language is a secondary one: by far the overriding aspect is its ease of use to the user.

6.2.4 Further considerations—procedural and non-procedural languages

From the inception of computing there have existed the alternative approaches of these two types of language. Both types have been in existence since the third generation and, although the procedural languages have been in the majority, the 4GLs are more likely to be non-procedural than not.

The difference between the two types is summarised in the statement that a procedural language specifies the way in which a process has to be carried out, while a non-procedural one specifies what is to be achieved but not how to achieve it. The latter is also known as a goal-driven language.

A simple example illustrates the difference:

(1) Procedural:
Drive to the T junction.
Turn left and drive to the traffic lights.
Turn right at the lights, take the left lane and enter the tunnel.
Pay the toll at the end, and filter right on to the motorway.
(With much more to follow.)
(2) Non-procedural:
Drive to Birmingham.

This illustrates a number of the points listed in the specification above.

(1) The non-procedural version is certainly brief.
(2) It approaches the form of a natural language.
(3) It appears usable by a non-specialist.
(4) It is easy to understand.
(5) It is user-friendly.

Two points must be mentioned here. First, this is a simplified example, but it does serve to illustrate that non-procedural text is of immense use in meeting the specification of a 4GL. As will be shown later in this chapter, 4GLs make considerable use of the non-procedural approach.

The second point is that the term 'non-procedural' is a relative one. The boundary between the two types is both fuzzy and arbitrary. For example, a COBOL statement such as:

SORT A-FILE ON ASCENDING KEY A-NAME
USING B-FILE
GIVING C-FILE.

does not give much indication about how the sorting will take place and compared with, say, an assembly language, it could well be defined as non-procedural. However, COBOL is generally considered to be a procedural language. So it is necessary to be careful with the use of the terms.

6.2.5 The effects on software design and production

4GLs have a very significant effect on the production of software when they are used by specialists. Commonly quoted figures for the production of COBOL code by professional programmers state that 10–20 lines of proven code per day is a usual level of achievement. The corresponding figures independently reported for 4GL query languages such as Natural and SQL are five to ten times higher.

A recent survey of the impact of 4GLs reports some interesting and illuminating anecdotes. Under pressure, complete rewrites have been undertaken using 4GLs:

(1) A firm had reduced its capacity and workforce several times in response to a general decline in the market. All efforts to cut back the data processing department had failed, however, and the computer costs were approaching those of the reduced production departments. It was decided to close the department and start again.

A powerful minicomputer was installed and a 4GL was purchased. All of the systems were rewritten in the new language in a total of 15 programmer years. The original COBOL system had taken 75 programmer years.

There are cases to show that the effect on the programming backlog is very beneficial:

(2) A county council had accumulated a programming backlog amounting to 55 programmer years. Further, the pending work was mostly in the form of software required to maintain the existing system; that is, even when (and if) it was written the organisation would have done little more than hold its position. They decided to stop using PL/1 and adopt a 4GL. The effect was in fact to increase the backlog but its nature changed. Within a year the maintenance work was completed and this resulted in increased requests for new systems to improve the operation of the organisation. The users' previous dissatisfaction was replaced by enthusiasm for the computer when they found their requests for new software being satisfied quickly.

The third example is quoted from the data processing manager of the county council concerned:

(3) 'There is a Parkinson effect from all innovation. Every improvement we've ever made in programmer productivity has provided users with the opportunity to *increase* the backlog.

'The pre-4GL backlog was just the tip of the iceberg. Frankly, it was easy to manage. Now we have a problem. It's called user enthusiasm.

'Our original objective for 4GLs was to reduce the programming backlog. In fact it's gone up. And it's super. We're delivering so fast that user demand is now in line with corporate objectives. We're actually delivering what they want.'

It is now necessary to see how 4GLs achieve the effects on software productivity that are reported.

6.3 Query languages

A query language is one which is used for the interrogation and maintenance of a database; although it must be pointed out that the term implies a limitation which does not really exist. That is, although primarily designed for processing queries, a query language usually includes the facilities required for setting up and maintaining a database.

As far as this definition goes, any programming language can be used in this manner; COBOL, especially with its CODASYL enhancements, is used as a query language in many applications. As was mentioned earlier, it was at one time expected to be usable by the non-specialist.

Special-purpose query languages have grown with the spread of the relational database. This type of database uses a series of tables (relations) to hold the data in a normalised form. The data are then processed by forming

Machine-details		
Machine	Description	Hrly-rate
M1	Lathe	12.56
M2	Drill	14.32
M3	Mill	32.44
M4	Grinder	20.78

(a)

Job-details	
Job-no	Client
J1	Redd
J2	Greene
J3	Whyte

(b)

Hours-worked		
Machine	Job-no	Hours
M1	J1	19
M1	J2	32
M2	J1	71
M2	J1	80
M2	J3	26
M3	J1	41
M3	J2	92
M4	J1	17
M4	J3	84

(c)

Figure 6.1 Normalised data set for (a) machines, (b) jobs and (c) clients

new relations according to the user's queries. The process of normalisation is the means by which redundancy is removed and integrity is ensured in a data set. This is achieved by the removal of repeating groups from the data set and ensuring that every non-key item in a relation is directly and totally dependent on the key. The subject is treated in detail by Clare and Lucopoulos (see the bibliography).

The origins of query languages for such databases are found in the relational algebra in which set operations are carried out on the data. For example, consider the data structure in Figures 6.1 a, b and c. In this data set we have normalised relations, showing details of machines (Figure

Machine	Description
M1	Lathe
M2	Drill
M3	Mill
M4	Grinder

Figure 6.2 Projected relation

6.1 a), details of clients' payments for each job (Figure 6.1 b) and how many hours of each machine's time are chargeable to each job (Figure 6.1 c).

To operate on the data, relational operators are used and for the purpose of this explanation we will look at the two most common: the projection and the join.

Using these operations, specific data can be extracted from the database according to whatever selection criteria happen to be applied.

6.3.1 Projection

A relation consists of rows and columns. A row corresponds to a record in a file and a column holds all the values of a particular attribute (or field). A column is called a domain.

The projection operation creates a new relation (table) from an existing one. The new relation R [A,B,C] contains the domains A, B and C of relation R in the order stated, and with any resulting duplicate rows eliminated.

For example, in Figure 6.1 a, the projection,

Machine-details [Machine, Description]

gives the new relation shown in Figure 6.2 and the projection Job-details [Job-no] gives simply:

J1
J2
J3

Note also that the projection Hours-worked [Job-no] gives exactly the same result as Job-details [Job-no] because the duplicates have been eliminated.

6.3.2 Join

The join operation, [R1 * R2], produces a new relation from two relations, R1 and R2. The new relation has a domain which is common to R1 and R2. Consider the normalised relation in Figure 6.3.

Then, the join [R1 * R2] gives the relation shown in Figure 6.4.

Note that the 'joining field' is Musician and that only those attribute values appearing in that domain in both relations appear in the joined one. Williams appears four times because that value occurred twice in each joining field. The database says nothing about whether he played, say, trumpet for Ellington and cornet for Basie or vice versa, or even both instruments for one bandleader or the other. All we know is that there was the possibility that he played both instruments in each band.

R1	
Leader	Musician
Ellington	Williams
Brubeck	Desmond
Basie	Williams
Goodman	Krupa

R2	
Musician	Instrument
Williams	Trumpet
Williams	Cornet
Krupa	Drums
Hodges	Alto

Figure 6.3 Normalised data set for bandleaders, musicians and instruments

A join can also be carried out using a particular attribute value as one of the joining relations. That is, we can have a relation consisting of a single row and a single column, which means that it comprises only a single item. For example, in Figure 6.1 to find Redd's job number we can write:

[Job-details * 'Redd']

which will give:

J1 Redd

This is itself a new relation having one row. Call the new relation TEMP (see Figure 6.5).

Projecting the Job-no from TEMP gives TEMP [Job-no] which, in turn, gives J1, the required result.

Putting the two processes together and using parentheses for clarity, we arrive at our first compound query in relational algebra:

([Job-details * 'Redd'])[Job-no] → J1

R3		
Leader	Musician	Instrument
Ellington	Williams	Trumpet
Ellington	Williams	Cornet
Basie	Williams	Trumpet
Basie	Williams	Cornet
Goodman	Krupa	Drums

Figure 6.4 Relation produced by joining R1 and R2

TEMP	
Job-no	Client
J1	Redd

Figure 6.5 Joined relation using a single attribute value

It will be seen that ambiguities can arise if we have more than one common domain in the two relations being joined, and it becomes necessary to adopt a convention to identify the common domain to be used.

A convenient convention is to say that the rightmost domain of the left-hand relation is to be joined to the leftmost domain in the right-hand relation. In this way the domains do not need even to have the same name; their positions are all that matters.

If the domains are not correctly placed in the relations for this to happen, a projection is first carried out to reorder them.

For example, to find out which clients' jobs need the lathe, the processes are as follows:

(1) Find the machine number of the lathe. This requires joining the Description field of Machine-details with the value 'Lathe':

(Machine-details [Machine, Description] * 'Lathe')

Note the projection to put Description on the right-hand side of the relation to be joined.

(2) The expression in the parentheses is now a new relation. Call it TEMP1. It will contain the following:

M1 Lathe

(3) We now extract the value, M1, by projecting the Machine field:

(TEMP1 [Machine])

This consists only of the value M1. It is now joined to Hours-worked giving the relation (TEMP1 [Machine] *Hrs-worked) as shown in Figure 6.6.

(4) Project Job-no from this joined relation:

((TEMP1 [Machine] * Hours-worked) [Job-no]) → J1
                                                 J2

Machine	Job-no	Hours
M1	J1	19
M1	J2	32

Figure 6.6 Joined relation

(5) Call this TEMP2. Join it to Job-details and project Client.

(TEMP2 * Job-details)[Client] → Redd
                                 Greene

This is the answer to the original query. The complete expression, therefore, is obtained by substituting the expanded forms of TEMP1 and TEMP2:

((((Machine-details[Machine,Description] * 'Lathe')[Machine] * Hours-worked)[Job-no]) * Job-details) [Client]

6.3.3 Conditional join

The join construct can be enhanced to allow conditional operations to be included explicitly. For example, to show which machines have been used for more than 80 hours on any project, the expression might be:

((Machine-details[Description, Machine])
                    * (Hours-worked * '>80'))[Description]

Expressions in parentheses are evaluated according to the normal rules of algebra or, in other words, innermost first. This operation will lead to the result:

Mill
Grinder

It is apparent that these constructs are not user-friendly. There is a need for careful syntactic construction of the query and, even if this is done without error, the resulting expression is not easy to understand. However, the technique does demonstrate that a query can be formulated and, by inference, we may conclude that a method of processing queries in a non-procedural language can be devised. A necessity for this is that a means of syntactic and semantic analysis must be built into the software and hidden from the user. The means of analysing the natural language statements is examined in Chapter 7. Next we will look at how current 4GLs solve the problem from the user's viewpoint.

6.3.4 4GL query languages

As was stated above, most query languages are based upon the constructs of projection and join. A requirement of the language, if it is to be user-friendly, is that the constructs must be achieved transparently by the translator of the 4GL. The amount of transparency achieved is one measure of the ease of use of the language.

SQL

This is an acronym for 'Structured Query Language', a product of IBM which is designed for the manipulation of a relational database. As with most query languages, it does more than simply process queries and provides full facilities for the creation and maintenance of a database. For the purposes of this explanation, we will concentrate on the data retrieval facilities.

SQL uses a series of key-words in the formulation of queries. The resulting statements in the language approach a form of understandable English, although it is far from allowing free formulation of queries in a natural form. However, comparison with the statements using the relational algebraic form shows a considerable improvement in user-friendliness.

We will look at the last query in section 6.3.2 above, which finds which clients' jobs need the lathe. Since SQL allows the use of synonyms to reduce keystrokes, the following synonyms will be used:

Machine details → MD
Hours-worked   → HW
Job-details   → JD

The query then becomes:

Select Client from Job-details where
     JD.Job-no   = HW.Job-no
and HW.Machine   = MD.Machine
and MD.Description   = 'Lathe'

In this language the projections and joins are implicit in the query. There is a temptation to observe that you can't see the join . . .

SQL provides various standard functions: for example, to sort and display the list of clients, we could add the statements:

Order by Client.
Print.

The second example, to find which machines were used for more than 80 hours on any one project, the query is:

Select Description from Machine-details where
     MD.Machine = HW.Machine
    and HW.Hours > 80.
Order by Description.
Print.

NATURAL

This is another 4GL with facilities similar to SQL. It provides all of the functions necessary to build and maintain a database. It formulates its queries using a different syntax from SQL but the general form can be inferred if we again use one of the same two examples:

Find Machine-details with Description = 'Lathe'
Find Hours-worked with Machine = MD.Machine
Find Job-details with Job-no = HW.Job-no
        sorted by Client
Display Client.

The way this works is to scan each relation in the sequence of the statements and select those entries which satisfy the conditions. The succeeding Find statement uses only the selected data from the previous one. Thus the statements above form a single compound statement terminated by the full stop.

The action of the statement is the same, then, as those described in section 6.3.2 above.

It should be noted that generally unique field-names would be used in NATURAL, not the compound ones used here for comparison with SQL.

6.3.5 Conclusion

The two languages described in section 6.3.4 are representative of the type of powerful products currently in use. They also strongly indicate the direction in which languages must proceed in pursuit of ease of use and ease of understanding. Many other examples of 4GL query languages could be given but they all exhibit similar characteristics and so would add little to the reader's enlightenment at this stage. For an exhaustive treatment of the languages, see the bibliography.

It will be seen that the development of the 4GLs has not yet reached the stage where queries may be put in a totally free natural language form, but progress towards this state is being made.

6.4 Prototyping

Another area where 4GLs have an essential role is in the production of prototype software. Before examining the ways in which 4GLs are used it is necessary to examine the concept itself.

6.4.1 The prototyping process

In the process of system design, it is generally agreed and proven that the involvement and active participation of the user is a desirable phenomenon.

If the system designer can capture and hold the user's interest and enthusiasm for the project, there will be a better product and a more satisfactory state of affairs than otherwise would occur.

The traditional methods of systems analysis and design are inherently deficient in this regard; they tend to involve user participation at the beginning but there is then a period of time when the user might or might not be consulted on matters of detail before the product is delivered.

In many (it is to be hoped the majority of) cases the product will be satisfactory. It will fulfil its function and the user will be pleased and everyone will live happily ever after. However, in many cases this is only partially achieved and there is a period of modification during which design errors are corrected. This can be a costly process. It has been suggested that the relative costs of correcting an error are one unit at the design stage, ten at implementation and 100 at production.

The alternative approach is variously described as heuristic development, middle—out design (as opposed to top—down or bottom—up), infological simulation or, more simply, prototyping. It is a process in which, after the first level of refinement of the solution to the problem has been carried out, the designer produces a draft prototype of the software for the user to see and use. The user is then involved in the further refinements, with the production of a series of prototypes until the finished product is agreed. The process is summarised in Figure 6.7.

A particularly useful feature of the process is that it allows false starts to be made without disastrous consequences. Faults in the design are picked up when the user sees the product and, crucially, it encourages user participation; the user is identified with the system throughout its development.

Note also that the process is nowhere inconsistent with a methodical approach. The process of refining the problem still occurs. Decisions on the design of the data structures are made in the same way as in other methods. Documentation is still an essential feature of the process. So the characteristic of the method which distinguishes it from the others is the incremental approach towards the final production of the software.

A further important characteristic of prototyping is that in many cases the prototype is used on the actual data. The degree to which this is feasible will, of course, vary among applications but in some instances this process

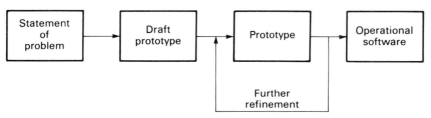

Figure 6.7 The prototyping process

assists in testing the software under stringent conditions and it also allows the user to see an early return on the investment in the project.

Care is necessary in these cases. This experimental aspect of prototyping requires monitoring to a high degree; the analogy might be drawn with a prototype airliner which will necessarily fly but will not be used to carry fare-paying passengers. From this we infer that a prototype which is being used in a system built from scratch will not usually be used as a live system; but to take the analogy further, a prototype system for packaging meals for airline passengers might well be used on them. Thus a prototype software system which is being added to an existing system and is for producing a new reporting or communications facility might well be used in a live fashion while its development cycle proceeds.

A final comment concerns the managing of a prototyping project. There is often the temptation to keep iterating to a better product. This phenomenon is not peculiar to prototyping and occurs in all sorts of application. However, prototyping, with its inherent cyclic nature, is particularly susceptible to it. Care must be taken to avoid the danger of never admitting that the product is finished.

6.4.2 Prototyping languages

When discussing query languages in section 6.3 above, we noted that many 3GLs can be used for that purpose: the same is true of prototyping. There is nothing inherent in the concept of a prototype which prescribes a 4GL to achieve it and, indeed, some forms of prototyping are carried out using Ada, APL and other 3GLs. However, if we consider the practicalities of the process and the implications in the statement used earlier, '... capture and hold the user's interest and enthusiasm ...' one fact emerges stark and incontrovertible: *the next version should be ready by tomorrow*. Prototypes are wanted quickly and this implies that the systems designer needs a language which can be used with a minimum of difficulty and which generally has the specification derived in section 6.2.3.

If, for example, a new report with range checks on data values and an intricate layout is required, the software writer does not want the bother of writing detailed data validation routines or of spending hours with a screen layout counting columns and lines to see whether the report is the right size for the display (or vice versa). What is needed is a language where all the processes are automatic and a default screen layout will be provided— enough for the user to perceive the structure of the software—and cosmetic finishing can be carried out when all else is complete.

6.4.3 Specific characteristics of 4GLs for prototyping

A number of characteristics have emerged over the period of time that 4GLs have been used for prototyping, and software designers seem to be in general agreement regarding their importance. The following list shows some of the most important:

(1) Database management (usually relational) facilities.
(2) Built-in query language.
(3) Default screen formats.
(4) Automatic validation and range-checking.
(5) Data dictionary. (This is a term which we have not used before. It refers to a structure in which all of the data names used in the software are listed together with their types, format details, description and place in the data structure. In this way the designer has quick reference to and ability to change the characteristics of any item in the system. An example is given in section 6.4.4 below.)
(6) Easy report generation.

Other characteristics are also specified (such as sorting and searching procedures, extensive help facilities, and good screen image printing) which are characteristics which lead to the easy production of working software. However, for the purposes of this discussion, we will stop at this point and look at an example.

6.4.4 Example—stock file

In this example we will look at the setting up of a stock file and the generation of a report showing the stock situation. The 4GL used is called SIMPLE and is a product of Prime INC. The system is implemented on a Prime 9955. It is driven interactively through a series of menus by means of which the user builds a database and can update it and generate reports in whatever form is required. The data dictionary is created automatically and default screen formats are supplied.

We will assume that the first level of the design has been carried out and a normalised data structure devised. The following processes will be examined:

(1) Set up a relation, STOCK, containing the following fields containing the items indicated:

STOCK-NO	(Stock number)
DESCR	(Description)
SUPPLIER	(Supplier name)
COST	(Buying-in cost)
SELL-PR	(Selling price)
QUANT	(Quantity on hand)
R-O-L	(Re-order level)

(Details of each field are shown in Figure 6.11)

(2) Insert data into each relation.
(3) Generate a simple report.

In using SIMPLE the processes are all driven by menus or prompts from the 4GL. There is no code. A comparison can be made by considering how much code in, say, COBOL would be needed to produce the same effect.

For the purpose of saving space, only a skeleton dialogue is shown and the screen format is compressed in width. The number of available screens of dialogue is large and the system has extensive help facilities which can be invoked at any stage throughout the processing. The replies are shown in bold type.

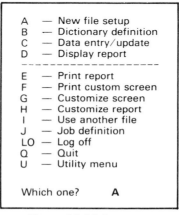

Figure 6.8 Main menu

(1) The program displays the main menu as shown in Figure 6.8.
(2) Selecting option A sets up a new file as shown in Figure 6.9.
(3) The file is now set up. The main menu returns and option B is selected to set up the fields in the new file as shown in Figure 6.10.

All the fields in turn are specified. At the end of the process, the screen display appears as in Figure 6.11.

In the complete version of SIMPLE, this display is wider and the type field is written in full; that is, Numbers, Text or Money. Specifying a

Figure 6.9 Use of the file set up option

```
Option B

You must name the key to your file:

              Key name STOCK-NUMBER

What type of key (Date, Text, Numbers)? N

Entry/display length (1-79 chars) 5

How many decimal places? 0

Description? STOCK SERIAL NUMBER

Would you like to (A)dd, (D)elete, (C)hange? A
```

Figure 6.10 Field definition

type for the field generates automatic validation of data input. Range-checking can also be built in.

(4) The next stage is to insert the data using option C. The system provides a default screen format which the designer may change in consultation with the user when the prototype is demonstrated. The default screen is shown in Figure 6.12.

Data are entered field by field and the record is stored. The system provides facilities to add, change and delete records and to browse though the file.

The file creation is now complete. The process can be repeated for any other files which the system requires and facilities exist for joining data from any number of files. In fact, the system allows the use of data sets with repeating groups but as this violates the rules of data normalisation its implementation is not advised.

(5) The last stage of this demonstration is to produce a report. This uses option D from the main menu and Figure 6.13 shows a report which lists the stock file sorted on stock number.

Field	Field name	Type	Length	Multiple values	Description
1	STOCK-NO	N	5	No	ITEM NO
2	DESCR	T	15	No	DESCRIPTION
3	SUPPLIER	T	20	No	SUPP NAME
4	COST	M	8	No	COST TO BUY
5	SELL-PR	M	8	No	SELLING PR
6	QUANT	N	6	No	NO IN STOCK
7	R-O-L	N	6	No	RE-ORDER AT

Figure 6.11 Data dictionary showing field details

```
┌─────────────────────────────────────────────────────────────┐
│                                                               │
│   Data entry/update                                           │
│                                                               │
│   Stock-no        Descr             Supplier                  │
│                                                               │
│   264 ____        RIBBON _____   BYTESMITH _____       │
│                                                               │
│   Cost       Sell-pr     Quant    R-O-L                       │
│                                                               │
│   12.34____  16.34____   43____   22 ____                     │
│                                                               │
│   [cr] to file this record                                    │
│                                                               │
└─────────────────────────────────────────────────────────────┘
```

Figure 6.12 Data capture using default screen

The prompt, 'Enter phrase(s), if any' is the point at which conditions can be specified. The one used, 'BY STOCK-NO', sorts the file on that field. The option allows virtually unlimited scope for conditions such as selected values (for example, 'On Stock-no, with Stock-no LT 1000') or for formatting (for example, 'By Supplier, by Stock-no break on supplier'). This last will sort on stock numbers within supplier and will insert blank lines into the listing as the supplier changes.

```
┌─────────────────────────────────────────────────────────────┐
│                                                               │
│   Which one? D                                                │
│                                                               │
│   Which fields do you wish to show? STOCK-NO                  │
│       DESCR     SELL-PR     QUANT                             │
│                                                               │
│   Enter phrase(s), if any: BY STOCK-NO                        │
│                                                               │
│   Stock-no Descr . . . . .          Sell-pr    Quant          │
│                                                               │
│       243    MONITOR                 75.32      122           │
│       264    RIBBON                  16.34       43           │
│       325    DRIVE                  122.04       34           │
│                                                               │
└─────────────────────────────────────────────────────────────┘
```

Figure 6.13 Report

6.4.5 Conclusions

The example in section 6.4.4 is necessarily a simplified one. The number of screens required to demonstrate a serious system would of course be prohibitively large in this text. However, it does demonstrate the essential features of a 4GL mentioned earlier. The system is written quickly, it allows easy modification and is simple to follow.

Prototyping undoubtedly has the advantage of involving the user throughout the development of the software and this is generally considered to be desirable. A corollary of this process is that there must be quick turnaround. That is, agreed changes must be implemented quickly or the user might lose interest. This in turn means that the language chosen must be reliable. The term 'quick and dirty' has been used to describe the process; but this has to be unacceptable. The use of 4GLs should permit the construction of software in a way which is both quick and clean.

It is a consequence of the nature of 4GLs that they produce more object code than 3GLs and that the object code is not always optimal in its form. The code produced often runs more slowly than a 3GL. The degree of slowness might or might not be crucial; if it is not, then the final version of the prototype becomes the production model. If speed is crucial, then the final version might be recoded. This still does not invalidate the process. Users report a similar increase in speed of development mentioned earlier in this chapter; that is, the development time using 4GLs is improved over 3GLs by a factor of more than five. Even if recoding is carried out at the end, there is still room for a time saving while at the same time knowing that the product is acceptable to the user.

Prototyping is a relatively new technique in computing. However, its use is on the increase and as the facilities of 4GLs continue to improve the likelihood is that its use will continue to spread.

6.5 Other types of 4GL and other uses of the term

At the beginning of this chapter it was observed that there are a number of different types of language which meet the definition in section 6.2 and there are a number of languages to which the term is applied but which do not meet the specification. Some of these are briefly considered.

6.5.1 Program generators

This type of 4GL, sometimes called an application generator, operates on the action list produced for a JSP specification. The 4GL is presented with the action list in a form of structured English and its output is a program in a 3GL (usually COBOL) which is then processed by a COBOL compiler. Program editing must be carried out at the 4GL level and any temptation to modify the intermediate COBOL code must be resisted because subsequent use of the 4GL will obliterate the modifications. Such systems have had varied success and have been widely used on IBM installations.

6.5.2 Expert system shells

The field of expert systems has seen a very rapid growth over the last few years. An expert system requires that there be a store of relevant knowledge—a knowledge base—and software for making decisions using this knowledge—an inference engine. Constructing the expert system requires that the person eliciting the knowledge (the knowledge analyst) work with the human expert to construct the product.

Many of the products are rule-based. That is, a set of rules is put together having the general form:

If ⟨condition⟩then⟨conclusion⟩.

An expert system is usually distinguished from a decision table processor in that it also deals in probabilities and in fuzzy logic, although it must be pointed out that there are some working expert systems which do not include this aspect. It will be apparent that the process lends itself to a 4GL approach since the constructs and processes will be very similar between one system and another. An expert system shell provides the means of building such a system without the detailed programming process required with AI languages or other 3GLs. Examples of shells are SAGE, Xi-plus, Frame Engine and LOOPS.

6.5.3 Artificial intelligence (AI) languages

AI languages, the best known of which are probably LISP and PROLOG, have been used for many years. Their essential characteristic is that they are non-procedural and for this reason they are sometimes referred to as 4GLs. However, in relation to the conditions derived earlier in this chapter to define 4GLs, they do not meet the criteria of user-friendliness and brevity of code. For this reason they must be excluded.

6.6 Summary

To return to a point made earlier in this chapter, there are many, often idiosyncratic, definitions of what constitutes a 4GL. Indeed, it was admitted that the definition used in this chapter reflects the authors' personal views. However, it must be accepted that if 4GLs are truly to be a new generation they must have significant characteristics which distinguish them from earlier generations.

Recent publications have pointed to Ada, C, MSDOS, UNIX and APL as 4GLs but examination of these products reveals that, although excellent, they are firmly based in 3GL technology.

As in many aspects of computing technology, there is a rapid rate of development and change in 4GLs. New examples appear regularly and vary greatly in areas of application and in capability. The price of a 4GL to run on a personal computer is often higher than the cost of the machine and this is perhaps an indication that they are in an early stage of their growth.

The necessary growth in user-friendliness and the need to approach natural language will ensure that over a period of time 4GLs will become as widely used as 3GLs are today.

No doubt the definition of a 4GL will remain vexed. However, if the purpose is kept in mind—that is, the language which makes computers easier for people to use—then you will know one when you see one.

6.7 Exercises

1 Investigate any 4GL—or so-called 4GL—which you have available. Is it suitable for use as:

   (a) A query language?
   (b) A prototyping language?

2 If it is suitable as a prototyping language, how do its characteristics match those listed in section 6.3.3?

3 For the stock file example in section 6.3.4 write in COBOL (or any other 3GL of your choice) the code for setting up and loading the file. How does the exercise compare with the use of SIMPLE?

CHAPTER 7

Summary

7.1 Natural language processing □ 7.2 Formal grammar specification □ 7.3 Conclusions

7.1 Natural language processing

The development of fourth-generation programming languages, as described in Chapter 6, shows an increasing convergence towards natural language. It is the belief of many people that the aim of language development is indeed such a convergence and eventually we will reach a stage where communication with the machine is achieved by means of language indistinguishable from that used among people.

Whether this is in fact desirable is by no means clear.

Natural language as a form of communication leaves much to be desired. Even when the English language is used properly, there are inherent characteristics which inevitably produce ambiguity, inexactness and downright confusion.

The difficulties arise from a number of sources. First, natural language has the whimsical feature of allowing one word to be both a noun and a verb or a noun and an adverb or, perhaps, all three (and maybe an adjective as well).

Consider some well-known examples:

'Police found safe under blanket'
'Fruit flies like oranges'
'Eighth Army push bottles up enemy troops' (wartime headline)
'Monty flies back to front' (wartime headline)

The analysis which humans carry out on such phrases is based upon context, experience, inference and intuition. The proportions of these vary from instance to instance and from person to person but the amount of what we might call informal processing which the human brain carries out on the data is considerable.

How, then, is this to be viewed with regard to the computer? Which of the essentially human processes mentioned in the preceding paragraph can reasonably be expected to be transferred to the machine? In order to examine the problem, it is useful to consider how meaning is extracted from text and to do this it is necessary to look at the idea of a grammar.

7.2 Formal grammar specification

A language is (possibly) best described by means of a formal grammar. This approach can be applied to natural or programming languages. In the case of the former, it is difficult to do completely, as demonstrated below; in the case of the latter, it is essential.

Defining a grammar requires a simple notation. There are two which are commonly used: Backus Naur Form (BNF), which was briefly encountered in Chapter 4, and syntax diagrams.

For the purposes of this discussion, BNF will be used. Syntax diagrams may be found in items listed in the bibliography.

7.2.1 The use of a formal grammar

BNF uses only three symbols:

::=   which means 'consists of'
⟨ ⟩   which hold an element of the language
| which means 'or' or 'alternatively'

To illustrate the use of BNF, consider a fundamental subset of English in which a sentence consists of a subject and a predicate. Within these there are nouns, verbs and articles. Further, the only words in the language are the nouns *dog, cat, mouse, student* and *lecturer*, the verbs *chased, caught, evaded* and *educated* and the articles *the* and *a*. The grammar would be as follows:

```
⟨sentence⟩       ::=  ⟨subject⟩⟨predicate⟩
⟨subject⟩        ::=  ⟨article⟩⟨noun⟩
⟨predicate⟩      ::=  ⟨verb⟩⟨direct object⟩
⟨direct object⟩  ::=  ⟨article⟩⟨noun⟩
⟨noun⟩           ::=  dog| cat| mouse| student| lecturer
⟨verb⟩           ::=  chased| caught| evaded| educated
⟨article⟩        ::=  a| the
```

The sequence in which the rules of the grammar are stated is not important. The rule set is continually scanned until an appropriate rule is found and can be applied.

It can be seen that all of the following sentences are valid within the grammatical rules:

A dog chased the cat.
The mouse evaded the cat.
The dog caught a mouse.
A mouse educated the lecturer.
The cat caught a student.

Clearly, a grammar of this kind can define the way in which a language is structured (that is, its syntax); but it cannot legislate for the meaning contained in a sentence (that is, the semantics). Inferring whether or not a sentence makes sense is a difficult process.

In defining a grammar for a natural language, difficulties are encountered very quickly. Suppose, for example, *aardvark* is added to the list of nouns. Immediately, it is necessary to add the article *an* to the list of articles. This is easy enough, but then the grammar allows the sentences:

An dog chased an cat.
A aardvark caught a mouse.

Obviously the grammar may be refined to trap the wrong use of the article, but it is becoming very unwieldy:

⟨sentence⟩   ::=   ⟨subject⟩⟨predicate⟩
⟨subject⟩   ::=   ⟨article1⟩⟨noun1⟩|⟨article2⟩⟨noun2⟩
⟨predicate⟩   ::=   ⟨verb⟩⟨direct object⟩
⟨direct object⟩   ::=   ⟨article1⟩⟨noun1⟩|⟨article2⟩⟨noun2⟩
⟨noun1⟩   ::=   dog|cat|mouse|student|lecturer
⟨noun2⟩   ::=   aardvark
⟨verb⟩   ::=   chased|caught|evaded|educated
⟨article1⟩   ::=   a|the
⟨article2⟩   ::=   an|the

Now, what about adjectives? First, modify ⟨subject⟩ and ⟨direct object⟩ (which have identical definitions) to include an adjective:

⟨subject⟩   ::=   ⟨article⟩⟨adjective⟩⟨noun⟩

(Forget for the moment the differences between noun1 and noun2.)
Add the definition of ⟨adjective⟩:

⟨adjective⟩   ::=   red|green|big|small|worried|brown|
                       spotted|hungry

More sentences become available:

A big dog chased a small cat.
The brown cat chased a spotted mouse.

However, it also allows such things as:

The green student chased a spotted lecturer.

Worse is to come. On many occasions, multiple ⟨adjective⟩s might be used, as in 'the big brown cat'. To accommodate this construct, the recursive definition is used as follows:

```
⟨subject⟩            ::= ⟨article⟩⟨adjectival phrase⟩⟨noun⟩
⟨adjectival phrase⟩ ::=
                ⟨null⟩ | ⟨adjective⟩ | ⟨adjective⟩⟨adjectival phrase⟩
```

This last definition means that a subject may have any number of adjectives or none between the article and the noun. In this way, the grammar allows such sentences as:

The big brown cat chased the small worried mouse.

But, unfortunately, it also allows:

The big small cat chased the blue brown dog.

Clearly, while it might be possible sensibly to define the syntax of a language (or at least a subset of it), the semantics—that is, the sense—is, as noted earlier, immensely difficult to analyse.

It is said that Noam Chomsky, perhaps the best-known authority on the subject, demonstrated the problem with the syntactically correct, rather beautiful and completely meaningless phrase, 'Green ideas sleep furiously'.

7.2.2 Application to programming languages

The discussion above has been concerned with the structure of syntactically correct sentences in a natural language. Clearly, the same arguments apply to programming languages. Fortunately, the morass of difficulties which accrue as soon as one tries to analyse even a relatively small subset of English does not occur with 3GLs and even current 4GLs can avoid most of them. For example, a SELECT statement (as used in section 6.2.4) might be defined as:

```
⟨SELECT statement⟩ ::= SELECT ⟨domain-name⟩ FROM ⟨relation⟩
                              WHERE ⟨condition-clause⟩
⟨condition-clause⟩   ::= ⟨condition⟩ |
                              ⟨condition-clause⟩AND⟨condition⟩
⟨condition⟩          ::= ⟨domain-name⟩⟨operator⟩⟨domain-name⟩
⟨operator⟩           ::= = | < | > | ≠ | ≤ | ≥
```

The recursive definition of ⟨condition-clause⟩ allows as many conditions as required to be ANDed together.

Grammars such as these form the basis of compilers. The compiler uses the rules of the grammar to test each statement during the process of syntax analysis (or parsing) and will reject any syntax errors during compilation. Obviously, a complete grammar will have to define components of the language down to the character level, so that the validity of names may be tested. For example, if a ⟨domain-name⟩ can be any combination of letters, digits and hyphens but must begin with a letter, the definition might be:

```
⟨domain-name⟩ ::= ⟨letter⟩ | ⟨domain-name⟩⟨character⟩ |
                       ⟨domain-name⟩-⟨character⟩
⟨character⟩      ::= ⟨letter⟩ | ⟨digit⟩
⟨letter⟩         ::= a | b | c | d | e...x | y | z
⟨digit⟩          ::= 1 | 2 | 3 | 4 | 5 | 6 | 7 | 8 | 9 | 0
```

Note that you cannot simply include the hyphen in the set of characters because to do so would allow a name to end with a hyphen and this is not permissible.

As a result of this, the grammar permits names such as job-no, size-in-shoes, j45, p23-t; but it will reject 4GL, temp--const, f45- and so on.

7.2.3 Bridging the gap

The gap alluded to here is the one between the traditional form of a programming language for which a complete grammar can be specified and a natural language for which—in all practical aspects—a complete grammar cannot be specified.

The preceding brief description of the use of grammars indicates some of the problems associated with specifying a language, whether it be a natural or a programming one. As was stated at the start of this chapter, the grammar of a programming language, if it is to be used to construct a compiler, must be complete. Otherwise, the compiler is unable to decide whether a sentence is or is not valid. Completeness also implies freedom from ambiguity. In the example in section 7.1, 'Police found safe under blanket', ambiguity arises because the word 'safe' can be either an adjective or a noun. So, in a formal grammar for the English language, the word would appear in both categories. If a word in a programming language were to have two meanings, then a sentence containing that word would be capable of interpretation in at least two ways and the compiled code would be unusable.

The question arises: where do we go from here? It is not a new question and has been asked on many occasions. One of the earliest references to it was in a 1970 conference on 'Man–computer interaction' where C. Longuet Higgins presented a seminal paper entitled 'The Monkey's Paw' which dealt with the literal-mindedness of the computer and posed questions which are only now beginning to be answered. The questions relate to the ways in which we are going to compromise the need for exactness in the programming language specification with the fuzziness of natural language and people's liking for it.

The answers are not altogether satisfactory. At least, not yet. It is certainly within the capability of the current technology to produce a 'clever' compiler which can draw inferences from a statement and decide upon its most likely meaning, but this leads only to further questions.

The development of non-procedural languages includes a large increase in the use of interpreters rather than compilers. This means that code is executed without there being a compiled program; that is, each statement is analysed and executed without there being an object code version in existence. A corollary of this is that the separation between code and data is fuzzy and the scope for inference is increased. Thus, it might be perfectly proper for a query system to infer that the question 'Find all red-headed employees who speak Serbo-Croat' would include people with auburn hair speaking Macedonian; but it is a totally different matter if an air traffic control system considers it safe to assume that a signal of the flight path of a 747 is not a light aircraft on an unauthorised route.

The extent to which a clever compiler—or any clever software—will be reliable is an unknown in this regard. There is still a reluctance by humanity at large to accept the computer as a control device. This is in spite of the spread of computing brought about by the personal computer; paradoxically, the acceptance of the machine at a personal level appears to generate no corresponding acceptance at a more global one. Every day we are subjected to amusing(?) anecdotes on the idiocy of systems. On the day that the London Stock Exchange implemented its new system there was a system failure which lasted for an hour; the resulting newspaper headlines ranged from the derisive to the hysterical. Clearly, reliability of large systems is of crucial importance as far as the image of computing is concerned and the introduction of clever systems has attendant risks which have to be carefully watched.

That such systems will arrive is not in question. The trend of the development as described in the three preceding chapters is towards natural language and it has been shown earlier in this chapter that this carries the overhead of inexactness. Paradoxically, at the same time, there is a school of thought which suggests that software must be subjected to formal proof in order to demonstrate its correctness. The formal proving of a program requires exactness to a high degree and there is some scepticism about the exact formal proof of correctness for other than very simple programs, due to the combinatorial explosion of the pathways through the program.

Whether these doubts are justified remains a matter of speculation. At the time of writing, reports from IBM Federal Systems Division indicate that formal proof of large systems is feasible and is being used; how the process will accommodate the fuzziness of clever software is another question, but one which will no doubt be answered in due course.

(As was mentioned in Chapter 2, formal methods of program proving are considered to be outside the scope of this book and the reader is referred to the bibliography.)

7.3 Conclusions

In the last four chapters we have studied methods and trends in the production of applications software. The processes examined have ranged from current structured methods to speculative and clever systems, the implementation of which is in only a very early stage.

A number of conclusions may tentatively be drawn about this subject. First, the diversity of programming languages continues at a high level. The number of languages, both third and fourth generation, is still high and although many of them will drop into obscurity (as have many of the languages devised during the last 20 years), it seems likely that a sort of 'steady state' of programming languages exists. Thus, as one language vanishes another forms from the emptiness of space to take its place.

It is to be hoped that improvement in the ease of use of languages will continue. In Chapter 6, the discussion on prototypes indicated that moving the software closer to the user is a desirable trend; and many believe that this is the way all software should go. To balance this view, it must be remembered that this was also the intention for COBOL—and it did not happen because of the complexity of the language. It is possible that there are inherent levels of complexity in the design of computer systems which will forever be outside the remit of the user and for which the specialist will always be needed. No doubt, also, there will always be a genre of specialists who will be devoted to perpetuating this state of affairs ...

Another important consideration is that processors will become faster and more powerful and consequently more able to deal with the less-than-optimal code generated by languages of the fourth generation and beyond. Optimising code and saving memory space, already considerations of decreasing importance, will be of negligible significance and so designers of software will be able to concentrate on making their products more user-friendly.

PART III

Software implementation

CHAPTER 8

The initial approach: planning ahead

8.1 Ground rules

Before planning software implementation, it might be better to plan about the planning. This is somewhat like the entry in the dictionary which reads:

recursive *adj See* RECURSIVE.

To implement a solution to a software problem, one needs somebody (or somebodies) to do it. One also needs a computer system to do it to. The solution will be implemented using some computer language which will be available to the computer system. This will necessarily be the subject of a certain amount of design planning beforehand. The design will then be followed to achieve the final computer program, which will subsequently be tested. It is worth noting that there is a tendency for programs to be *verified*. This is like the proving of a mathematical theorem. Instead of trying it out in a large number of cases to weed out all obvious mistakes afterwards, more care is taken beforehand.

The framework of this chapter will assume that there is a product to be made. This means that none exists in a form suitable to be bought. The problem may be that the product is so new that it doesn't exist. Alternatively, it might exist, but be sufficiently expensive as to be beyond the available budget. Perhaps the computer system upon which an old version existed has been superseded, and it is time to rewrite the product completely. There may be other reasons, but those are some of the more obvious ones.

If this appears overly fussy, beware! Once upon a time, an application program was written for a computer and duly used. Later, the computer system became too expensive to run any more because new computers became available which were cheaper. To avoid rewriting the program (and other similar ones, it must be admitted), a computer system simulator was written. This simulated the action of the old computer on the new computer system, and all was well. However, in time the new system in its turn became obsolete and was replaced. This time, the simulation was done in the computer hardware and firmware (this is usually called emulation). Now the original program, unchanged, was being simulated, and the simulation was emulated: all to avoid rewriting. By now the original program documentation had been lost, and only the operating instructions remained! Not very good, perhaps, but true. Surely, if a system *should* be rewritten, it *will* be rewritten: and that is the purpose of the discussion in this chapter.

The unit of implementation will be assumed to be a program, even though this is not always the case. For convenience, it will suffice. One might assume that the purpose of computer programming, by its very name, is the production of a program. However, it may be that the operation is sufficiently large as to require a suite of programs; or it may be sufficiently small as not to require anything more than a small subprogram. If it is sufficiently large, more than one person may be required to write it, but if there is only a little work to be done, it might not even require one programmer's full-time attention. The context will make the situation clear.

8.2 Allocation of personnel

One of the aspects of planning ahead is to decide how long a particular job is going to take. Also, the kinds of people who will be involved in its implementation have to be chosen. To achieve the solution of a problem on a computer requires a computer program. Some computer systems appear to write their own programs by the use of program generators, but we know that this is not what happens in reality: the responsibility for the task rests ultimately with human beings.

The writing of programs is a creative operation, and one which has been closely studied. If the size of a completed program is known (perhaps in terms of lines of code), then the amount of human effort needed can be accurately assessed. If a particular task is going to occupy ten man-months and one person is allocated to perform it, then it will take ten months. Plans may then be made accordingly.

If more than one person is employed in the operation, it should take less time: if two people are used, it should (strictly) take five months. After all, if it takes twenty minutes to travel ten miles at thirty miles per hour, it should take ten minutes to travel the same distance at sixty miles per hour; and so on.

However, experience tells us that this need not be quite the way things work in practice. If we could increase our velocity to 600 miles per hour, the ten miles would be covered in one minute; but if we allocate forty people to the ten man-month job, it is extremely unlikely to be finished in a week. Hence the measurement in these terms does not follow a linear scale. One might reasonably regard the concept of uniform man-months to be somewhat of a myth, but it is a convenient approximation. Its non-linearity does not stop it being a useful way of looking at overall task planning.

There is another problem which needs to be dealt with to keep a reasonable grasp on the 'real world'. In any team enterprise—and any sizeable job is going to be dealt with by a team rather than an individual—not all team members are of equal productivity. If the team is to be properly cohesive, it will need management of its organisation. Any effort directed into management will necessarily have been diverted from the original task. Management operations will cover a large number of skills, not necessarily connected with the direct production of the program. They have sometimes been likened to the oil in the mechanism: without oil, the system would soon seize up. The oil in a car's gearbox has no part in the propulsion of the vehicle, but disaster would strike very soon if it were not included. It should also be inspected regularly to make sure that it is still working correctly.

To implement a computer program, a number of individuals will have to be suitably selected. They will then have to be formed into a team to perform that task. They will have various levels of skill and will each have a function within the team. With proper planning, the time and effort required will be known; and a completion date and a costing will be available before any work is commenced.

8.3 Selection of operating system

When a task is to be performed by a computer, it is usually possible to make a choice from among a number of computer systems. Taking an example from another field, if one wished to travel between two places in London, one might (among other things) walk, or cycle, go by bus, or taxi, or underground, or even use one's own car. It would probably depend on a number of factors, such as the time available, or whether one had a bicycle or a car, or whether there was a convenient bus route, and so on. The situation in the computer case is similar.

The situation as far as computers are concerned is more complex than it would have been a few years ago! Before microcomputer systems became widespread, one used *the* computer, and that was the end of it. Insofar as *the* computer had the *one* operating system, that was the end of that, as well. Therefore there was no choice in the matter and no selection could take place under the user's direction. If one were *buying* the computer and its operating system, that was different—but it was not a common situation.

Now the position tends to be more flexible. In any reasonably large firm, there will be a choice of computers ranging from mainframes through minicomputers (and super-minis) to microcomputers of varying sizes. If networking facilities are provided, the flexibility tends to be even greater. Even in small firms, there may well be a choice of microcomputer systems. Added to this, there will be a choice of operating systems.

Indeed, for any one computer, there may be more than one operating system available. This may, on larger computers, appear as a choice to be made when initialising any task (for instance, batch processing vs. interactive usage). Or it may be according to the time of day—it is not uncommon for interactive jobs to be executed during the daytime, with batch processing proceeding overnight. Some computers have dedicated operating systems and some change them frequently.

This flexibility does not apply only to mainframe or super-minicomputers. It takes very little time to change operating systems on a standard microcomputer system which has different microprocessors available within its hardware. The change from MSDOS to CP/M might take no more than changing a switch position to access different ROMs; and the choice here is becoming steadily greater.

Given this flexibility, there still remains the exercise of matching the operating system and its computer. Once again, the choice may be a simple one: to propose the *single* apposite framework for the task in hand. If there is a single operating system supporting teleprocessing, and teleprocessing is an absolute requirement, then it takes very little time to select that system. The difficulties only arise when a choice is to be made among a number of possibilities which actually offer all of the facilities wanted.

This may appear to be a trivial statement, but the obvious need to select 'Number One in a Field of One' is sometimes the subject of much agonised thought—as if there *were* a choice. The matter of *how* a choice is to be made, when a real choice exists, is not discussed here. This is a difficult subject: but as long as the awareness exists, then the discussion is not a wasted one.

8.4 Which language shall we use?

This is a problem allied with that of the previous section, and each may very well influence the other to a greater or lesser degree. If the computer system does not support a particular language, there is little use in including such a language in a menu for that computer. It might be possible to add a language to the system, by buying or leasing an implementation of it. Under such circumstances it will, of course, take the same status as those already provided.

It is worthwhile investigating language classifications in this context. This is, in itself, quite a problem. There are several 'splits' which can be made, and some possibilities are illustrated in Figure 8.1 (not to scale!).

For the most part, languages can be classified into these categories, or into similar ones. There are specialised languages for simulation and for system implementation. Some general-purpose languages attempt to be 'all things to all men'. Some languages are available in essentially the same form on many different computer architectures, while some are specific to one particular aspect of one particular computer. These categories are certainly liable to overlap—PL/1 is an example of one which was designed to bridge the gap between 'commercial' and 'scientific'. However, for a particular requirement, it should be possible to choose from an appropriate menu of computer languages.

It is relatively easy to pick a short list of languages from among a set of menus to satisfy a particular need. Under ideal conditions, the short list will consist of just one candidate, and that will solve the problem. If the number remaining after selection is zero, the conditions must be relaxed and the operation repeated. If more than one remains, the criteria may be made

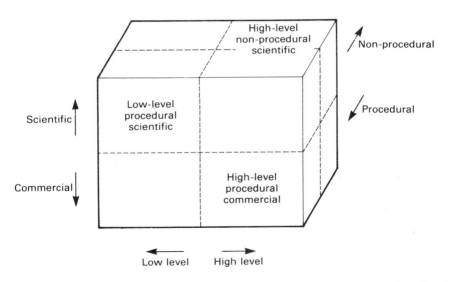

The figure suffers from all of the usual inadequacies of attempting the representation of a three-dimensional object on a flat page! But this can be overcome, by anyone uneasy about it, as a Karnaugh Map.

Figure 8.1 Language classification

more specific. When the selection yields precisely one suitable answer, the operation has been successful.

However, this method may still fail to yield an acceptable single language. Then other characteristics of the available languages must be used to enable a decision to be taken. Among these may be the efficiency of the result. This may be in space or speed terms if the application is in a critical area in these respects, or it may be in rapidity of implementation if there is a requirement for prompt availability. Perhaps portability will be relevant if there is the likelihood of future utility on other computer systems; and so on.

8.5 What is the best design method?

A number of design methods have already been discussed in Part II of this book. Following the analogy suggested in section 8.4, it should be possible to pick a best one. In the best mathematical tradition, we should really start by showing that at least one exists. Fortunately, this has already been done. Now it remains to demonstrate the *need* for one.

It is possible here to appeal to anyone who has tried to implement software without a design method. However, if the problem solved was sufficiently simple, the answer is often given that all that was required was to write down the solution. Programming is creative work, even though '... there is no new thing under the sun'. 'Common sense' tells us, however, that if the problem is sufficiently large, it will need a formal design method.

How, then, do we decide on the best method? This is probably best done by analogy, because the truly scientific way cannot be taken. It has been said that 'if you can't measure it, it isn't science', but until there are proper ways of evaluating the worth of particular methods which work *consistently* and *reproducibly*, analogy is all that is available. Some experts may have sufficient experience to select a 'best method'. However, they may find it extremely difficult to communicate precisely the way in which they do it. This is where 'expert systems' may be of help to us in the future. Others may have recourse to intuition, which is possibly the same process. However, to most of us, a set of rules of thumb may be as much as we can hope for. Which brings us back to analogy.

So, have we seen a problem of this nature before? What did we do last time? What were the strengths of our approach, and what were the weaknesses? What would we have changed (always supposing that we could have done so)? This sequence of questions works only if the answer to the first one is 'yes'. We are now looking at a method for finding a method, which is again somewhat recursive. However, this meta-method can be tackled. It will probably present itself as a checklist of questions similar to those above.

It may be possible to view the overall task of picking a design method in one of two generalised ways. These might well be described as top–down and bottom–up, by comparison with parsing techniques in compilation. 'Top–down' would involve inspecting the problem to be solved and refining it into sub-problems. This continues until each sub-problem is sufficiently well defined to be subject to a known design method. 'Bottom–up' would start with a (number of) design method(s) and applying this (or these) to various aspects of the problem until it was solved. In cases, one must be aware of the nature of the problem to be solved and of the various design methods available.

This still suffers from the shortcoming of not being very scientific, according to the definition given earlier. It now resembles much more closely, however, an engineering approach to the task. Faced with a number of nuts and bolts to be adjusted, we rummage through our toolkit. When we have found a set of spanners of the appropriate size, we use them in the correct fashion. This approach has been termed 'software engineering'. The whole idea of 'the right tool for the right job' is the rationale behind the name.

A word of warning, irrespective of whether you pick the top–down or the bottom–up approach: don't be misled into trying the same design method slavishly in every situation—not all nuts yield to the same spanner. Use the correct one. If you can't find it straightaway, don't ruin the system by attempting to use one of the wrong size or shape—the right spanner is in the box somewhere; and don't try and use a method with which you are not familiar—that's another way into deep trouble.

8.6 Implementation strategy

When a new building is being erected, the architect doesn't decide where to put it and then send a few bricklayers on site to get on with it. Imagine the chaos! A lot of detailed planning work has to go into such an operation if it is to run with even a minimum of smoothness. Of course, the architects certainly do not concern themselves with the doings of every bricklayer— that would be far too detailed—but they do have to set out overall timetables and ordering of materials. All the time, though, they have to pay attention to many external factors which do not concern individuals further down the line.

How do they go about it? The key notion here is that of strategic planning. Overall planning is completed in advance, before committing anything to tactical operation. In the solution of a large problem, there is likely to be an implementing team, and several people working on the planning. 'He finds out what to do; draws up the orders; and I sign 'em. Division of labor!' With a large problem, strategic considerations demand that approach.

It is the same thing with planning software implementation. Here, the overall plan will need to have a timetable. It will need to give movements and duties of implementors, even if there is only one actual person involved. The environment is the problem to be solved. If the problem is small, there may only be one part-time programmer. Or there may be one or more *teams* of programmers if the problem is a large one—and have no doubt about it, some problems are *very* large. One operating system of the 1960s (IBM's OS/360) received some 5000 man-years spread over just its first three years of implementation. By simple arithmetic, a task of that magnitude must have taken at least 1300 implementors. In fact, it took considerably more, and that was with a very well ordered strategic approach. There is more about this aspect in Chapter 10.

So, in order to perform properly in the task of implementation, the framework must be organised in which that task is to take place. The resources have to be arranged to be available before they are used. The scheduling of implementors and computer systems must be taken in hand, but not (at this stage of development) in too much detail. One of the dangers to be avoided at this stage is for operations to be considered which are too small or detailed. Such early refinement would inevitably direct attention away from the things which are presently much more important.

The result produced by this operation is a well-integrated framework which is then ready to have its details filled in. This application, by the way, corresponds directly to a top–down plan. The overall planning has arranged that the correct number of implementors will find the correct amount of computing power in the right place at the right time. The various subtask implementors will know how they fit in with each other, and they will then be able to concentrate on the completion of their subtasks with confidence. They will know their place in the whole structure and will have only their own immediate details to worry about.

Another advantage of the approach using this mechanism comes to light when the implementation is actually carried out. The implementation strategists will be able to inspect each subtask's progress and accuracy with ease. They will not need to know all of the internal details. Any shortcomings will be dealt with in terms of a single defective task. It may be necessary to check the subtasks dependent on such a defective item, but without descending to the level of too much detail. This principle of feedback of correct strength at the correct level applies in all well-designed machinery. When properly applied, it avoids trouble at the earliest possible stages.

8.7 Implementation tactics

Let us now turn our attention from the broad front of implementation to the finer details. What this means, precisely, depends on whereabouts in the system we are. It also depends on the size of the problem which was being solved. The level of strategic planning may correspond to the breaking down of a multi-man-year task, or it may have been a request for a particular procedure to form part of a program. In the former case, the team will now perform further refinement to produce portions manageable to individuals; in the latter case, there is no need for further refinement at the strategic level.

At this point, therefore, it is assumed that there is now a single person engaged in the relevant implementation. What should have been supplied at this point? The implementation strategists are well aware of their strategic needs and make their intentions absolutely clear. Hence the programmer would know the purpose of the program and its external interfaces. This may be in terms of its input and output transfer requirements, or perhaps as parameters to be passed into and out of it. More information might be given. The program's place in the whole structure might be defined (Figure 8.2): but that isn't essential.

There may, though, be other factors to be considered by the programmer. Standards of documentation, language, operating system, or planning method might be enforced for reasons of uniformity. In such situations, the programmer would necessarily follow such standards. There are reasons for such enforcement, even if they are not immediately obvious. Reverting to the analogy, it is not necessary for an individual bricklayer to know *why* a particular wall has to be built. If directives are not followed, however, there is the distinct likelihood of failure in the overall operation. Such a chain of cause and effect may appear somewhat extreme, but can be per-

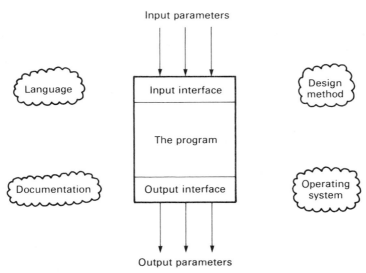

Figure 8.2 The program's place

suasive. 'A little neglect may breed mischief, ... for want of a nail ... the rider was lost.'

So now it is up to an individual to commence the detailed planning of a particular indivisible piece of the software. This will continue by well-defined pathways. The data structures will be defined; the algorithms to transform the initial data to the final results will be produced; from these the program itself can be written. The data structures correspond to the variables of the program, and algorithms to the program code.

During all of these operations, it is essential for the programmer to record what is being done, and why. If any errors occur, it is then feasible to trace them to their source. Similar ones can then be avoided in the future. If those inaccuracies are a result of ambiguous or erroneous specification, they may affect other programmers and there may be a feed through of errors into the overall system. This is one of the several reasons for insisting on documentation which is accurate *and* up-to-date. Out-of-date information is not merely a nuisance, but positively harmful.

8.8 Validation of implementation

What is the result of the programmer's work? It is a program to carry out the task originally specified. Nevertheless, how can we be sure that the program will do what it was meant to do? Does it fulfil the requirements, or does it fall short in some respects? Or perhaps, does it even do too much? So the next stage, after implementation, is to make sure that the customer gets what was ordered.

The trend towards the production of verified programs, rather than relying on debugging, has already been noted. However, this is not satisfactory on its own. There is no substitute, finally, for demonstration to show that what has been delivered is what was wanted. It is better to view these as two aspects of the same process, complementing each other. Each is well worth discussing, as each should appear naturally as a part of good implementational techniques.

Starting with the verification of programs, a brief explanation follows. The method relies on the recognition that during any process, certain things remain fixed. This may, at first sight, appear somewhat of a contradiction. It is, in fact, not particularly strange when the concept is understood. Consider, for instance, the operation of sorting a number of items into order. One fixed aspect of the situation is certainly the number of items. If we gain or lose some during a sorting operation, there is surely something wrong. As has been said elsewhere, 'I counted them all out, and I counted them all back'. Of course, there is a more restrictive condition governing the sorting process. Any item coming into the process must also exit from it, although not necessarily in the same place. For program verification, a suitable fixed condition (known as the 'invariant') is selected. This is then shown to hold at chosen points throughout the program under consideration. This is, of course, a very short description, but there are many books on the subject for those who might wish to learn more.

One of its aspects is more immediately relevant to the task in hand. It relates directly to the invariants described above. To apply it, first identify, at a suitable position within the program, a condition which must hold at each time that that position is reached. A simple piece of program code may be inserted to check that the condition is indeed true at that point. It should then produce an apposite error message if the condition test fails. A typical example concerns a sorting program (see Figure 8.3). A point is chosen within the data to be sorted, so that all data 'below' that point have keys less than all data 'above' the point. It is a relatively simple matter to arrange such a test, although it may be time-consuming in operation. However, which is better? A program which works correctly, if slowly, or a rapid program producing incorrect results?

In practice, the position is not as black as that. It is simple to arrange for the verification code to be active only during program testing. Before the program's actual use, the code would be made passive. This may be done by transforming all such tests into comments after the testing has proved successful. If the language permits it, advantage may automatically be taken of such facilities. This is sometimes known as a debugging feature.

Program testing to remove mistakes, usually referred to as 'debugging', is probably a more familiar validation operation. This consists of passing test data through the program and checking the results which emerge. If they correspond to correct values for those particular data, then no errors have been identified. If there are discrepancies, then there are errors which need to be corrected. (The possibility that the check values are themselves incorrect is not admissible here!)

The production of correct results from an incorrect program is not ruled

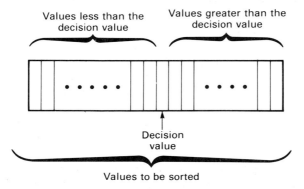

Figure 8.3 A sorting program

out by this method. It may merely be that the incorrect portions have not been exercised by the test data given. For this reason, the use of test data alone is not really a satisfactory method of validation. Essentially, it is only one of a number of unfortunate possibilities. If large programs are to be tested in this way, the volume of test data required may be extremely large. Even so, this may still do little more than scratch the surface.

As an example of this, the validation of compilers may be carried out by passing standard programs through them. The answers which the compiled programs yield are then themselves checked. It is a kind of piggy-back, or second-hand way of doing the job. For validating ANS COBOL compilers, the US Navy supplies such programs. There are some 250 programs within the testing suite. This may seem quite extensive, because some of the test programs are over 1000 lines in length. Unfortunately, in this case, the compiler which these programs have to validate takes (typically) some 15–20 man-years to implement, so it isn't really quite as good as one might immediately expect. However, it *is* all that there is, *and* it has official backing. A similar situation obtains for Pascal compilers, and the same comments are relevant in that case also. It does allow for a measure of uniformity, however, which is better than nothing at all.

In the absence of test data kindly supplied by someone else, where do such data come from? The answer is obvious: they must be produced by the implementor(s). It would not be reasonable, though, to write a program and *then* to embark on the production of the test data and results. If the task is other than of trivial size, such an unstructured method would be very difficult to implement properly. Inevitably, parts of the program would get tested many times, others not at all. The former would cause no trouble, if a little wasteful, but the latter certainly could. Therefore, the test data and results must be produced in parallel with the program implementation. As each part of the program is written, the testing information should also be produced, while the key points are still fresh in the mind. Then the data are all assembled ready for the test, at the same time as the program is ready to be tested. A neat solution to what might otherwise be a somewhat tedious chore.

If there is only one program to be validated, the job is done; but if there are more than one (in a complex system), the various parts have to be put together. The implementation strategists must assemble the subgroups of the grand design into successively larger groups. Testing and verifying must be a continuous operation. As each item is validated, it can be added into the framework. The result is a fully validated product: surely a Good Thing.

8.9 Continuing development

At last—the program has been written, and validated as correct. It has been passed to the customer, and all is well; and that should be the end of that.

In reality, though, it is usually merely the beginning of things. In this imperfect world, operational matters seldom behave as we would like them to. There will be changes made, for a number of reasons. Despite our best intentions and all of our hard work, some errors will inevitably have slipped through. Or, as happens far too often, the customer will have a change of mind and will require changes to be made to perfectly good programs. In either case, there is a need to alter what has already been produced.

What is there available to make it possible to make these changes? There is all the documentation which has been produced: it contains all the planning details, both strategical and tactical, and all the testing schemes; it is all up-to-date, and reflects accurately the state of the programs at the moment. If the problem concerns a previously undetected error, then its nature must be discovered before anything further may be done about it. If the test data are defective, in that they failed to find the error, they must also be altered. This will usually involve additions, rather than alterations as such. In this way, test data can become quite voluminous; and the program can then be corrected and re-released.

If the change was as the result of a change in the customer's requirement, the situation is not quite so clear-cut. There may be a need for a considerable amount of redesigning. (It should be pointed out that 'there is no such thing as a *small* change'. The effect on test data alone can be extremely large. One of the difficulties encountered is in convincing the customer of this truth.) It may be possible to limit the effects of a change to a single program or it may spread over several, according to what needs to be done. If the whole system is affected, there is probably a good case for redesigning from the beginning. No matter how awful this may appear in prospect, it should not be avoided. There are too many live systems made up mostly of alterations, because this had not been done. The result is a poorly documented inefficient system which is extremely difficult to work with.

If the changes can be localised, the situation is better, and may well be undertaken without a complete redesign. However, the same caveats apply as applied previously. Once the change has been made to the design, the test data will need redesigning. Just as they were originally designed during the initial system preparation, so they will need to be available when they are wanted. The documentation describing the program's function will be updated, but the original work will not be scrapped. It still has the useful function of giving the reasons *why* certain choices were made. In the lifetime of a much-amended job, the historical documentation alone can become quite unwieldy. It will still remain extremely useful and should not be discarded merely because of its age. If the bulk becomes too great, there is always microfilm.

For obvious reasons, the documentation may be considerably affected by changes in the implementation, but the way in which it is presented may be of use in comprehending those effects. Consider the purposes of documentation. For the users of the system, it describes what to do to use it, without being too specific about how it all works. For the originators, it provides a set of validation documents to show that it performs correctly according to its specification. For maintenance workers, who might have to make further changes, it gives the methods and rationale used in its detailed implementation. These three parts of the documentation might well be provided as separate items, because they might need changing separately to reflect the changes made during further development. However, it is important that all of the parts of the product are kept in step with each other all the time. The alternative is a recipe for disaster!

8.10 Exercises

1 Estimate the time which will be needed on a 10 man-month job if

   (a) 1 person
   (b) 2 people
   (c) 4 people
   (d) 8 people
   (e) 16 people

   are available. Plot your results on a graph and comment on the result. What assumptions have you made to arrive at your answers?
2 Compare the planning operation described in (1) with any other with which you are familiar. What are the differences? Why are they present?
3 List the operating systems with which you are reasonably familiar and add a few lines of description about each one.
4 Make a list of the computer languages with which you are reasonably familiar. Extend each entry with a list of suitable attributes (some of which are suggested in section 8.4: but this is by no means exhaustive). You might also include characteristics which are not directly part of the languages in question, but which may be related to their implementations. Collect languages with common attributes into menus: if there are many selection criteria in common, merge the menus appropriately to give a more widely applicable result.
5 How is debugging carried out in any language with which you are familiar? How might it best be arranged in languages which do not have an explicit debugging facility incorporated as part of their implementation?

CHAPTER 9

Software construction tools

9.1 The constructor's environment

'No man is an Island, entire of it self' is a sentiment particularly relevant to any implementor's state. When the implementor is part of a team, this is particularly true. Even if this is a solo mission, however, it remains valid. 'If I have seen further it is by standing on the shoulder of giants' applies to us all. This chapter describes not the personnel environment, but that of the operating system and the system software.

This can be seen as the *inevitable* interface between the programmer and the outside world. Unless one is the most primitive of system programmers, there is no direct contact with, for example, the disc drive hardware commands. It is a long time since any serious programming was done utilising binary patterns to represent instructions or data. Hence, attention must be concentrated upon the *appearance* of the system as presented by its relevant interfaces.

At what level of the operating system are these interfaces encountered? As in so many other cases, it all depends on the job which is being done at the time. A COBOL programmer, for instance, does not need to know precisely where on a disc the relevant data are stored, as long as they can be accessed consistently. On the other hand, a programmer using assembly code for disc access on a microcomputer may need to be very aware of the precise track and sector involved. In any case, a lively appreciation of the exact interface must be available to the programmer.

It is also important that the appropriate instructions be made available to the programmer, in any case. This defines the interface needed—if there are not the requisite commands, then the job cannot be done. In many cases, the situation admits no alternatives and the language is adequate: COBOL is a reasonable example of this. There are, however, certain tasks that cannot be accomplished in COBOL for various reasons, and in such cases it would be necessary to change the environment. This might be done in a number of ways, according to the requirements, of course.

However, the environment is not just that of the program instruction interface, important though that may be. Source programs are frequently stored on a backing storage medium (typically on magnetic disc). From here they have to be translated into a form suitable for execution. If a program contains errors, it needs to be corrected by some means. Once translated, it usually needs to be operated upon further before execution. A minimum requirement is that it can be loaded into the immediate access store of its target operating system. While being executed, it is desirable to monitor its progress in case of errors. There are many utilities of one form or another which can further smooth the path to completeness. It is to these that the main attention is given below.

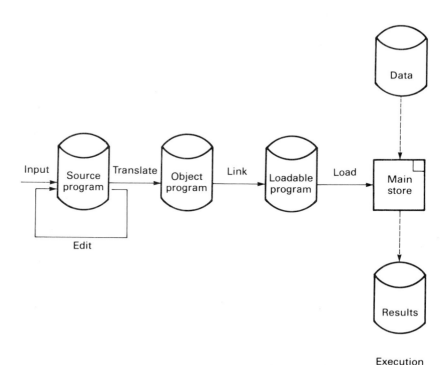

Figure 9.1 Program preparation

To describe the parts, it is useful to have a diagram expressing their various relationships to each other. Assuming that the relevant files are held on magnetic disc media, of whatever type, a system chart may best illustrate the situation.

If errors are detected at any time, it is possible that much of the cycle shown in Figure 9.1 will need to be repeated, starting with editing of the source program. Hence, a start will be made with that part of the system which first claims a programmer's attention.

9.2 The need for tools

When a computer system is switched on initially, it contains no programs of any kind in its immediate access store. Therefore, to make a start, a set of instructions must be inserted in a form acceptable to the processor. Unfortunately for human beings, this has to be in a binary format—0s and 1s only. It is, of course, possible to write programs in this form, but it is not very efficient. So, one of the most useful software tools and, arguably, the most fundamental is one to translate programs from human-orientated form to one which is machine-orientated. It is not easy for modern programmers to appreciate the profound effect that such tools had. Fortunately a tendency to take such things for granted does not obscure their worth. However, that is really only the beginning of the tool kit.

In the same way that programming is no longer carried out in binary form, so there is no need to duplicate work unnecessarily elsewhere. Some programmers with exceptionally long memories can recall the tedium of preparing programs for paper tape or card media. The source text (there is no need to retreat further in time here) was not always correct first time and sometimes corrections had to be made. To amend a card pack, the cards in error were removed and correct ones inserted. In this respect, very much after the style of a line-orientated source text editor now. Of course, if one were sufficiently unlucky as to drop a card pack ...! Not pleasant, but not absolutely disastrous.

When paper tape was the chosen medium to hold source text, however, it could not become out of order by being dropped. Although it might be difficult to wind into an orderly form, the information could not be deranged in its order. The difficulty occurred if changes had to be made. A number of subterfuges were helpful here. Typically, if a character had no holes punched, or all holes punched, it was ignored. Hence, characters could be deleted (typically, using a hand-held device) quite easily. However, it was very difficult to *add* extra characters, or lines. The tape could be cut and separated, and a new section inserted, if done very carefully. Sharp knives were in some demand in those days; and specialised sticky tape was remarkably popular.

This, of course, is no way to encourage efficient production. The tools which have done very much to ameliorate a programmer's lot are simple text editors, with which everyone should be familiar. They may deal with complete lines at a time after the manner of card pack editing; they may deal with blocks of characters, as if mimicking paper tape work; they may be able to access the text randomly or be strictly sequential; they may be very user-friendly, using screenfuls of information at a time; they may be keyboard driven, or use a mouse, and so on; but they fulfil a fundamental need.

User-friendliness is not the only criterion by which to judge utility so, as a third example, consider linkage editing. This is the process of gathering together separately translated part-programs to make a complete unit. Once again, the profundity of the operation may not be immediately appreciated, but if the whole program is very large there are many advantages which accrue. When the total program exceeds (for instance) 10,000 instructions, it is an imposition to retranslate the entire program in case of one amendment. This is not meant to imply that the correct way to write a 10,000 instruction program is all in one piece. Monolithic programs are not at all a good idea if they are other than extremely small. (If this seems to be too much to worry about, consider a computer language translator. In such a situation, 10,000 instructions is definitely on the low side for a commercial venture.) Hence the way to solve the problem is to split the program into a proper number of separate procedures. These can be structured to be translated independently and combined later. When alterations have to be made, a single procedure only is affected, which allows changes to be made more rapidly and with less complication.

All of these examples demonstrate the desirability of proper software tools for the efficient production of programs. There are, of course, many other desirable utilities typically available within well-structured operating systems. It will not be possible to describe every one of these, but some will be discussed in more detail below.

9.3 Program text preparation

As has already been said, one of the principal programming interactions is with program source text files. These have not only to be prepared initially, but also amended as necessary. The principal software tool for this task is a text editor, but there are other relevant operations (Figure 9.2). While these secondary tools may not apparently be so popular, they can be of great utility. Even a tool as simple as a word-orientated sorting package may be surprising in its power.

The first input of text may use a medium prepared off-line: possibly magnetic tape or magnetic disc. However this is obtained, a simple software

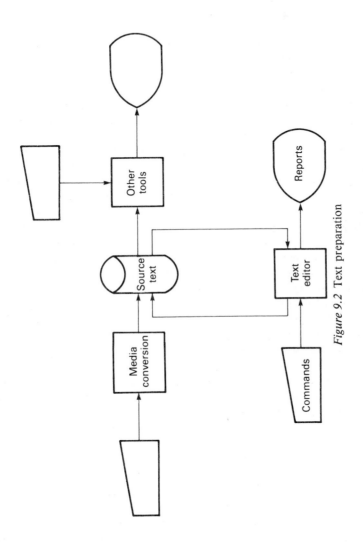

Figure 9.2 Text preparation

tool will be needed to transfer it to its on-line storage. Such a tool might have one of several names: 'media conversion package' or 'peripheral interchange program' are typical of these. It may be that input is under direct data entry, which is a more immediate use of such a tool. However, it should be remembered that such a program exists: it is too easy to take such tools for granted.

Once established, further operations on the text will take place under the control of some kind of editor. It is possible, of course, that such an editor will be used in the initial input. Suitable reflection will suggest whether this is more or less desirable, perhaps. In any case, such editors have come very much to be the workhorses of text preparation and are generally available in three styles, according to the commands which they can usefully accept: character editors, line editors and screen editors.

The simplest of these are probably the line editors. These have the appearance of being record orientated, where each line of a text file is a single record. Lines are often of fixed length, perhaps 40 or 80 characters. The files are amended by insertion, deletion or replacement of single lines, or blocks of lines. It is sometimes possible to introduce the contents of another text file at a given position, as a specialised kind of insertion. Such editors are sometimes provided as built-in facilities within language processors, most typically in BASIC language systems.

Character editors frequently have the same facilities as line editors, but also allow editing within a line. The same basic operations are provided: insertion, deletion and replacement, of characters and of blocks of characters. The details to be considered frequently differ from the similar line editors. For instance, the possibility arises of producing lines of any length by successive insertions. Because of this, the treatment of lines as such becomes less important. A 'newline' character may then take on a proper meaning of its own, rather than being implicit, as is the case for the record-orientated text of fixed line length.

At the next level of sophistication comes screen-orientated editing. This provides a 'window' into the text of a file, and anything visible through the window can be edited (see Figure 9.3). This depends for best effect on the provision of a suitable terminal to accept the editing commands. Within the visible area, characters or lines may be amended; and the window may be moved around within the file. The most flexible access is provided when movement may be to anywhere within the file, although not all editors allow this.

Following the preparation of text files, what can usefully be done in terms of text processing alone? A typical computer-based system might attain efficient production through judicious use of macros which are, in effect, shorthand forms of frequently used pieces of text. Following the initial text preparation, before it is submitted for translation (for instance), these shorthand forms are expanded into their appropriate appearances. The facility of expanding macros, using a macroprocessor, can *impose* uniformity where it is needed. Thus, if a certain instruction sequence is used frequently, it can be implemented as a macro. This saves labour; and if a change has to be made to the sequence, it is made universally by a single amendment.

As another example, consider a concordance generator. This is designed

```
Graduate Careers in Computing

... This expansion in the use of
computer systems has led inevitably
to the requirements of increased
familiarity with computer systems so
that the equipment may be used in
its moist efficient way. Because of
this, the opportunities have
increased for those who understand
not just the systems as provided,
but also the applications for which
they are being used.
```

```
An overview of those areas into
which computing has a direct input
yields three categories for
consideration.  They may loosely be
identified with the hardware, the
software, and the applications.  The
builders of the machines are
concerned with the first category,
and have to do with areas such as
Electronics, Electronic Engineering,
Instrument and Control Technology,
and Process Control and
Instrumentation.  They represent the
```

```
hardware aspect, and are largely
connected with the design and
assembly of the machines which
everybody else is to use.  The
software providers form the middle
group.  They make it ready for
others, and typically have job
titles to do with Computer
Programming and Computing.  The
users of computers fall into the
last category, ...
```

Figure 9.3 The editing operation

to process text considered as a sequence of words, suitably delivered. Its task is primarily to count the occurrences of all the different words in the text file. The output is typically a list of all of the words sorted into lexicographical order, together with a count associated with each word. Thus, it is similar to the cross-reference listing as given in some language translators. It is a powerful tool for discovering mis-spelt words and identifying variables used only once, among other things.

Finally (although there are many other tools which would be described if there were room), program text formatters are simple and powerful. Their task is merely to lay out programs in a standard form and to list the result. For instance, in a Pascal program, blocks could be indented in a standard way. In this manner, not only may the programs be presented in a fashion pleasing to the eye, but gross errors are easily detected. It is not even particularly difficult to implement such tools and they are worth the effort in very many cases.

This is no more than an introduction to a subject of considerable size. For a fuller description, there are well-structured texts which discuss not only other ideas, but also give their implementations in full detail. These are recommended for further reading and fuller investigation.

9.4 Program translation

Once the text has been prepared, it has to be translated (see Figure 9.4). The software tools for this task go under various names: compilers and assemblers are two of the most popular. Traditionally, the assemblers deal with low-level languages and the compilers with their high-level counterparts. To avoid any bias, the term translator will be used throughout.

The result of translation is an object program or module. For various reasons it is seldom directly executable, but requires further processing. After translation, a program's human-understandable characteristics have been exchanged for their computer-related equivalents. There have been many descriptions given of translators from theoretical and practical viewpoints, so that these details will not be pursued. The emphasis in this section will concentrate on their aspects as tools and on their appearance to the user.

In its simplest form, a translator does no more than the mere translation. It would almost certainly not be generally acceptable in this form, however. Human beings are fallible and prone to error. Hence a translator that failed to indicate an unsuccessful translation would not be satisfactory. Users should expect that their errors will be reported in a sympathetic and exact fashion, so that they may be corrected with a minimum of difficulty. Translators which collapse at the first error in a source program, or fail to report accurately, should not be tolerated.

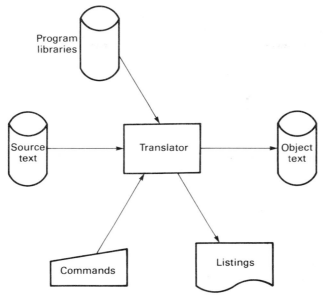

Figure 9.4 Translation

Error reports are usually the minimal text listings output from a translator. With a suitable set of commands, many other listings become available. The simplest of these is probably a source listing: an echo of the text input to the translator. This should not be taken too much for granted, as the translator's viewpoint is not always what we expect. It might be a corrupted text version which has unexpectedly become available. Then, the file name will have the correct value, but the contents will be wrong. In addition, useful information, such as line numbers, might be appended. Again, it might not seem much, but it may be useful.

It is often useful to know about the usage of variables within a program. One of the facilities provided by good translators is a cross-reference listing. In this, every occurrence of each variable is listed, usually lexicographically sorted. It is important to note that this is not quite the same as a concordance generator. In a program containing the fragment

print (' time = ', time); /* print time */

a concordance generator would report three occurrences of 'time'. A cross-reference listing, however, would only report one.

High-level language programmers have no need to reference the detailed instruction code into which their programs are translated. That would defeat the purpose: that of machine independence. Low-level languages, which are machine dependent, are different. Therefore, one of the listings available to a low-level language translator relates to the translated result.

This is a listing, usually printed in octal or hexadecimal format, of the object program. This is often allied with a symbol dictionary, which gives the machine store addresses which correspond to the user-defined labels. This is to enable machine-dependent alterations to be made. These are somewhat old-fashioned, but useful to system programmers on certain critical occasions (Figure 9.5).

```
Program prime (Input,Output);

{The program repeatedly asks for the input of an integer
 and prints out its smallest factor,
 or says that the integer is prime}

Var factor, maxfactor   : 0 .. 65535;
    number              : Integer;

Begin { Start of main loop }
    Repeat
        Repeat
            writeln;
            write ('Input an integer (up to 9 digits)',
                    ' (0 to finish): ');
            readln (number);
        Until number >= 0;

        write ('Smallest factor of ', number : 1, ' is ');
        maxfactor := round (sqrt (number));

        { Treat the even and odd numbers separately }
        factor := 2;
        If odd (number) then
            { Try all odd divisors
              up to square root of number }
            Begin factor := 1;
                Repeat
                    factor := factor + 2;
                Until (number mod factor = 0)
                    or (factor > maxfactor);
            End;

        { Now decide whether prime or not }
        If (factor <= maxfactor) and (factor < number)
            then writeln (factor : 1)
            else
        If number <> 0 then writeln ('Prime')

    Until number = 0;

End.
```

Figure 9.5 A typical program listing

If there are pieces of program text which are frequently used, some translators allow these to be incorporated into programs by the use of built-in macroprocessors. They bear the same relationship to their independent counterparts as do integrated cross-reference listings to concordances. (Each of the independent text-processors was described in the previous section.) The common source text incorporated in this way should not be confused with object text added at later stages. This process combines the source texts, and translates the result purely in source program terms.

9.5 Execution and debugging

Once translation has taken place, the object text has to be submitted for execution. This may take place in one or more stages and, in each case, the appropriate tool is applied.

If the final execution is to be deferred, a separate linkage editor is used. This is also known as a collector, consolidator or composer, among other things. It takes the object text which is output by translators and tidies it up to be ready for loading (Figure 9.6). This two-stage process is employed because the translator's output is not necessarily immediately ready to run.

To be fair, the output of a translator is very often fit for immediate loading. However, if there are much-used portions of program code, they need not be translated repeatedly. Linkage editing offers a way to avoid this. Not only can common program text be added before translation, by

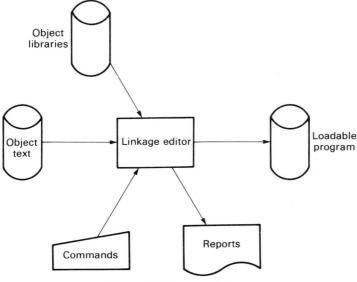

Figure 9.6 Program linkage

macroprocessing facilities, but pretranslated object text can be incorporated at the linkage editing stage. When one considers the number of times that low-level input or output routines are invoked, the facility makes a great deal of sense. The result, anyway, is a loadable program.

At this point, a program loader is called into use. This may be part of the underlying software, which is further discussed in Chapter 12, or may be made available in some other way. In any case, its job is to transfer the loadable program from wherever it resides into the computer's immediate access store. The program is then ready for execution. In some systems, the functions of the linkage editor and loader are combined into a linking loader. This is more useful for programs under test, as the intermediate stage is avoided, and the program is loaded immediately ready for use. If the program is required many times in its final form, it is more efficient to use the tools separately.

There is an added virtue in the use of linkage editing. It allows programs to be developed in small parts (often called procedures or sub-programs) which can be linked together after translation. In this way, if an error is detected, only part of the program needs to be corrected and retranslated. As the units under consideration are smaller, there is less likelihood of further errors being introduced. In some cases, the different sub-programs may even be written in different languages, which allows each one to use the language suited to the particular part of the application.

At the end of program loading, no matter how it is accomplished, the program is ready for execution. It is possible that the next operation is the execution itself. This is satisfactory only if there are no errors in the program logic. If there is anything unexpected during execution, what happens next? This is dependent on the operating system, if any. If a control program (part of the operating system) is present, it may take corrective action, but in a computer acting as a control system in its own right, there may well be no control program present. This demonstrates two things: the danger of embarking on unstructured development and the importance of software testing tools. This applies even when the operating system is present. It is better to anticipate trouble and take avoiding action than to suffer the consequences of the alternative.

The use of debugging tools at this stage should be self-explanatory. They appear in many levels of complexity. The simplest ones function as a safety net. They are activated only in case of trouble, usually terminal. Not for nothing is a tool of this type known as 'post mortem'. It may give no more than an indication of the point in the program where an error occurred and a reason for it. A typical message might thus be 'DIVIDE BY ZERO AT LINE 42'.

More extensive information might be made available. The value of every variable may be listed, although the output under these circumstances could be extremely voluminous. Poor tools of this nature may give only computer-relevant information with little relation to the program source text. Advanced tools may even allow continuation after correction of the effects of the error. The situation leading to the message given above might allow the program to execute further after setting the result of the division to some extremely large value.

This may appear a reasonable way to continue, but if the program does not terminate in an execution error, yet gives incorrect output, such tools

```
Snapshot


0A43:0000           FA B8 EA 0C 8E D8-B8 31 0D 8E D0 BC 00 01    z8j..X81..P<..
0A43:0010  FB B8 70 04 A3 12 00 8C-06 56 00 26 A1 2C 00 A3    {8p.#....V.&!,.#
0A43:0020  62 00 BE 80 00 26 8A 0C-32 ED E3 15 46 26 8A 04    b.>..&..2mc.F&..
0A43:0030  3C 3D 74 10 3C 20 74 04-3C 09 75 05 49 7F ED 33    <=t.< t.<.u.I.m3
0A43:0040  C9 EB 44 90 33 DB 49 74-2E 46 26 8A 04 3C 20 74    IkD.3[It.F&..< t
0A43:0050  26 3C 09 74 22 2C 30 7C-28 3C 09 7F 24 03 DB 72    &<.t",0|(<..$.[r
0A43:0060  20 8B D3 03 DB 72 1A 03-DB 72 16 03 DA 72 12 32    .S.[r..[r..Zr.2
0A43:0070  E4 03 D8 72 0C EB CF 0B-DB 74 06 89 1E 46 04 EB    d.Xr.kO.[t...F.k
0A43:0080  BB BA                                              ; ;


AX=0000  BX=0000  CX=2ED2  DX=0000  SP=0100  BP=0000  SI=0000  DI=0000
DS=0A33  ES=0A33  SS=0D31  CS=0A43  IP=0003   NV UP DI PL NZ NA PO NC


Trace


0A43:0003 B8EA0C       MOV    AX,0CEA
0A43:0006 8ED8         MOV    DS,AX
0A43:000B 8ED0         MOV    SS,AX
0A43:0010 FB           STI
0A43:0011 B87004       MOV    AX,0470
0A43:0014 A31200       MOV    [0012],AX              DS:0012=0000
0A43:0017 8C065600     MOV    [0056],ES              DS:0056=0000
0A43:001B 26           ES:
0A43:001C A12C00       MOV    AX,[002C]              ES:002C=0A30
0A43:001F A36200       MOV    [0062],AX              DS:0062=0000
0A43:0022 BE8000       MOV    SI,0080
0A43:0025 26           ES:
0A43:0026 8A0C         MOV    CL,[SI]                ES:0080=01
0A43:0028 32ED         XOR    CH,CH
0A43:002A E315         JCXZ   0041
0A43:002C 46           INC    SI
0A43:002D 26           ES:
0A43:002E 8A04         MOV    AL,[SI]                ES:0081=20


Snapshot


0A43:0080           64 00 E9 A6 00 8B-1E 46 04 D1 EB 03 DB 81    d.i&...F.Qk.[.
0A43:0090  FB 00 02 77 07 BB 00 02-89 1E 46 04 26 8B 16 02    [..w.;...F.&...
0A43:00A0  00 8C D8 2B D0 F7 C2 00-F0 75 0B D1 E2 D1 E2 D1    ..X+PwB.pu.QbQbQ
0A43:00B0  E2 D1 E2 EB 04 90 BA F0-FF A1 12 00 03 C3 72 04    bQbk..:p.!...Cr.
0A43:00C0  3B D0 77 06 BA 93 00 EB-64 90 89 16 10 00 FA 8C    ;Pw.:..kd.....z.
0A43:00D0  D8 8E D0 8B E2 FB 8B D1-A1 12 00 A3 58 00 A3 5A    X.P.b{.Q!..#X.#Z
0A43:00E0  00 8B 1E 10 00 2B D8 2B-1E 46 04 72 D7 89 1E 5C    .....+X+.F.rW..\
0A43:00F0  00 06 33 C0 50 8B EC 8B-DA 8B CA 83 C3 04 81 E3    ..3@P.1.z.J.C..c
0A43:0100  FE FF


AX=0A20  BX=0000  CX=0001  DX=0000  SP=0100  BP=0000  SI=0081  DI=0000
DS=0CEA  ES=0A33  SS=0D31  CS=0A43  IP=0030   NV UP EI PL NZ NA PE NC
```

Figure 9.7 Snapshot and trace

are not of much use. This corresponds to selection of an inappropriate tool. The correct tool for such an application would produce a 'snapshot' of the program variables at suitable points. In this way, any deviation from correct results would be easier to identify.

This, too, is not necessarily the full requirement. For correct program execution, not only must variables take their correct values, but the path taken through the program must be correct. To identify that this has been done, a 'trace' of the execution is required (Figure 9.7). A software tool with this effect might provide a report of all lines executed, in due order. Or it might report each procedure label as it was passed, which is less voluminous. In any case, either of the two latter tools, if not used with great care, might produce an overwhelming amount of results.

The latter observation leads to consideration of the constitution of correct volume. It is of no use whatsoever to present many lines, or even pages, of results if they are not going to be inspected. Ideally, the only items to be produced would be those in error. This would correspond already to knowing where the error existed, which cannot be the case. Hence the amount must be such that it can feasibly be inspected and accurately assessed. If it can be prepared automatically, and comparison can take place under computer control, so much the better. This is particularly applicable when a new program is written to supersede an existing one. In such cases, the use of suitable software tools of this nature is almost automatic.

9.6 Helpful utilities

There are many other software tools available, often grouped under the heading of utilities. They take no direct part in program preparation and execution but, nonetheless, their presence is very important. They are intended to provide support to the main activity and to guard against various difficulties which might arise. Some of them have already been mentioned, and those explanations will be amplified as necessary.

Some of the more obvious ones are file comparison utilities. Their function is to compare two files and report if they differ. In essence, these are very simple, but there are various ways in which differences may be reported. If the files are read record by record, reports may be issued listing the record numbers only, or the contents of the records which differ may also be listed. If the files are not in readable character format (for instance, object text files) the differing records may be converted to octal or hexadecimal format before presentation. The level of user-friendliness may be increased, so that if source text files are being compared, program comments are omitted from the comparison. A more advanced form is able to avoid reporting multiple mis-matches, if a single record in one file is missing.

Another utility operation already mentioned is that of copying. This may be as simple as transferring one file to another of the same type, record by record, but it may actually be more complex, although outwardly simple. If a serial tape file is transferred on to a serial magnetic disc file, there is little extra complication. If, however, the magnetic disc file's organisation is indexed sequential, much more work must be done. It is very likely that the extended processing will be inherent in the operating system primitive operations, but it still has to be done.

This type of processing will typically allow concatenation of files. In this way, program text files may be built up a few records at a time and combined later. This has the advantage of minimising loss in case of system malfunction. If text files are initially prepared by direct data entry, it is often preferable to limit input to small volumes and then to juxtapose them afterwards. The problem of computer or human error also leads to the use of similar copying to produce duplicate versions of important files. In this way, if a critical piece of data is lost, it may be retrieved from the copy (usually known as an archive or backup). Archival utilities are often invoked automatically. In some cases, the entire store of files is copied daily; or changed files only may be copied. Copies are typically kept on magnetic tape, for economy.

Other copying-type utilities may be taken even more for granted. Of this nature are pseudo-off-line operators, also known as spoolers (SPOOL stands for Simultaneous Peripheral Operation On-Line). These are used to simulate slow peripherals used by several programs, without duplicating the actual devices. For instance, consider printer spooling. Every program's printing commands are diverted so that output is to (for instance) a magnetic disc file. (Each program has a separate file for each simulated printer.) In this way, programs are able to execute whether or not a printer is actually available to them at that time. Subsequently, the files are printed by a despooler utility, whose only task is printing spooled files, which enables a greater use of the computer's processing facilities.

Utilities are also available to allow the efficiency of programs to be measured. Such utilities interact with the computer's operating system, or in effect *are* the operating system, and time the execution of programs. If the elapsed-time clock is inspected before execution commences and again after it ceases, it is easy to evaluate the time taken. More sophisticated timing utilities will count only the time spent in executing instructions, ignoring time spent waiting for peripheral transfers. In each case, program timings may be compared.

It is also possible to calculate timings internal to programs. If the programs are produced from separate parts (see section 9.5), the separate procedures may be timed independently. In this way, the appropriate utilities, known as profilers, can detect where most time is being spent within programs. This will allow the maximum optimisation to be directed where it will do most good. In critical cases, certain procedures may be rewritten in a low-level language. While this is not generally recommended, for reasons of implementors' efficiency, specific treatment of this nature may be admissible.

9.7 An integrated approach

It is much better to plan ahead than to react to difficulties as they arise. Therefore, the employment of utilities should not be viewed as an attempt to use such software tools merely because they are there. It is better to adopt a fully-considered method, using such tools as are necessary. It is unlikely, for instance, that any users apart from translator writers will have need of syntax-analyser generators! For these reasons, a suggested application program implementation route will be given.

Most of the route is straightforward (Figure 9.8). Initial text preparation will be undertaken by specialised staff. The text is then introduced by the appropriate media conversion tool (unless of course it was input directly). This may appear to be overly fussy: why should not the programmer input the program? However, one seldom develops the specialised data preparation skills required for efficiency, except by being that specialist. This method avoids the misuse of programmers' time, which can more usefully be spent in other ways.

What happens next? Another media conversion tool can be used to list the text, and obvious errors may be identified. Alternatively, if the text is that of a program, and not test data, it may seem that the best next step is to submit it to the appropriate language translator and produce its source listings at the same time. This effects two jobs in one: very desirable. It has to be admitted that not all translators' diagnostic messages are particularly marvellous, however. A better path might first employ a program text formatter to improve the initial layout; this will also highlight any major structural errors quickly. This would be followed by a program syntax checker, which is a software tool resembling a translator. It differs in its intent, however: instead of its main task being the production of an object program, a syntax checker aims to provide very thorough diagnosis of program errors; its major aim is intelligibility.

At this point, unless you are one of those extremely rare people who gets it right first time, corrections will need to be made. A suitable set of editing commands will be drawn up to effect the corrections but, unless they are few and trivial, they may be entrusted to other hands. As noted above, programmers' time is valuable. This method may appear idealistic, but in terms of efficiency it should not be dismissed out of hand. In any case, after the alterations have been made, the same checking as before may be used.

The next item for single programs might well be the use of an interpreter,

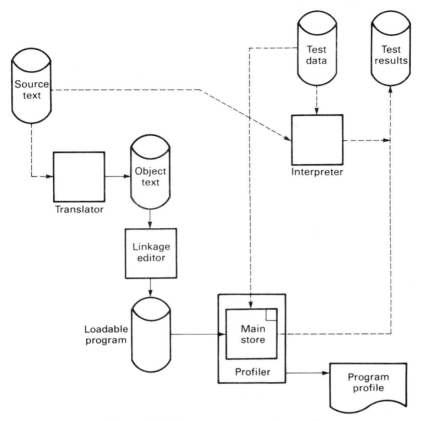

Figure 9.8 The program generation cycle

rather than immediate translation. This software tool accepts the source text of a program and executes it statement by statement, instead of translating it in its entirety. It is usually very much slower in execution than a translated program but, as it necessarily has access to all of the source text, its run-time diagnostics are much more useful. It is best used to detect execution errors so that corrections may efficiently be made, as suggested above.

Only when the results are fully satisfactory should the program be translated. It then takes its final form, and is submitted to a profiler. Critical sections may be optimised, to allow for efficient resource use. This path is given diagrammatically in Figure 9.8.

This planning ahead should apply in every case, not just in the use of software tools. The implementation of any system is necessarily eased by the use of suitable tools, hence their importance, but there is never any excuse for the omission of forward planning.

9.8 Exercises

1 Assume that you are a COBOL programmer who needs to write a program which is to access a database. How might you accomplish this? (Standard COBOL does not support database operations.)

2 How might source text be organised efficiently on a magnetic medium? With a chosen organisation, investigate how the text might be referred to during editing, and consider the problems of replacement, insertion and deletion of characters and of lines of text.

3 Make a list of the text-related software tools available to you under the operating system with which you are most familiar. Write a few sentences about each one, describing its environment, its use and any special points about it.

4 What commands are available in the text editor(s) with which you are familiar? How efficient are they, in human-orientated terms?

5 With reference to a translator with which you are familiar, how useful and how user-friendly are its diagnostic messages?

6 It has been said that one never really knows a translator until all of its error messages have been sampled. How many different error reports can you persuade your favourite translator to produce? (You will need more than one source program, but it is more of a challenge to achieve a maximum mixture in a minimum of programs!)

7 In block-structured languages, particular problems apply to the usage of variables. Certain other problems also apply to languages allowing qualification of names (for instance, COBOL and PL/1). What are the problems in each case?

8 Investigate the software tools available to you which fulfil the debugging function. Are they easy to use? Have you any recommendations you wish to make to their implementors?

9 Design an algorithm to compare two files record by record, and report how they differ. Ensure that your algorithm avoids multiple reports if a single record is missing from either file.

10 What kind of information needs to be attached to each file within an operating system to allow only such files as have been changed (since the last archival) to be archived?

11 Compare the implementation path suggested in section 9.7 with the one you usually utilise. If they are not the same:

(a) Where do they differ?
(b) How do they differ?
(c) Why do they differ?

CHAPTER 10

The software implementors

10.1 Implementation and psychology

It has already been observed that without people there can be no implementation. It follows, then, that the personnel involved cannot be isolated from implementational considerations. However, there are different kinds of people, exactly as there are different areas of implementation, and if the one can be matched to the other, so much the better.

In matching components from two different areas, each should be able to be assessed in some way. Psychology, defined by the *Concise Oxford Dictionary* as the 'science of the nature ... of human mind', indicates that the worth of the implementors can be assessed in some way. It might be argued that this is not necessarily exact; but it provides a reasonable initial basis from which to work.

To start with, the kinds of people available differ widely. Some are particularly good at writing programs, but not so much so at system design; some are experts in system analysis, but do not interact well with operating systems; and so on. Of course, there are some exceptional individuals who are strong in all areas—but they are few.

In the same way, some people work better on their own, while others are natural team members; others are better leaders than subordinates. Because of this, before any implementation is undertaken, it is proper that the implementation manager arrays his forces appropriately. Of course, the problem has other aspects to concern the manager and these depend largely on the way in which original work is done. (This ignores, for the time being, the problems of system maintenance.)

In a system being implemented for the first time, rather than achieved by alterations to one which already exists, analysis and design are abstract processes. This fact has to be recognised, and they have to be undertaken as such. In this way, design is more nearly akin to the composition of a piece of music and the playing of it, rather than the assembly of a car. Creative work of this kind is usually thought of as a solitary activity. Quite often, in practice, it is. Some parts of the creative process are commonly so private that not even the creator's conscious mind is allowed to know what the unconscious is doing until it has finished!

However, it is not always or necessarily such a lonely undertaking. Certain phases of creativity can usefully be handled by teams: so-called 'think tanks', groups of people assembled specifically to generate ideas. While teamwork in analysis and programming is not always praised so highly, the principle remains the same. In the field of implementation, it has become sufficiently commonplace as to attract little excitement. Nevertheless, it is a significant aspect of a manager's task, when appropriate, to identify the need for such a team and then, of course, to assemble it in order for it to execute its functions.

This is not a plea to treat the thinkers of original thoughts as if they were hot-house plants. There is much of the work which can be done in a methodical fashion, but from time to time some of the processes must be carried out creatively and this must be taken into account in the working environment. Following the earlier image, one would hardly attempt to compose a symphony in an assembly area for cars. (And we don't think that assembling a car would be very practical in a concert hall, either.) Therefore, another aspect of the manager's task is the provision of suitable working conditions.

This is not merely a function of a place to put one's pen and paper. Any flat horizontal surface might seem adequate but, perhaps, noise, or unreasonable temperature, or draughts, might render it unfriendly. It must be possible for the implementor to *concentrate* on the job in hand. There would be good lighting, an equable temperature and fresh air; and the specialised tools of the trade would be available. This might appear obvious, but better productivity can be realised when such things are taken into consideration. In the implementation of computing systems, as elsewhere, more work is done by those not worried by extraneous matters.

A recently published report discusses this problem area, and it is worrying to discover that much of a programmer's 'so-called workday is made up largely of frustration time'. It is not surprising that programmers whose workplace is congenial typically perform significantly better than their colleagues in less fortunate circumstances. It follows that it is in the interest of all to secure sensibly appropriate working conditions. Any reasonable expenditure to arrange this is usually soon recouped in such cases.

10.2 Working alone or together

During the course of implementing a piece of software, a particularly important question needs to be answered. Is it better to entrust it to one implementor, or is it better for a team? In some cases, of course, the answer is obvious, while in others the various possibilities must be looked at more carefully. The problem, which was introduced in Chapter 8, is here treated more fully.

If the problem to be solved is a very large one, a team will necessarily be needed. If it is very small, one person may well be adequate. That does not mean, however, that it would be correct to assign a single implementor to such a task. For instance, after the problem has been solved, the implementation can be presented apparently matching its specifications. People, however, tend to see what they expect, rather than what is necessarily present. A simple example of this is shown in Figure 10.1. Hence it is usually advisable to have one's work checked by somebody else—teamwork.

Ultimately, most correctly undertaken production is the responsibility of a number of people. Some one-person software houses have been successful, but the bulk of useful work does not fall into this category. It is preferable to apportion the design to one area, the programming to another, and the testing to yet another. In this way, erroneous preconceptions may be identified and corrected more readily.

The above description is one of an interesting ideal situation, which must sometimes be modified in practice. Often the testing is split between the designer and the programmer. In operations which favour the use of programmer/analysts, all three tasks may become the responsibility of one implementor.

In fact, of course, all work is ultimately done by individuals, however they are organised. This is acknowledged in the previous section, but there are other aspects of the situation. Individuals have a number of attributes which are generally relevant in their work in implementation. Among these are abilities to withstand stress and to adapt to changing conditions, which apply in all circumstances. If organisation in a team is contemplated, such things as ability to work with others and to take on leading or subordinate roles must be added.

I love Paris in the
the springtime

Figure 10.1 How carefully do you read?

The ability to withstand stress is a desirable attribute. As the due date for completion of a project approaches, so the strains on the implementor(s) increase. If an implementor is unable to adjust to the situation, the quality of the work will probably suffer. This can lead to increasing stress levels and may have most unfortunate outcomes. Those who can adapt well to changing conditions are less likely to suffer from such effects. It is a generally desirable trait, however, as the discipline of computing has always been subject to rapid and far-reaching changes. Individuals who cannot adapt tend to use outmoded and less efficient techniques, to their detriment.

If the implementation is to be performed by a team, it seems reasonable that the team members should be able to work with each other. This can sometimes cause difficulties. Traditionally, programming has been largely an individual task. Many programmers, therefore, are happiest working on their own and tend to be less productive when employed as one of a group. In many teams, there is a feeling that there are more leaders than subordinates.

It is possibly one of the observations that can be made, that in any team there will be more members who would prefer to lead. The difficulty then arises in the selection of a suitable leader. Typically, the skills which make up a good programmer do not correspond to good leadership. People are not programs, after all! If this is not recognised, poor teams may be made up. A number of solutions have been proposed to this problem and will be discussed later in this chapter.

10.3 Personnel selection

Not every qualified person is the right one for the job. There are qualities other than competence which are needed. In the absence of trained and experienced workers, though, there is not likely to be much good work done. Yet even the best trained practitioners of the tasks cannot produce anything without working. So the requirements of staffing, when personnel are selected, are threefold. For the staff involved in any job there must be

- the *right* number
- of *active*
- *trained* and *experienced* people.

This section will look at some of the kinds of people involved and some characteristics which they might reasonably be expected to possess.

Somebody has to provide overall direction to any job to be done. Such a person might typically be called a manager. Perhaps the title given will be somewhat more descriptive, as in the case of a data-processing manager, or programming manager, but the task will principally be one of organisation and direction of people and operations. To do this, a manager will need not only to be able to plan a campaign in the first place, but to be sufficiently resilient as not to stop when things go wrong.

It is undeniable that things do go wrong, sometimes even necessitating the complete redesign of an overall master-plan. A good manager will need imagination, suitably disciplined, and a proper resourcefulness. There is also a requirement for a good overall understanding of the technical problems involved in each solution to be implemented. The rationale here is not that the manager will be expected to deal with the details of the work in person, but that he or she must not be placed in a position of total reliance on subordinates—progress reports need to be inspected and questioned with understanding.

A good manager should be able to learn rapidly; innovation must be *properly* used and directed. It would be too easy for less experienced subordinates to apply new techniques overenthusiastically, even to the detriment of an entire project.

It might be argued that one does not often get the opportunity to select one's manager. This may appear to be true, but each new employment position is just as much the selection of a manager by the employee as that of a new worker by the employer. This points out the importance of doing it properly. Surely no-one wants to be part of a team which is poorly constructed. There is no monopoly on competence, or the lack of it, in any team member. Working in a poorly-managed team can be extremely unpleasant and should be avoided if possible.

A good systems analyst and designer has somewhat different characteristics. In this case, technical ability is very important. The analyst's task is in planning and communication. This communication is two-way, and will entail sympathy and sensitivity as well as accuracy. The major tasks of an analyst are to find out, carefully, what needs to be done and to draw up the plans for doing it. For this, the environment in which the system is found must be well understood. A proper sense of perspective is invaluable. Responsibility second only to the manager's is needed, sometimes (inaccurately) described as maturity. An awareness of the entire system environment is important—no system operates in isolation.

The designs of the analyst, under overall managerial control, have to be realised. In a computing software context, this is the task of programmers. These are the people who take over when a suitable level of detail has been reached and produce the actual program code. Such personnel must be technically able and well acquainted with the software 'tools of the trade'. There is an attitude found too often which equates 'cleverness' with technical ability: this temptation should be avoided. What is needed is practical skill, and proper competence rather than absolute perfection (but the programs *must* follow their specification). Programmers need to be dependable, stable and orderly in mind, with clarity of thought. Much programming is shared, and achievement takes place based on a group rather than an individual. Nevertheless each member must be able to take the appropriate strain at critical times so that difficulties, as well as successes, can be shared.

Where do such people come from in an organisation? Recruitment may take place from within or from outside. In the first case, it might better be called retraining, although there are distressing attempts to apply the same techniques to personnel recruited from without. If a need is identifiably short-term only, vacancies might be filled by specialist contract workers—this applies more often to programmers than to other people.

How are people identified as suitable? There is usually an advertisement made, followed by one or more interviews. Requests may be direct person-to-person, by printed advertisement (local or national), or through a recruitment agency. Interviews may be personal only or may include technical and aptitude testing. There is no fixed way in which any of these are carried out, but personal contact can be most useful on both sides. In this way, employees may also investigate any potential employers, as has been suggested earlier, at the same time as the employers are evaluating the prospective recruits. One wouldn't want to be unhappily employed if it could be avoided.

Some things to look for are obvious: pay, working conditions and similar material items; but less tangible items are also important. The staff turnover rate may provide a good indication: if it is too high, it may be because of internal friction, blocked promotion paths or merely boredom; if it appears too low, the cause may be managerial lethargy, lack of stimulation, or unused and unappreciated talent. It is always worth finding out about staff development policy and training, too.

10.4 Performance and its measurement

Work must proceed at an acceptable rate during implementation, and it must be possible to show that it is acceptable. If an implementation manager has to estimate the time taken to complete some portion of a task (or perhaps all of it), he must have a measure to apply. The unfortunate part of such a measure is that an implementor might then be required to produce a particular rate; but if it cannot be measured, it cannot easily be managed either.

Among the measures which have been proposed are included lines of code written, volume of object code produced at compilation, number of executions attempted, and volume of documentation produced. These are measured as achieved in a given time, and the result can then be used as a suitable evaluation factor. There are a number of problems associated with this kind of assessment, classified into two types: external and internal.

The external difficulties occur when trying to compare different areas of measurement. If a programmer is assessed at (say) 200 lines per month, and a testing implementor at 40 executions in the same time, are these in any sense equal? The problem can become more difficult when the kinds of work appear more nearly similar. Is 200 lines per month of COBOL in any way the same as 200 lines per month of assembler code? Or the comparison may be attempted between original programs and amendments to existing ones. Is it easier to write 200 lines of COBOL for an original implementation or to produce 200 lines of COBOL updating an old program?

The internal difficulties are also quite difficult to reconcile. One programmer's 200 lines of COBOL might achieve a different amount of work when compared with a similar measure from another programmer. If one implementor's assembly language draws heavily on macros for some reason, does this make the production rate higher or lower than one which does not?

Measures of compiled code may be more helpful in terms of utilisation of computing power: the more code, the more powerful it ought to be. This does not necessarily reflect on the *implementational* work, however, and management should be able to assess this aspect. Think of some of the very high-level language systems (program generators) now available. A small number of lines of original source code can produce large and powerful result programs. Does this imply that the writers of the source text are worth significantly more than COBOL programmers?

Within these scales of measurement, all of the values produced relate to a certain volume of work produced in a given time. There is no account taken of the quality of the work produced. If the volume measured is large, but of poor quality, the *real* measure of productivity is low. Hence there must be some way of allowing for this. For example, it is far better to have a small high-quality manual than a large book which is difficult to use.

10.5 Implementor communications

In earlier discussion it has already been pointed out that some tasks are too large for a single implementor. It was also suggested that while other tasks exist which are not too large, there may well be reasons for allocating more than one implementor for their treatment. At that point, the implementational unit becomes a team. Within the team there is then a need for interchange of relevant information. There will always be a requirement for external communication—jobs to be done must come from somewhere. In such cases, exterior personnel will have to specify their needs to the team in some way. An outline of such a system is given in Figure 10.2.

The amount of work involved in communications will not be a simple linear function of the size of the task in hand. Internal communication

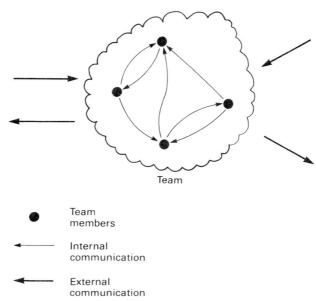

Team

●   Team
      members

◄————   Internal
      communication

◄————   External
      communication

Figure 10.2 Internal and external communication

pathways can, if not carefully chosen, proliferate out of all reasonable bounds as the number in a team is allowed to increase. Between any two people, two paths exist (one each way). There are six between any two or three people, which rises to fifty-six in a group of eight. This does not necessarily mean that large teams cannot work; just that communication must be controlled.

A simple way of accomplishing this is to split large teams into smaller units. As an example, what happens if a team of six members is split into groups of three? The paths fall from a maximum of thirty to a maximum of fourteen: six in each of the two groups, and two between the groups. This is diagrammatically described in Figure 10.3.

This assumes that where there is too much internal communication required, the 'real' work suffers. However, at some point in large tasks, such a limit will inevitably be reached, even though this is not necessarily at a team membership of six.

Good external communication can be made more difficult if the dangers of the situation have not become obvious at an early stage. Ideally, communication should take place between external personnel and one team member only. In that way, misunderstandings outside the team, about who knows what inside the team, are minimised. The converse applies, of course: it is preferable that specification is given by one person only because, again, there is less likelihood of confusion about what was said; but it is not necessarily easy to enforce team discipline on outsiders!

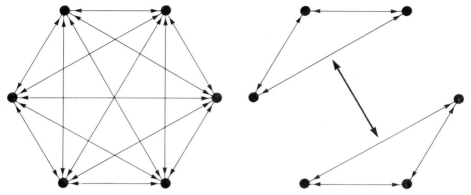

Figure 10.3 Management of internal communication

How is this communication to be carried out? It is reasonable to assume that it will appear in at least two forms—spoken and written. It is, however, important in any carefully run project to be sure of what has been said. For this reason, spoken communication can generally only be treated informally. Even so, it is not entirely out of place. It might otherwise be too easy to shelter behind a large amount of documentation. The use of the telephone, or of casual conversations, should not be discounted. A *simple* request is not worthy of too much extra work, but if it has important consequences it should be transcribed as soon as that can conveniently be done. There are too many instances of unconfirmed spoken statements being used to the detriment of the overall result.

There is also the utility of formal meetings. These may be internal, but may also involve people external to the team. They should lead to the production of accurate documentation of those things agreed at the meeting. Also, the actions to be performed should be identified following the decisions taken. Misunderstandings are more likely to be detected, and they can more easily be dealt with, if many minds are working on them simultaneously and in the same place.

Written communication, then, will be of several types. Some can be quite formal, such as a specific project requirement; other parts may merely be working notes, made day-by-day during the implementation. It is very tempting to treat the first kind with great consideration, but not to worry too much about the second. It is quite possible, though, that at some future time some of the intermediate working will become important for some reason: it might be desirable to know the reasons why a particular alternative was chosen; the *order* of certain decisions might give insight into the relevant process. Hence a dated (and even timed) record of implementation might well be a useful adjunct to communication.

Many of the problems of informal written communications can be dealt with by proper use of computer systems. The use of computer networks for passing information between team members allows automation of many useful operations. For instance, if a recipient is not currently present or available, any messages may be held pending his or her return. All messages can be date- and time-stamped as a matter of course and their receipt can be acknowledged automatically. Multiple destinations are as easy to arrange as single ones, and a permanent record may be kept, available to all at a moment's notice. Even the necessity for team members to work geographically close together is of less importance under these conditions. Each member, ultimately, may work in the environment which is most agreeable: cottage industries indeed.

10.6 Team organisations

Implementation teams, like any other teams, need to be organised. It is unreasonable to expect a group of people spontaneously to form a useful entity. The first part of organisation is the managerial environment to arrange this. This is most often arranged hierarchically, with various levels of management reporting upwards. Within a software environment, the structure may well resemble that given in Figure 10.4.

Within each team, a similar organisation might also be set up. The team leader would report to the project manager, although in some cases (such as Team 3 in Figure 10.4) they might be one and the same. Reporting to the

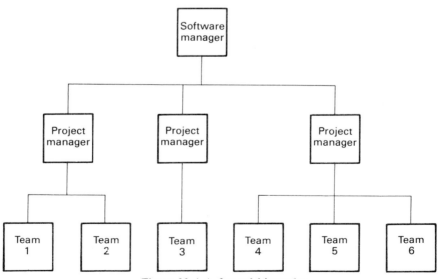

Figure 10.4 A formal hierarchy

team leader would be the senior analyst and senior programmer. The analysts would report to the senior analyst, and the programmers to the senior programmer. Thus, when a problem was presented to the team, the project manager would instruct the team leader. The team leader would brief the senior analyst and senior programmer and they, in turn, would organise their respective staff.

This remarkably formal hierarchy is not, however, always the most productive way of organising the team structure. Typically, the senior programmer is the best person available at the programming task, but already some of her available time has been used in organisation. Thus the most valuable programmer is already not being used efficiently; the same applies, of course, to the analysts.

Another difficulty arises owing to the nature of the implementational task. Before any programming can begin, a significant amount of analysis must already have taken place. Because of the dependence of some parts of an hierarchically organised structure on the others, the team as a whole is not able to function at its maximum rate. The immediate cause is the specialisation of some of the tasks. The solution to this, then, is to address the problem from its dependence on specialisation. If all of the implementors can be made *less* specific in their direction, it is possible that more work could be done overall in a $\ $ n time. This could happen because fewer of the team members would wait for others to complete their tasks before starting. In this case, programmers and analysts would take on part of each others' roles and become programmer/analysts.

The arrangement in Figure 10.5 shows the more egalitarian organisation to which this approach leads. This does not mean, though, that a given member analyses part of the problem and then goes on to produce a program for that part. It may well be preferable to avoid over-attachment to particular sections of the solution. One tends to be less critical of work in which one is heavily involved. If typical individual implementors can be made less possessive of their work, the result is usually an improvement in

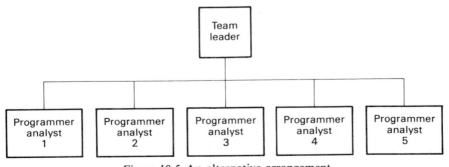

Figure 10.5 An alternative arrangement

accuracy. The converse argument should also be addressed. There must be a strong team identification so that there is still a well-directed feeling of responsibility about the work to be done. It is not acceptable that the result could become nobody's business by a process of dilution.

This method only works at all well if teams are small. The team takes on an identity of its own, and members work towards the good of the team rather than the individual. Each implementor's style is known throughout the team and may be (reasonably painlessly) modified, if necessary. This is especially useful as well-established members leave and are replaced: continuity may be maintained while the replacements are being integrated.

From these ideas, other organisational arrangements have arisen which, however, draw heavily on the positive aspects described. The smaller team is preferable to the larger one, if the work can still be done; the specialist is better than the generalist, if this can be arranged. These points are carried forward into the next section.

10.7 The 'chief programmer' concept

A number of difficulties may arise in a team organised on egalitarian lines. Among these is the loss of precisely those strengths which would normally arise from the particular expertise of each of its members. Lincoln, Jefferson and the American Declaration of Independence notwithstanding, all men are not created equal. Some, like Orwell's animals, are more equal than others. The best results would be achieved by allowing the real experts to achieve their full potential. The other team members would employ their particular talents to allow this to happen.

The extent of the difference comes to light when one compares, for example, the expert programmer with one less expert. The difference in productivity between a good programmer and a real expert may be as much as a factor of five. The programs from the latter are finished more rapidly, have fewer errors, and are easier to understand and to modify. Quite often they are simpler in approach—good programs are not unnecessarily complicated.

These ideas have led to the concept of the 'chief programmer' team: the expert is left free to do what he does best; everyone else does everything else. In general, every team member takes up different specialisations. This allows more concentrated work to take place and leads inevitably to better results. External distractions are minimised, because one of the specialists undertakes the general exterior communication. The need to 'change gear' to amend documentation disappears: all of this is dealt with by the specialist. And so on.

The following personnel are identified:

The chief programmer. She is fully responsible for all design, programming, testing, integration and installation.

The assistant programmer. He is the backup in case of trouble. He is fully familiar with all stages of the implementation and, under normal circumstances, will assist the chief programmer and verify her work.

The administrator. She deals with all external matters not directly concerned with the implementation.

The toolsmith. His job is to make sure that all of the software tools required by the chief programmer are ready whenever they are needed.

The documentation editor. She takes all of the original documentation provided by the chief programmer and makes sure that it is up-to-date at all times, properly indexed, cross-referenced, and so on.

The language and system expert. He is ready to answer all questions on any detail of the languages or the systems being used.

The librarian. Her task is to keep all files, both machine- and human-related, in step. All listings and program logs are under her control, for instance.

The tester. All testing is under his control. He is responsible for objective assessment of the project at all times.

In addition to these eight specialists, there should be extra support staff to enable them to function efficiently. These will include secretarial support and program coding support, among others. The whole will also need a considerable amount of computer support, but the entire system can be extremely productive.

In some smaller teams, some of the members may 'double up', taking more than one of the special tasks. For instance, the librarian and the tester may be the same person. The overall tasks have been identified, though, and this particular outlook in itself allows great use to be made of the available strengths.

It is not the universal panacea. Some organisations are not set up in such a way as to allow the formation of these types of team. There are also difficulties associated with precisely the expertise required to permit the structure. The worth of a chief programmer, and her general psychological make-up, will make her extremely desirable to outside bodies. For considerations of these and other problems, reference should be made to other texts.

10.8 Implementor/computer interfaces

The implementors in a well-equipped team will use the computer system in a number of ways, but this does not take into account who actually does each part of the job. Some of the input is straightforward: program source and other text files have to be initialised and updated; commands have to be given to produce executable programs from the human-understandable versions; the actual execution of programs has to be put in proper order.

While all of this takes place, there is information flowing in the other direction. Computer systems do not necessarily obey Newton's Third Law: action and reaction are not always equal and opposite when computers are used. Anyone with a program obeying an endless loop has observed that. However, in well-regulated use, input is designed to provoke corresponding output. Program listings and execution logs are produced; files of results are presented for inspection; statistics relating to machine usage are output to the various interested parties.

In all of the instances mentioned above, however, no mention of the *method* of input or output has been given. Each reader may well have an appropriate image in mind. It would be a good idea, though, to contemplate some of the alternatives. Not all input comes, either directly or indirectly, from a typewriter keyboard and, in any case, not all keyboards are necessarily of the same layout. It does not follow that the output must be sent to a screen or to a printer. While it is undeniable that a large amount of input and output is of this nature, there are alternatives.

It may seem somewhat tangential to investigate methods other than the most widespread ones. Nevertheless, consider the rapid changes which have taken place in computing styles over the previous 25 years and, it may reasonably be assumed, will continue to take place in any 25-year period. Some of the less controversial means of input include non-'qwerty' and digital-only keyboards, but the use of touch-sensitive screen techniques, 'mice' and so on, is definitely on the increase. It is not too soon to prepare for spoken input and its attendant difficulties.

Output mechanisms of various types are also available: the use of colour, both in screen and printed form, is widespread; graphical output, as well as text, is common; musical, and in restricted areas, spoken expression is no longer experimental, but easily available. Comparison of the expected ways of machine/man communication with what has actually taken place can be instructive. The simple replacement of watches with dials by those with digital output is remarkably significant.

Even with all this taken into account, the way in which commands are given must be well understood. It is in this area that the use of the correct software tools can prove very productive. To give two similar examples, the proper use of the function keys of microcomputers, and of macros in job control languages, can lead to considerable time saving. It makes sense for an implementor to transfer a much-used task to one of these mechanisms. The alternative is often repetition of the same sequence of simple commands. And that is precisely the area in which computers are strong.

The output interfaces are also important. The emphasis is less on speed and economy of space than heretofore. The widespread availability of relatively cheap computational power has seen to that. What is of more weight is the clarity and accuracy of communication. The need to prune communication to a bare minimum is a thing of the past. Hence implementors must be well aware of such necessities.

10.9 Exercises

1 In as objective a way as possible, assess your own attributes as a worker and (possible) member of a team. Where would you be best placed within a team (be honest!)? Where would you be happiest working? Why should these have any relationship with each other?

2 Consider your normal working conditions. Tabulate their attributes and comment on each item. Do they correspond to those which might reasonably be expected to allow you to achieve the best results?

3 By suitable enquiries, establish the common career paths available within the computer industry. How do these correspond to the three short job descriptions given within the chapter? What, in your opinion, is the career path which you are likely to follow?

4 During your implementation operations, you have had to perform in a number of different ways. Assess the relative difficulties of the various areas covered, and suggest measurements which might be fairly applied to each of them. (You should be able to identify at least five different headings for this exercise.)

5 In the calculation for the number of interactions among members of a group, what formula has been used? If 'n' members are arranged into 'm' teams, how may the number of paths in total be minimised? (This is easy to tabulate, and not difficult to solve with a suitable program!)

6 Consider the communication which took place during the implementation of any program which you have produced. What proportion was spoken? How would you improve (if possible) the way in which it was done?

7 Draw an organisation chart corresponding to the chief programmer team concept. Consider the flow of control and information along each of the pathways between each of the specialists, and compare this with any other system with which you are familiar.

8 Describe the input and the output interfaces, both physical and logical, which appear in computer systems with which you are familiar. Comment on each one, suggesting improvements you would like to see. Suggest, in those cases where you can, how those improvements might be made.

CHAPTER 11

Embedded systems design and implementation

11.1 The use of embedded systems

The previous chapters have paid particular attention to the people and the tools involved in the software production process. It has been assumed—tacitly, perhaps—that the computer on which the software was being constructed was the same as that for which the software was being written. This is, however, not always the case. There are a number of possible explanations for this, but the cause is very often the same in each instance. The system developing the programs is friendlier (which usually means bigger, and more expensive), and of a more general nature, than the one on which it is finally to execute.

Since the advent of the microprocessor, though, more and more computers have been physically built into their applications. This allows them more easily to monitor and control the system of which they then form an integral part. Typical domestic examples of this are in cars and washing machines, but many larger systems are of great importance in applications such as the monitoring of environments for chemical plants and in similar areas in the nuclear industry.

The general nature of these embedded control systems means that they are used in some form of process monitoring, evaluation or control. There is a strong implication that the associated operation is an industrial one, rather than commercially based or business orientated. This arises largely from the speed of response required when the application relates to a physical process, and the computer system is made to form an essential part of the operation. This does not always mean that the task is a large or complicated one, but that it must be done quickly and reliably. In some cases, there is a variety of simple tasks to be carried out: for example, controlling the operations of a number of flow valves. But the keynote is that the job is a dedicated one—the controller is special purpose, not (as in most familiar situations) general purpose at all.

In these situations, the devices are more typically microprocessors than microcomputers, having only a small amount of memory included. They play a leading role, however, for without them the job could not take place. The storage is kept to a minimum (why pay for something that isn't going to be used?), but there will probably be specialised hardware interfaces to enable the processor to access the devices it is to control. These might well include stepper motors, atmospheric sensors or other similar exotic pieces of equipment which will be controlled. The system is then thoroughly embedded within the application, and contact with the human part of the world (if any) is by some simple display. This could be a terminal of some description, but is more likely in many cases to be a 'dials and switches' human–machine interface. See Figure 11.1.

This is a 'hidden away' kind of existence and creates a development problem for the would-be implementors. How can the physical system be created and tested?

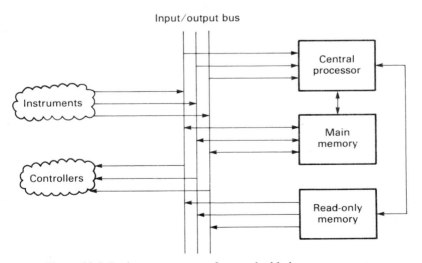

Input/output bus

Central processor

Instruments

Main memory

Controllers

Read-only memory

Figure 11.1 Basic components of an embedded computer system

11.2 Development of embedded software

The normal way in which software is produced using a general-purpose mainframe, mini or microcomputer starts with the transcription of the program on to a medium acceptable to the system. This may be by use of a terminal, key-to-disc or other similar procedure; but it is then assumed that the computer accepting the program will be the one upon which it is to be executed. Thus, the host configuration (the one upon which the operation is developed) is the same as the target configuration (the one upon which it will be run).

In order to allow a reasonably easy development, the host system should provide:

(1) A medium to hold system software, utilities and stored programs under development (both source and object forms). This will probably be a magnetic medium of some kind, such as disc or tape.
(2) Media for input and output, on which coding can be presented and diagnostic messages and listings returned. The former may be done directly via a keyboard, but paper forms are usually better for the latter.
(3) Sufficient main memory and backing storage to allow the translation software and software development tools to carry out their tasks easily and efficiently (see Chapter 9).

While these features are readily available within the general-purpose systems mentioned above, they are not found in the specialised embedded systems which are the subject here. Because of this, the host configuration will have to differ from the target configuration. Therefore the question must now be asked: how is software to be developed on a host machine for eventual dedicated execution within a target system which might differ greatly from it?

11.3 Development of embedded hardware

While this book is really about software and its development, there is so much explicit interaction between the software and the hardware in embedded systems that a general discussion about the configuration of the system's hardware is essential. Indeed, so much are the two aspects intertwined that system implementors for embedded systems usually have to design both the software and the hardware. Just as standard programming languages are used for providing software, so there exist standard building blocks for the hardware. These include processor chips, interface chips, sensors, motors and so on.

So, the total system building operation involves:

(1) software building on a host configuration;
(2) hardware construction from the component level;

(3) the embedding of the software within the target hardware; and
(4) the embedding of the computer-based system into the total application.

Two questions now arise: How is the hardware to be constructed and tested without actually embedding the system into its application? and How is the software to be embedded within the target hardware in order to test the system?

It might appear tempting to apply rigorous design techniques to the development process and so avoid as many of the errors as possible, followed by putting everything together to see what would happen. (After all, it seems to work with conventional software, doesn't it?...) There are a number of reasons which suggest that this might not be the best way, though. For instance, the physical application to be controlled might not yet exist, or it might be dangerous (chemical plants are not always very pleasant places to be near when things go wrong). Or it might be prohibitively expensive to arrive at the correct answer by a set of approximations: the equipment being controlled might be damaged by errors in programming, and some of those devices are extremely costly.

11.4 The design and implementation process

If the application being developed uses the same host and target systems (the 'conventional' case), the software development cycle appears as in

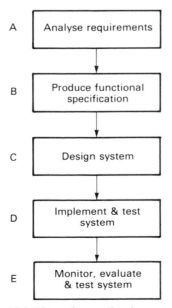

Figure 11.2 The software development cycle

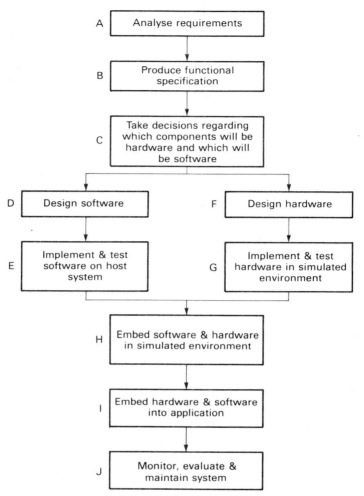

Figure 11.3 The embedded computer system development cycle

Figure 11.2. Of course, the diagram has been simplified a little by leaving out some of the feedback loops, but the overall picture is a linear one.

For an embedded computer system, the layout is somewhat different, as shown in Figure 11.3, where again the feedback loops have been omitted in the interests of clarity.

It is obvious that the two diagrams differ greatly, even though both describe a system development procedure. Figure 11.2 depicts what is essentially a software-only development, whereas Figure 11.3 involves both hardware and software. Many of the stages in both diagrams are dealt with in other chapters of this book; but the operations D, E, F, G, H and I in

Figure 11.3 are dealt with here. They relate directly to the questions posed above, in sections 11.2 and 11.3. However, since the main purpose of this book is to consider the software processes, these will be looked at in more detail than the hardware: that will only be inspected at a tactical level.

Once a functional specification of the system operations has been produced, a number of implementation decisions must be made. By the time that this occurs, most of those decisions affect the hardware/software interface, and they are mostly to do with the position of that interface within the system. In other words, which parts are best to realise in hardware and which in software? To enable the designer to do the job, he or she must be as aware of the present capabilities of the different pieces of available hardware as of the various software components. Thus, familiarity must be assumed not only with the different chip-sets and interfaces, but also the software utilities. With this information, alternative implementation strategies can realistically be evaluated.

Without going into hardware details, the trade-off between the two can be summarised by statements and questions such as:

- If you can do it in hardware, it will be faster
- Software implementation gives more flexibility
- Does a suitable chip already exist?
- Custom-built chips are expensive, but may be cheap enough in volume
- Is it cheaper to design a special chip or to write special software?
- Is the timing so critical that a hardwired approach must be taken?
- Is software flexibility important for future system development?

Also, broader questions must be investigated, for instance:

- Is it one processor for each task, or can multitasking be done?
- How is the system backup to be undertaken?
- How are functional system units to be corrected when they are in error?

11.5 Case study—implementation of an embedded system

11.5.1 The process to be implemented

To illustrate some of the points mentioned above, the system described in Figure 11.4 will be used as a case study. It represents part of a continuous chemical process which is to be computer-controlled.

The process centres round a vat in which the chemical reaction takes place. It takes place continuously and is fed by three kinds of chemicals (called somewhat boringly, to protect their anonymity, X, Y and Z). The operation is controlled by sets of sensors and actuators under the control

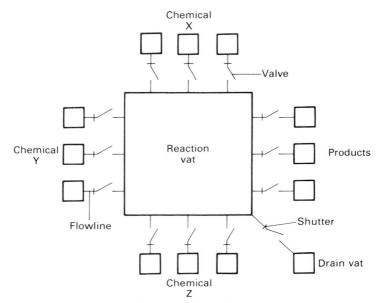

Figure 11.4 Part of chemical process

of the computer system. The functions of the sensors are to measure the physical level of the mixture in the vat, the temperature of its contents and the purity of the products being formed. Using this information, the system has to decide whether any alteration should be made to the temperature of the reaction and about the input flow rates of X, Y and Z. It then has to act upon those decisions. The latter operation is controlled by valve and shutter mechanisms set in each of the three input lines: the valve allows a variable amount of the relevant reactant to be introduced, and the shutter can be closed if none of that particular chemical is required or if a close-down is requested.

However, this is not the only decision it has to take. If anything should go wrong, it must also deal with that. If any of the equipment malfunctions, such as an inlet valve failing to work properly, it must make appropriate adjustments to the remainder of the system. It may deal with such relatively simple changes by small reconfigurations, but exceptional circumstances may demand exceptional measures. In such cases, emergency dumping of the contents of the vat may need to take place, and the system must be able to initiate such an operation if it becomes necessary.

More far-reaching decisions must be taken when necessary: if the input reservoirs need replenishment (stock control), if completed products are to be removed for shipping, or if any defective equipment is to be replaced or repaired, the system must be able to summon human assistance. This, too, comes under the heading of 'exception handling', or at least it is to be hoped so. After all, an automatic control system is supposed to be installed to relieve human beings of the boring and repetitive work which it undertakes. However, subject to the requirements of overall plant safety, it is better that the reaction be maintained than that it be shut down. There are financial considerations even in such an avowedly technical world.

11.5.2 The functional specification of the control system

The system has been defined rather broadly and loosely so far and, in practice, a functional description would be more detailed and precise than this. Let us, nevertheless, assume that the system has now been defined adequately at the functional level and go on to discuss the remaining stages indicated in Figure 11.3. It is time to make the necessary decisions regarding the hardware and the software configurations which will be required for the implementation.

Let us, therefore, explore some of the questions which arise in the case study and investigate the kinds of decision which might be taken. A full functional specification will describe how often measurements have to be taken and how often adjustments will need to be considered. It will also have indicated where the basic sensing and control equipment (such as level monitors and valve assemblies) will be located within the physical application. The functional characteristics of the devices themselves will also be known. So, what are the types of decision which have to be made now?

Consider the main process vat: the role of the embedded system here is mainly one of monitoring. The functional specification will include the sampling rates associated with the level of chemicals within the vat, the reaction temperature, the constituent proportions and the product purity. However, before setting out on the implementation itself, some preliminary work will decide the size of the task.

Given the sampling rate and the number of sensors, it is easy to estimate the volume of data to be stored and processed. While this might not be particularly critical for many general-purpose computers in use today, in a process control system the storage requirements are more stringent. For example, if an average value of a particular reading is needed during the control of the system, will it be sufficient to keep a running average or must all of the data values be kept for a more complex function to be calculated? If sampling takes place 10,000 times each second, and data must be held for one hour, there must be storage for 36 million items—not an easy undertaking in any operation.

To be fair, a sampling rate of 10,000 per second is somewhat on the high side for this application: it is not as if it were an atomic reactor or any similar process. However, the calculations needed to work out the volume of data must still be made. In this way, we can be sure that the computer system specified can deal with the problem, without being too extravagant with its resources. The level in the vat, and its temperature, is not likely to vary drastically over short periods, so that sampling at 10-second intervals will probably suffice. If any value approaches a critical area, the sampling rate can be increased, but it is unlikely to exceed once per second.

For sampling every 10 seconds at each sensing point, therefore, allowing for storage during a 24-hour period and assuming that raw data are held, we have:

6 times per minute × 60 minutes × 24 hours = 8640 data items per day

with a small increase for each sensor monitoring a point which 'goes critical' during the day. This requirement is well within the capability of main memory for many microcomputer configurations, as long as appropriate archiving takes place to suitable backing media when necessary. This backing storage requirement would need to be added to the system specification, of course: it would be embarrassing to detect extra requirements and then not to include them.

With such a sampling rate, even an extremely complex analysis could be carried out at the same time. A relatively slow microprocessor, with a one microsecond cycle time, could probably allocate up to 800,000 cycles and still allow generously for system overheads. It is more likely to have too much time than too little. This shows up a popular misconception about real-time systems—that the processors involved are necessarily under pressure. While there may be some time-critical sections, only exceptional circumstances are likely to cause hyperactivity.

11.5.3 Designing the system

Given the functional specification, and following the above reasoning, it is now ready to commence the design work. For simplicity, it will be assumed that the sensors can be connected directly to their processor(s). Knowing the sampling rates and the general complexity of the analysis algorithms now enables the processor requirements to be put together. The previous paragraph suggests that processing will not be too time-critical, and so it is probable that a single processor with a suitable amount of main memory will suffice to deal with all of the raw data to be input. A more time-critical application than the one under consideration (see Figure 11.5) might require different processors for different sensors.

It is now time to check one of the other questions asked in section 11.4—how is the processor to be backed-up in case of failure? This decision can be quite complex, but will almost certainly require a second processor which can be brought into use (probably automatically) should the first one fail.

The next problem is one of interfacing. The functional specification

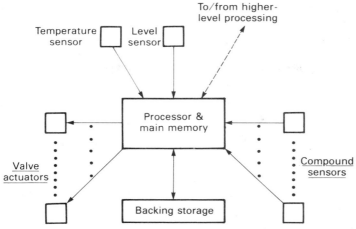

Figure 11.5 Main process vat connections

describes the physical characteristics, and descriptions of the available hardware (chips, and so on) will rapidly tell us whether the current hardware will satisfy the requirements. If not, economic or timing decisions (or both) will have to be made. It may be summarised as: are the chips to be custom-designed or would it be better to implement a mixture of special software with existing chips? Custom-designed chips have an initial design cost which is disproportionately high if only a few are built—the more there are, the cheaper each one is. On the other hand, specialised hardware will probably be faster than the software alternative: but is the extra speed needed?

How much backing storage will be needed (if any)? If there is a 'higher level' machine to which data may be transported at regular intervals, there might be no need at all. If this is not so, though, the maximum capacity will need to be calculated, together with access time considerations and organisational capabilities. With this information, the type and capacity will be able to be decided.

A connection to the 'higher level' processing is included in Figure 11.5, as suggested in Figure 11.4. This involves the control of the whole system, rather than just the vat monitoring, which is merely a subsystem of the whole. Other subsystems might include the control of the flows of the various chemicals used, collection of the product, control of the vat drain line, and so on. These subsystems are linked to make up the whole process. For example, the flows of the chemical constituents will depend on the composition of the contents of the main vat. Similarly, the product collection subsystem also needs to know the current composition of the vat contents to decide whether any products should be drawn off and collected.

Each subsystem will have its own particular task to attend to, but the system manager will orchestrate these together. The system manager is the 'higher level' process mentioned above and is commonly implemented using a database on the 'parent' machine. (This is not necessarily a database in any but the widest sense of the word: it may be no more than a serial file if nothing more complicated is needed.) Each subsystem may then query or update the relevant part of the database using its connection to the higher level; but now there is a further piece of design to be undertaken. The database must be included in the design work, and the data in the database must be structured appropriately. The access rights and relevant protocols must also be taken into consideration to ensure that the data retain their integrity: and suitable data analysis techniques are well covered in a number of well-established texts.

The database will be maintained within the higher level system, and so it is also necessary to decide on its configuration. There are three items which contribute to this:

(1) The maximum data flow between each subsystem and the parent system. This is needed to determine the communication line speeds.
(2) The maximum total data flow between every subsystem and the parent. This will allow the parent's request-handling capability to be specified.
(3) The total size of the database and its frequency of access will allow its organisation to be determined. If access time is not a critical factor, disc storage may be used exclusively. If, however, this is not the case, some main memory might be set aside in addition to any backing storage used to form dedicated buffers for the data.

The demands on the parent database might well not stop there. There may be a need for human intervention from time to time (on an exception basis, surely), and the data may then be seen as part of a management information system. This would provide up-to-date product information for whichever managers might need it, prior to possible alterations in the system's operations. The functional specification will have defined these requirements, and the system must be capable of meeting them. In hardware terms, this might include a local area network with workstations attached. The human–machine interface might profit from the use of graphical displays, and decisions concerning the necessary packages would also have to be undertaken.

It is quite possible, through this discussion, that the process shown in Figure 11.4 is only a part of a much larger application. Under such circumstances, the necessary interconnections will form part of the functional specification. The provision of the relevant connections will then form yet a further part of the decisions to be taken. This may well build up a local area network still further, or include it as part of a wide area network.

Finally, throughout all of the planning, sight must not be lost of the backup of historical data needed, and the fail-safe requirements which must also be met. This last part might stem from processor failure, or from component or physical damage. It is a complex problem, and concerns adaptive control and the efficient handling of exceptional conditions. However, once all of the decisions discussed in this section have been taken, it is time to embark on the design phases of production.

11.5.4 Software design (Operation D in Figure 11.3)

This is the point at which software development is ready to commence. Chapters 3 to 10 of this book deal with this aspect, and it is important to recognise that the same methods, tools and techniques apply to the design of embedded systems as to any others. The overall approach may be modified somewhat, however, because of the real-time nature of the embedded system, by the requirement that processes will have to work in parallel, and by physical constraints, as discussed earlier in this chapter.

Following the previous discussion, we may assume that a single processor will be used to implement the control of the system described in Figure 11.3. Design mechanisms have been discussed in the course of Chapters 3 to 7 of

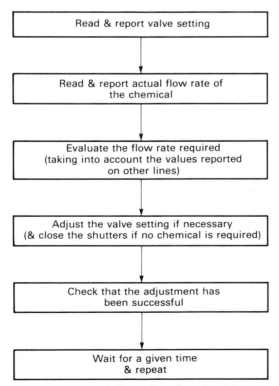

Figure 11.6 Skeleton flow line algorithm

this book, and one of those (or a similar one) will be used at this point. The real-time nature of the application, with its attendant parallel processing, adds in extra factors.

For each flow line, the requirement can be described by the outline given in Figure 11.6. There are obvious interactions between the different flow line processes, because each one accesses information relating to the other two. This is carried out, of course, via the parent's database facilities. Thus, while the required flow rate for line C is being evaluated, the current rates of flow for the other lines are of great interest (see Figure 11.7). A problem might arise, though, if the rates of flow on lines A or B are also being changed (remember: these processes are taking place in real time and in parallel). For short spaces of time, the data being held might be subtly incorrect or slightly out-of-date.

Hence, there is a synchronisation requirement . . . To accommodate this, the easiest solution is to impose a constraint on all data used during processing, of not too complicated a nature. A suitable candidate might be: 'All data items used are stable at the start of a control iteration, and will remain so during that iteration.' This simple approach will solve the problem, and simple solutions are always to be favoured above complicated ones! But how are the monitoring and control algorithms to be structured?

The algorithm described in Figure 11.6 is really three algorithms, one instance being applied to each flow line. Let these be called Algorithm A, Algorithm B and Algorithm C, according to the flow line to which each

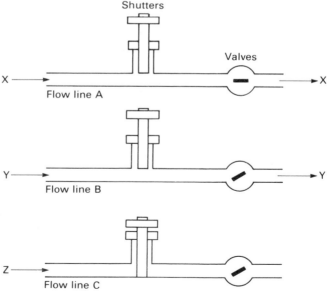

Figure 11.7 Flow lines in the case study

Initialise;
Loop until closedown__condition;

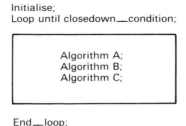

Algorithm A;
Algorithm B;
Algorithm C;

End__loop;

Figure 11.8 A uni-processor solution

refers. Following the earlier assumption that processor time is not critical, the overall monitoring and control could be undertaken as described in Figure 11.8.

This way of implementing the solution might well prove adequate, but there are problems which might arise. For instance, what would happen if one of the flow lines were fractured, or if the activities on one of the flow lines became critical in some other way? In the first case, recovery or close-down activities would need to be initiated: and if recovery were possible in some way, the algorithm for that flow line would need modification to deal with the changed circumstances until repair had been effected. The second case should change the overall scheduling so that the corresponding algorithm was executed at greater frequency for as long as the condition lasted.

Although the software for which the design is suggested in Figure 11.8 could be adapted to meet the requirements discussed, an alternative way of looking at the problem would avoid some of the more obvious complications. A parallel processing implementation is outlined in Figure 11.9.

The software design described uses multi-tasking features which are now becoming more easily available in high-level languages. Modula 2 and Ada are two of these, allowing processes to be defined, and then executed, in

Initialise;
Loop until closedown__condition;

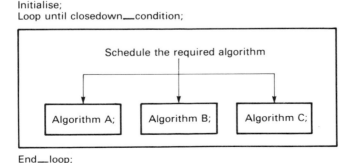

Schedule the required algorithm

Algorithm A;   Algorithm B;   Algorithm C;

End__loop;

Figure 11.9 A parallel processing solution

```
MODULE ProdandCons;

    FROM   Processes IMPORT
               StartProcess, Init, SEND, WAIT, SIGNAL;
    CONST  DataBuffSize  = 30;
           ProducerSize  = 200;
           ConsumerSize  = 200;

(* N.B.   The two latter definitions are guesswork ... *)
(*        They may lead to failure during StartProcess *)
(*        and will consequently have to be increased   *)

    TYPE   DataBuffIndex = [1 .. DataBuffSize];
           DataBuff      = ARRAY DataBuffIndex OF CARDINAL;
    VAR    CircularBuffer                              : DataBuff;
           BuffNotEmpty, BuffNotFull                   : SIGNAL;
           TakeFrom, AddTo                             : DataBuffIndex;
           I                                           : CARDINAL;

    PROCEDURE Producer;
    VAR NextValue : CARDINAL;

        PROCEDURE Put (Value : CARDINAL);
        BEGIN
            WAIT (BuffNotFull);
            CircularBuffer [AddTo] := Value;
            IF AddTo = DataBuffSize THEN
                AddTo := 1
            ELSE
                AddTo := AddTo + 1
            END (* IF *);
            SEND (BuffNotEmpty)
        END Put;

    BEGIN
        LOOP
            (* At this point, the Producer invents a CARDINAL *)
            (*          which it inserts into NextValue        *)
            Put (NextValue)
        END
    END Producer;

    PROCEDURE Consumer;
    VAR NextValue : CARDINAL;

        PROCEDURE Get (VAR Value : CARDINAL);
        BEGIN
            WAIT (BuffNotEmpty);
            Value := CircularBuffer [TakeFrom];
            IF TakeFrom = DataBuffSize THEN
                TakeFrom := 1
            ELSE
                TakeFrom := TakeFrom + 1
            END (* IF *);
            SEND (BuffNotFull)
        END Get;
```

```
BEGIN
    LOOP
        Get (NextValue);
        (* At this point, the Consumer processes the CARDINAL *)
        (*              which it finds in NextValue            *)
    END
END Consumer;

BEGIN
    Init (BuffNotEmpty); Init (BuffNotFull);
    TakeFrom := 1; AddTo := 1;
    FOR I := 1 TO DataBuffSize DO
        SEND (BuffNotFull)
    END (* FOR *);
    StartProcess (Producer, ProducerSize);
    StartProcess (Producer, ProducerSize);
    StartProcess (Consumer, ConsumerSize)
END ProdandCons.
```

Figure 11.10 Program example

parallel. They incorporate the necessary communication and synchronisation operations, which previously had been found only in low-level languages.

The solution given solves one of the problems which was identified earlier: if a flow line becomes or is made inactive for any reason, this is catered for with no run-time overhead. The appropriate instance of the algorithm is merely inhibited from being scheduled and entered, and thus becomes inactivated, until the flow line again becomes operative. To attack the other difficulty, that of requiring one of the processes to assume a high priority if its associated operation enters a critical phase, is similarly easily adjusted by attention to the scheduling process itself.

While this description does not itself do more than introduce the subject and indicate further reading, it provides a framework for the approach to design of software. The knowledge that the facilities exist to implement the consequent designs is of considerable assistance, and allows decisions to be taken in that design procedure.

11.5.5 Software implementation (Operation E in Figure 11.3)

Now that the design is complete, the implementation and testing of the software on the host machine may take place. Since this does not involve the target machine, the normal software development cycle can be invoked. In this way, all ordinary programming mistakes (mis-spellings, syntax errors, and so on) can be easily corrected. The difficulties arise in connection with the possible errors which might occur at run-time.

This may be tackled using an emulator designed to mimic the target system's behaviour. Even so, this will not detect all of the possible mistakes. Because the final system also depends on the hardware with which it is to interface, much of the final software debugging cannot be done until the software and hardware are being integrated together. Nevertheless, the following software tools and hardware provisions will be necessary to allow those parts of the implementation phase already identified to be carried out:

(1) An editor for program source correction (and possibly also for initial input of the source).
(2) A translator (assembler or compiler) to produce object code.
(3) A linkage editor (or linker) to construct complete programs from the separate object modules.
(4) Backing storage to hold all program modules (source, object and executable modules, and any system programs also required).
(5) An emulator processor (or sometimes a simulator program) for the initial run-time debugging.
(6) Displays, and possibly hard-copy peripherals, to present the results.

Now the software is ready for the integration operation with the hardware and, after that, for embedding within the application to be controlled.

11.5.6 Hardware design and prototyping (Operations F and G in Figure 11.3)

Because this book is principally about software, this description will not be a long one. It starts with logic design which, just as with software design, is a 'paper exercise' and can be done at a desk. It uses standard published information about hardware and draws on the designer's knowledge of the objectives to be met. This procedure is now being assisted more and more by computer-based integrated support environments, which may also make the software interface design considerably easier.

The circuit modules are then connected to form a prototype system. This operation is sometimes known as 'breadboarding', after the support medium which used to be used for early electronic circuit experiments. The tools are familiar to the hardware implementors: oscilloscopes, voltmeters and their like, logic analysers, and so on. These can detect the more gross hardware errors but, as in the software case, the final debugging can only take place when the hardware and software are integrated.

11.5.7 Hardware and software integration (Operations H and I in Figure 11.3)

This is the critical stage, of course. To make it a little worse, unless the software is working, one cannot test the hardware; and, naturally, vice versa!

Because of this, testing at this stage is both dynamic and interactive. It may be better to solve hardware design difficulties by modifying the software, or the other way round, than by attacking the problem directly. Quite a change from the more conventional programming techniques.

The most important testing method is in-prototype test, also known as in-circuit emulation or user-system emulation. The host system's emulator is connected to the user's prototype hardware by a suitable probe. The former replaces the latter's microprocessor and supervises the running of the system. In this way, the usual testing techniques used in software testing (stepping, tracing, inspection of variable contents etc.) may be applied in this rather different case. Break points may be set if debugged areas are to be traversed, which may also be important if the processor must necessarily run at full speed through a part of the program.

In the same way, transfer may take place from the host system to the target system in stages, a small part at a time as each is verified to be correct. Perhaps the interrupt manager might be transferred first, followed by input/output drivers, and so on. It is better to do the job in this order, taking the most fundamental parts of the operating system first (because that is what is really under discussion here). A real-time trace may be applied to this smallest of systems to verify that it is indeed functioning correctly. In this, a logic analyser may scan the contents of the address and data busses continuously and copy their contents to its store for later analysis. Using this approach, only the most important events are checked at first—after all, if they don't work, nothing else will. Events within the system may also be used to trigger capture of data: logic analysers can be sophisticated computer systems in their own right. Finally, when it has made all the transfer, the software can be 'burned' into a programmable read-only memory (PROM) for existence independent of its host.

The software/hardware integration may thus be described in three stages:

(1) *The emulation stage.* The user program, in loadable form, is executed on an emulator processor using the host's I/O system and clock. This allows use of a target processor of the correct type without the need for external hardware.

(2) *The prototyping stage.* The user program is tested with the prototype hardware. As before, the program executes on the emulator processor, but all I/O functions are performed by the user's prototype. The host system arranges the appropriate memory mapping to cater for the split in systems. The prototype usually also provides the clock.

(3) *The target stage.* Memory and I/O are performed on the target system, and control is maintained by the user from the host system's emulator.

The target system has now been produced under control of the host, with all the convenience which that implies. It has been tested as fully as it can, and is now ready for its independent existence.

11.6 Summary

This chapter has discussed the nature of embedded control systems and the ways in which they differ from the more conventional software products usually associated in people's minds with computers. The example supporting the description is taken from real life, even though it is not a particularly complicated process. Using this as a foundation, it is quite feasible to develop other real-time dedicated control applications.

The use of parallel processing in such an application is a natural way of using the power and capabilities of the computer system in a disciplined but flexible fashion. Later, in Chapter 13, the run-time support requirements will be further explored. These complement the real-time nature of some of the problems already met. The problems of embedding software and hardware within an application, together with the integration required of the two parts, will not be dealt with further, however.

11.7 Exercises

1 List ten common processes which have at least one microprocessor embedded into them. What role does the computer-based part of each play?
2 In the context of the case study, as described in subsection 11.5.3, discuss the decisions which must be taken in:

(a) The monitoring and control of the management of chemical X; and
(b) The operation of the drain vat.

3 Discover what is meant by an Integrated Project Support Environment (IPSE) and discuss this with respect to products currently available.

PART IV

Run-time support and maintenance

CHAPTER 12
Underlying software

12.1 Applications software and system software

Software occurs in two essentially different forms, which might be thought of as separate shells or as similar to skins in an onion. The outer shell is the software produced to solve customers' problems, and is often called applications software. This software assumes that something else exists to enable it to run within a computer system and, indeed, to be produced in the first place. The enabling mechanism is usually software of some form or another, known as the system software.

This system software appears in many forms and for many reasons, some of which are:

(1) To provide users with a reasonable interface to the computer system. In the early days, computers often communicated with the outside world using banks of switches for input and rows of lights (some in pretty colours) for output—that is, when they weren't punching holes into cards or paper tape! All those who fancy continuing in this fashion are welcome to it, of course, but have applied some few years too late.

(2) To allow software system builders to write programs and parts of programs in high-level languages. This also represents a tremendous step forwards because, as was discussed in Chapter 6, early computers (those without system software) communicated all instructions in numeric

form. In this way, the number 01021032058 might well have been decoded into four parts, 01 021 032 058, and then obeyed as 'ADD the number in location 21 to the number in location 32, leaving the result in location 58'. Just to make this a little more obscure, it would all have been stored in binary form anyway. With the advent of system software, although the computers still obey instructions of this form, they are written in languages easier for humans to understand and use, and only translated for the machines' use. Computers don't care . . . The outcome is easier use, better productivity, understanding, portability, maintainability, and so on.

(3) To automate the management of software production. This especially applies when a project demands many programmers in the writing of many inter-dependent pieces of software. This management task, and some of the tools used to help in its solution, has already been discussed in Chapter 9. In this way it is easier for individual programmers to create the software and for project leaders to manage the overall system production.

(4) To provide the support during the testing and live phases in the life of a piece of software to enable it to be run on its target system. This run-time support and maintenance is of great importance, and this chapter deals with the background to the system support software and some of the general techniques used in its production.

There are many books giving information about system software, some specialising in the translation of high-level languages. Even though this book describes the design, implementation and support of software, it addresses itself more to those aspects on which users will typically spend more time—the applications. This does not mean that system software is in some way elite, or that system programmers, who produce it, are some rare breed which should be nurtured carefully. They equally need to analyse their problems before starting design and implementation, so where is the difference? If their specifications are not what the rest of us are more used to ('. . . we need a compiler for ISO Standard Pascal . . .'), they are still as important to them as ours are to us.

Sometimes their ideas may be particularly important—many of the software tools in common use were developed by system programmers to make their own lives easier. Some suites of system programs have been so large that the tools which appear no more than convenient to the outside world were absolutely essential in their realisation. However, system programmers are also prone to mistake, and some of the problems which arise from errors in system software can be much further reaching than any others.

12.2 The place of underlying software

The main topic for this chapter is concerned with run-time support, and the tactical maintenance of software. Because of this, more attention will be paid to the actual running of programs. If, instead of the image of an onion suggested above, the picture is one of a building—foundations, ground floor, and so on—then the applications software is one of the upper stories. It is supported by the system software, which is in its turn dependent on the hardware of the system (see Figure 12.1). The immediate interface for the support of an applications program is thus the software system, and this suggests the title above.

This does not mean that the underlying software is just another term for the operating system of a computer. For a full specialist text on such systems, there are many contenders. It is of far more interest here to concentrate on those parts which are central to the run-time support: the basic requirements and the tools to realise them.

It is reasonable to enquire here about the desirability of any treatment of underlying software in this book, and the answer may most easily be given by considering the continuing development of computer systems. During the two decades from about 1960, programmers usually implemented their software, for both applications and systems, using computers already bought. These were very often mainframe machines running with standard operating systems. In such circumstances, applications programmers did not particularly need to have a deep understanding of the workings of the underlying software: the user interface was as much as was necessary, but seldom any more. As in driving a car, you have to know the 'rules of the road' and where to insert the fuel, but knowledge of the engine is not essential.

While this situation has not changed very much for systems of the larger size, increasing use is being made of smaller custom-built or 'one-off' applications. Implementors of such systems will need to know not only the straightforward interface details to produce their software, but will need to specify and purchase the appropriate hardware and its support systems. The software is then installed, with the hardware, as a complete system. The configuration of a whole system will sometimes entail the production of the underlying software, although this may already exist in some cases. Even

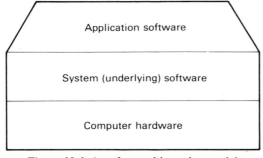

Figure 12.1 A software hierarchy model

then, evaluation of the different possibilities must be undertaken, and a similar understanding is essential.

In some cases, which need not be particularly unusual ones, a device driver for specialised peripheral hardware might be needed, or alterations might be required in the scheduling algorithm for different processes in the operating system. In some extreme situations, mainly for industrial control, a complete run-time support system might have to be implemented. The awareness of underlying software at an appropriate level is now needed in enough application implementations for its consideration to be included here.

12.3 The evolution of underlying software

Early computers, such as those used to about 1960, could only execute one program at a time. This situation, also common on many microcomputers today, is termed uniprogramming. In such configurations, only one part of the system was active at any one time. For instance, either the processor was executing instructions or one of the peripherals was in use, but not both at once. This was because the control unit (an early name for the central processor) was in complete control of every part of the system individually, and it could only do one thing at a time.

In a uniprogramming environment there could be no contention. Programs could not get mixed up about which one would be serviced next, because there was only one program, and so it had the undivided attention of all of the units making up the system. Because of this, there was no need for any underlying software to keep everything under control and resolve contention. This is very similar to the way in which personal computer systems work today, which reinforces the analogy suggested above.

There was some contention, however: in any pattern of use, how was selection made for the next program to be run? (As in many schools today!) The solution was probably a familiar one—the prospective users formed a queue and performed their computations in due order. Each one would have the programs and associated data in a box (storage on paper tape or punched cards, remember), and load and execute as his or her turn came. Human nature solved the problem, although sometimes it did degenerate into 'Biggest person first' . . . (This off-line scheduling has been made more automatic and, one might hope, fairer by the underlying software, and is discussed at greater length in Chapter 13.)

These early systems were extremely simple as far as their underlying software was concerned. In modern terms, also, they were remarkably slow: a minimum time for an addition was 64 microseconds (thus, 16,000 per second) while multiplication took 2 milliseconds. Perhaps the two go together, but those are certainly very different from today's figures. (The performance characteristics are those of the English Electric DEUCE.) When one considers that the prime output peripheral (a card punch) worked at 100 cards per minute, some of the other problems also become a little more obvious.

The processor speed, even in those days, was thus several orders of magnitude greater than that of the input and output. This tended to suggest that the most critical resource was the control unit, seen in its role of instruction processor. Because of the disparity in speeds, the typical pattern of operation consisted of a short burst of (relatively) intense processor activity, followed by a long wait for a peripheral to become ready for its next operation. The direct implication of this is that while the processor was working, the peripherals were of necessity idle; and, not unnaturally, vice versa.

Computer designers were somewhat concerned about the way in which their expensive machines were not being used to their best advantage—why couldn't both parts be used at once? If output, for example, could be made to operate at the same time as the processor, considerable time would be saved. The answer was obvious, in hindsight, but at the time it was necessary for the technology to catch up. Two major breakthroughs in the way people thought about computer processing were needed: the interrupt and processor-independent devices.

The interrupt is a way of attracting the processor's attention when it is doing something else; and processor-independent devices are those which will work without continuous supervision from the central processor—for such is it going to have to be called. (These are dealt with in greater depth in section 12.4, below, and Chapter 14.) The actual breakthroughs were made in the late 1950s, and resulted in computers becoming more efficient in their throughput and in the utilisation of their resources. In fact, the cost was one of increased complexity, but has proved its worth.

To improve the usage, more than one program found itself in the computer system at any one time, even though only one of the several could be using the processor at once. In this way was multiprogramming born, but at the expense of the introduction of contention. If there is more than one potential user of a non-shareable resource, there might be an argument: and there it all began ...

It was, indeed, worse than that. Each program wanted its peripherals at the appropriate time and had to have guarantees that no other program would (or could) interfere. If several programs wished to fit into the main memory at the same time and there wasn't enough room, how would the difficulty be resolved? Control and management became most necessary, and the tasks were allocated to the underlying software: what else could react at a speed sufficiently rapid?

From those early beginnings have grown the systems in general use today. They are much more sophisticated than their ancestors, but still recognisable as their descendants. Chapters 13, 14 and 15 describe them in greater detail.

12.4 Interrupts and multiprogramming

If an interrupt is one of the necessities enabling multiprogramming to take place, it will be best if it is defined more carefully. An interrupt is an attempt to change the current state of the system; further, it occurs when one of a particular number of events takes place within the system. This might appear somewhat too theoretical to be of much use, but consider the analogy of a telephone call to a programmer working in an office. This is an attempt to get him or her to stop whatever is going on at the moment and do something else. When the new operation has been carried out, the original work can be resumed, if necessary. Of course, the interruption might be of sufficient importance as to cause the former task to be ignored permanently, but it might be something that can be dealt with there and then. It depends on the nature of the call.

In the context of computing, consider the multiprogramming system shown in Figure 12.2. Three activities are taking place concurrently (i.e. at the same time):

- the order code processor (OCP) is executing program A
- device Y is transferring data for program B
- device Z is transferring data for program C

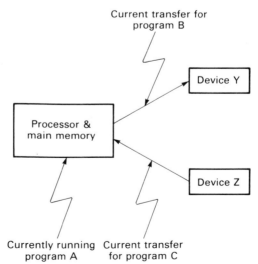

Figure 12.2 Multiprogramming three activities

The term OCP is used to highlight the difference between it and any other processor which might form part of the system. It has previously been referred to as the control unit, but the level of sophistication of the computers under consideration is now supposed to be greater than formerly. This defines the overall state of the system, but it is sometimes useful to look at the programs individually.

In terms of the three programs, then:

- program A is active, using the OCP
- program B is suspended, awaiting device Y to complete its transfer
- program C is suspended, awaiting device Z to complete its transfer

(There is another possible program state, although none of those under consideration finds itself in it. This is 'runnable', which occurs when a program is waiting for a transfer to finish, but is not allowed the use of the OCP at this time.)

A number of changes could take place to alter this situation, some of which include:

- program A could initiate an input or an output, and be forced to wait until it had finished
- the transfer using device Y could finish
- the transfer using device Z could finish
- the operator could commence communication with the system, and introduce something quite different to be done

When any one of these or a number of other situations arose, its presence would be signalled to the OCP by an interrupt to enable it to be dealt with appropriately.

The changes which could take place for each of the examples above might thus be, respectively:

- program A is switched to the suspended state
- program B becomes runnable
- program C becomes runnable
- the system enters into communication with the operator. What happens after that is not absolutely clear, because there are a large number of possibilities, and the action will depend on the nature of the communication.

In the first case, another program will have to be selected to become the active one. In this, as in the other three instances, there will be contention for the use of the OCP and, of course, the underlying software will have to sort that out.

12.5 Categories of interrupt

It is clear that interrupts can come from different places. To make the description of how they are to be dealt with easier, they will be divided into seven categories. This also corresponds to the way in which the underlying software perceives them, for consistency of programming.

12.5.1 Input/output transfer

The program currently running has started a peripheral transfer, but cannot now continue until it has been completed. The program has therefore to be suspended and not re-entered until the transfer is complete. This will take place independently of the program, under the guidance of the underlying software. In practice, the operation is usually taken over on behalf of programs by the underlying software and the whole made into a self-contained request. Such a request is sufficiently different to deserve a specialised interrupt of its own. (Chapter 14 deals with this in more detail.)

12.5.2 Operating system call

A common operation is to request some information or other standard service from the operating system: the input/output request is a special instance of this. It may take the form of 'What time is it?' or 'What other programs are present in the system at the moment?' The underlying software will intercept the request and either deal with it itself, if the operation is sufficiently easy, or schedule another program to perform the operation on its behalf. In some systems, this method is also used for the input/output request.

12.5.3 Program error

Well, everybody makes mistakes ... *Errare Humanum Est*, as somebody once said. Perhaps careful attention to the ideas of this book will at least render the problem less likely. However, this is a different kind of interrupt—something has gone wrong.

A commonly held view is that interrupts and errors are more or less synonymous, but it is already clear that this is not so. We may hope that errors do not go unreported, and many (but not all) do lead to an interrupt. There are many possible sources here, including:

- an incorrectly formatted data area (unlikely, we hope, for careful readers)
- an attempt to reference part of an array outside its bounds
- an arithmetic operation leading to an overflow

● an attempt by one of the programs to write to (or read from) part of the main memory not belonging to it

In each case, the underlying software will either have to stop the operation or take corrective action. What happens after that depends on the philosophy which attended the design of the computer system.

12.5.4 Page exception

In any computer system, programs address different parts of the main memory according to the tasks which they are carrying out. Under a virtual memory management system, this sometimes leads to attempts to use parts of the data store which are not immediately available, so provision must be made for this. In fact, it leads to this type of interrupt.

At this point, the underlying software acts to ensure that the correct data item is found, and all is well. In practice, it improves the flexibility of the programs, but may slow them down a little. The topic is discussed at greater length in Chapter 15.

12.5.5 Device communication

The idea of using the underlying software to ease the task of input and output has already been mentioned. It is central to the way in which multi-programming works, but there is one other facility which makes the system efficient. To avoid the processor continually checking all of the peripherals with transfers outstanding, an interrupt is arranged whenever any transfer terminates.

This form of communication from a device is a termination interrupt. When it is detected, the underlying software can change the relevant program's state from suspended to runnable, so that it once more can enter into contention for the OCP! It, too, is a particular example which corresponds to the normal and error-free operating of the system. Also included in this category of interrupts are those which signal errors detected by peripherals requiring attention. These range from the relatively innocuous 'I've run out of paper' to the rather nastier 'One of my read/write heads just scratched the disc surface'. The spread of possibilities is wide here, and may best be followed up in fuller texts.

12.5.6 Timer

Most computer systems have an internal clock, usable for many purposes. The three most common are:

● to keep the time-of-day correct; this is a common piece of information for programs which has to be maintained

- to select the next contender when the active program has done a reasonable amount of work (this scheduling operation is discussed in Chapter 13)
- to check that a device is not taking too long performing an operation: for instance, if a valve has been told to close, and has not responded that it has done so within (say) 5 seconds, there might well be something wrong which will have to be remedied

12.5.7 Operator request

This too has been mentioned above. It is used to affect the system's operations by human intervention. Examples of requests, which sometimes look suspiciously like commands, might include 'the time is now 18:15' or 'Program Number 3 is misbehaving and must be terminated'.

Operator messages of this nature lead to some operating system action when the underlying software has finished decoding their meaning. The action may be trivial, as in the first example above, or it may have extremely complex repercussions, as in the second.

12.6 Priorities and the underlying software

At any moment, not every possible event has equal importance: and the same is true of interrupts. In a real-time process, the processor might be instructing a set of valves in their correct settings when an interrupt from a printer arrives. The response would probably best be interpreted in human terms as: 'I understand, but I'm rather busy at the moment. I'll be with you as soon as I can.' If the interrupt was from an alarm sensor, though, the response of the system would probably be more along the lines of 'Drop everything, I'm on my way'.

This shows that, while the interrupt idea is an important one, it can stand a little improvement in some of its detailed implementation. A set of priorities (Figure 12.3) to be associated with the interrupts is the basis of the enhancement. This may be carried out in one of a number of ways, the precise mechanism varying from architecture to architecture; but the idea remains the same.

The division into categories already made above is a beginning, but sometimes finer gradations might be of assistance. Thus the 'device communication' category might be subdivided according to the type of device under consideration, perhaps by channels or controllers.

The implementation of such a scheme is widely used and may be summarised as follows.

With each priority and category of interrupt, associate a particular hardware signal. (This is, in fact, already the case, if one pauses to consider it.)

Figure 12.3 Priorities . . .

If each of these is signalled by a bit in a predetermined hardware register, and the bits arranged in order of importance, it is a rapid operation to decide on the importance of the interrupt as soon as it is sensed. This register is commonly called an Interrupt Flag Register (IFR); but as this is a software book, the details of circuitry will be assumed.

When, therefore, an interrupt occurs, one of the bits in the IFR is also set automatically. Nothing should happen, though, unless the interrupt is judged to be important enough in the current context. This is often arranged by the inclusion of a second register known as the Interrupt Mask Register (IMR). This is set, not by the hardware, but by the underlying software program in some predetermined way. These two interact in a simple but powerful fashion.

When any program is made active and begins to use the processor, the IMR is set up with a bit pattern corresponding to those bits in the IFR which correspond to important interrupts, and with those only. After this, the interrupts are ignored unless the result of a bitwise Boolean 'And' operation gives a non-zero result—or, in other words, if the interrupt bit in the IFR finds a corresponding bit in the IMR (see Figure 12.4). This suggests that every program has associated with it a mask bit pattern filled with precisely those interrupt bits which represent more important processes. This

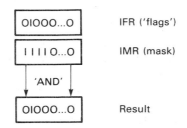

OIOOO...O	IFR ('flags')
IIIIO...O	IMR (mask)
'AND'	
OIOOO...O	Result

Figure 12.4 An important interrupt

important operation may thus be carried out in a simple but powerful way or, as a mathematician might express it, elegantly.

One point of interest concerns error interrupts. In any process, errors associated with it must be considered important, and thus cause entry into the underlying software if detected. If not, it seems obvious that errors might go undetected! Because of this, great care has to be applied into deciding on the priority of interrupts for any specified process—this is a particular area where great problems may arise from simple slips in logic.

The stage is now set for the entrance of the principal player in this scene—the underlying software—but how is it to effect that entrance? How does it become activated?

'...I can call spirits from the vasty deep'

is all very well, but

'Why, so can I, or so can any man;
But will they come when you do call for them?'

must still apply. Also there are some other little matters which must be attended to.

First, it must be possible to get back to the place we came from, and in the same effective state: a timer interrupt should hardly corrupt any other program's operations in the general way of things. In this way, programs can be suspended and resumed and their owners be none the wiser. Because of this, on entry to the underlying software, all working registers liable to be used must be put in a safe place for subsequent restoration. There is a similar safe place associated with each program, often referred to as a process description record, and the values its contents may contain include:

- program counter
- IMR value
- values of working registers
- relevant pointer values (for instance, the stack pointer)

The hardware arranges for these values to be stored, and the underlying software must then commence execution at its first instruction. This may be easy because it is always found at the same place regardless of any other programs carried within the system. In this case, the program counter is merely loaded with this known fixed value, and all is well. It does suffer from a certain lack of flexibility, but it is easy to achieve.

Alternatively, this may be done at one remove: instead of the instructions themselves starting at a known position, their address might be placed in a specific place or even in a reserved register. While this may appear unnecessarily complicated, it has the advantages of flexibility, and may even allow for alternative entry points, according to various external considerations, with very little extra effort. See Figure 12.5.

Main memory

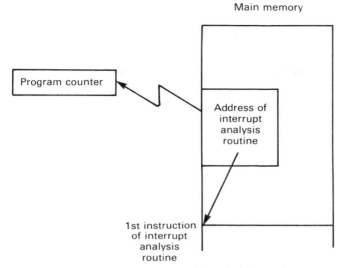

Figure 12.5 Indirect entry to the underlying software

In whatever way, the interrupt analysis phase of the underlying software is being executed. The hardware has done its work, and the system software is in control. The overall structure of that software is dealt with in Chapter 13 but, as a preview, it can be said without prejudice to have a beginning, a middle and an end. (Unlike Schubert's Eighth Symphony, which has a beginning . . .)

12.7 Exercises

1 List the system software components with which you are familiar. In each case, briefly describe their purpose(s) within the system.
2 For one of the components of the system software, write a brief criticism (remember: criticism doesn't only concentrate on the negative points . . .). Using your criticism, suggest how the component might be improved.
3 List as many different interrupts as you can and suggest (with reasons) the categories into which they fall.
4 For each member of the list of interrupts, describe the action which the underlying software should take when the interrupt occurs.
5 Divide the list of interrupts into two parts: those which are independent of the OCP and those which are not. State your reasoning carefully in each case.

CHAPTER 13

Processor management

13.1 Computer processors

The parts of a computer system are given in outline in Figure 13.1. The computer memory is discussed in Chapter 15 and the peripherals in Chapter 16. The remaining parts are often taken as one and called the central processing unit, or CPU. Strictly, the order code processor (OCP) and arithmetic-logical unit (ALU) are separate. In general, each computer system has one of each, very closely connected. It is possible, though, to encounter systems with more than one ALU for each OCP, or vice versa. Some specialised systems, indeed, have more than one of each.

In any case, it is convenient to treat the OCP/ALU as one unit, and this will be assumed to be the processor (unqualified) in the following discussion. It is capable of accepting data and performing calculations using them; it directs the operations performed by the memory and the peripherals; it accepts data from them as necessary, so as to continue its operations; it is usually the single most complex part of the computer system; it is often viewed as the most expensive; it is also often assumed to be the most rapidly performing part of the computer.

Much of the effort invested in the production of computer systems is aimed at making the maximum use of the processor's capability. The rationale underlying this relates to the relative speeds of the parts of the computer. The times within which the memory and the processor respond

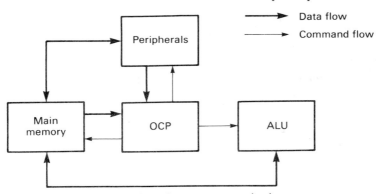

Figure 13.1 Computer organisation

are 'electronic' and measured in microseconds or nanoseconds. The *effective* response times of the peripherals are generally much greater, often being measured in milliseconds or seconds.

As shown in Figure 13.1, the peripherals receive their commands, as might well be expected, from the processor. If the latter is capable of issuing such commands once every microsecond, but they are only accepted every millisecond, there is potentially an imbalance. This represents an average, of course. If a continuing ratio of 1000 processor commands to one peripheral command is maintained, the two areas will continue in excellent balance, each working at its maximum speed. But if this delicate situation occurs only as an average, there may be temporary imbalances from time to time.

To attain maximum throughput, moreover, assumes one thing more. This is that once it has received a command, the peripheral in question will have no further interaction whatsoever with the processor until it is ready for it. It is difficult, though, for this situation to be maintained. How is the processor to know whether the peripheral is capable of receiving another command without disturbing its operation in some way? Hence the functions provided by a computer output peripheral (for instance) must go beyond the mere acceptance of an 'Output this character' command. Simple peripherals, therefore, must be able to respond to a question to give details of their status and availability.

A more complex peripheral should be able to respond more constructively, and this is often achieved by attaching a small independent extra processor to it. With the low cost and easy availability of microprocessors, this is a sensible extension and represents the continuing evolution of such peripheral implementation. Typically, a single extra processor will be used to extend the power of a number of similar peripherals. This is not difficult to arrange, because of the previously mentioned disparity in speeds. Such a processor is sometimes known as a channel.

Hence the layout shown in Figure 13.1 should be interpreted, in some computer systems, in a slightly different fashion. The peripherals described may well be controlled by specialised processors to enable the OCP to concentrate on its own specialised task. In that way the imbalance in the speeds between the OCP and the peripherals may be smoothed out. It will not be eliminated, however: that requires a little more attention and construction.

13.2 Evolution and development

This, then, is how the processors' environment appears. The *central* processor, general-purpose in nature, has the major task of obeying the user's program instructions. Whenever it has a peripheral transfer to execute, it must either carry that out itself or transfer the responsibility to a *peripheral* processor. The latter is specialised to deal with its peripheral(s) only, with a limited repertoire of commands. In some cases it is very primitive indeed, with possibly only two commands: transfer information, or transfer peripheral status (busy or available).

However, whenever a transfer is wanted and the peripheral in question is not ready, what is the processor to do? The only possibility, assuming that (for instance) 'Output a character' is *really* what the programmer wants, is to wait until the appropriate output peripheral is ready. It can then accept the information, and the user's program can continue with its other computations. As shown in Figure 13.2, on certain occasions (* in the figure), some time passes while neither the output operation can take place nor can the calculation continue: that time cannot be utilised.

This occurs because as long as the processor is active, it must be obeying an instruction. An active instruction processor not obeying instructions is not easy to comprehend. Therefore, there is a need for the processor to be synchronised with the peripheral, and there are essentially two ways in

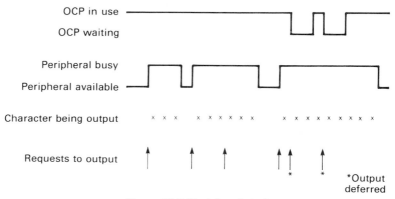

Figure 13.2 Peripheral timing

which this can be done. The first allows the processor to be halted (no instructions processed) until the peripheral is ready to accept more data. At this time, the processor must be restarted to perform the task. The second allows a 'dynamic halt' to occur, where the processor asks the peripheral a continuous stream of 'Are you ready?' questions, probably in a loop. This continues until it indeed becomes ready and the loop may be discontinued.

There is a danger in the first method, because the processor must not be halted unless it is definitely known that the peripheral is not available. If the processor could only be restarted by the *act* of the peripheral becoming ready, in that case the processor would never be restarted. Although some early computers used this approach and suffered the consequences noted, it has since been modified to avoid the danger.

Instead of the processor being halted, it is now allowed to proceed with another task. When the peripheral becomes available, the extra task is temporarily suspended in its execution until a later time, and the peripheral can now be used as required. This describes 'interrupt-driven' transfers in their essence, of which more detail is given below. The second method (continuous looping) is more akin to a 'polled' transfer.

To elaborate on a simple interrupt-driven system, imagine two tasks which require the use of the processor. They cannot use it simultaneously, so instead they use it alternately. One of them (call it task O, for 'output dependent') has a certain amount of output to perform, but the other task (task C, for 'computation dependent') has only computation. They will be organised so that task O transfers use of the processor to task C whenever it cannot make its transfer, and task C transfers it back whenever a transfer is again possible.

The problems involved are actually manifold, but the immediate mechanics of arranging the sharing of the processor are of interest. Task O must precede every output command with a status enquiry: if the peripheral is not available, control passes to task C. Task C must include a similar status enquiry every so often in its instruction stream so that control passes back to task O if the peripheral has become available. It is probable that task C involves a loop, and so the enquiry can occur somewhere within that loop. An outline of this is given in Figure 13.3.

The scenario is somewhat untidy. Every output command *must* be preceded by a status enquiry, and a change of tasks if the peripheral is busy. It therefore makes sense to incorporate the three actions into one and such tidying up is well within the capabilities of computer designers. Similarly, instead of incorporating explicit status enquiries within each computation-dependent program, arrangements can be made for the computer itself to transfer back to the 'output character' instruction.

The tidying requires a little more to get it right. How does each task know where it is (so to speak) when it starts again after the other task stops? A copy of the appropriate program counter must therefore be stored in a

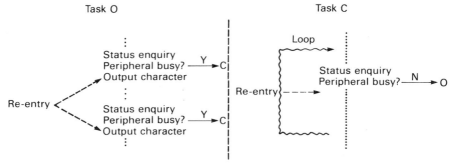

Figure 13.3 Task interaction

convenient place, ready for use at its due time. As each task is made to transfer to the other one, it stores its program counter in the correct place. It then finds and restores the other task's program counter to allow it to carry on. This is the origin of the 'interrupt', as each task interrupts the processing of the other.

13.3 A few definitions

Two words have been used above without definition, and it is fitting to deal with these, and others, a little more carefully. The items to be defined are all connected with the processing of computer instructions on an organised basis.

13.3.1 Task

This is an individual unit of processing and describes a particular form of organisation. Tasks may be active or dormant, according to whether they are being processed or not.

13.3.2 Process

A process is something capable of being attached to a processor and, thereby, being executed. A single task may consist of a number of processes, each of which is to be executed at its appropriate time. Processes belonging to a given task may be executed one after the other (serial processing), at the same time (parallel processing) or in a mixture of the two.

13.3.3 Procedure

This is the way in which tasks are specified. In macroscopic terms, a procedure is the unit of execution as far as its programmer is concerned. Some computer languages use the word to signify a subroutine.

13.3.4 Program

This is a collection of one or more procedures which has been constructed to perform a specific operation. Traditionally, this is the unit of performance.

13.3.5 Module

A module is a physical aggregation of one or more procedures or data structures upon which further operations may take place. Typical operations performed on modules include compilation, editing (for source text) and loading (for object programs).

13.3.6 Job

A collection of programs may be grouped together for submission to a computer system. In this form, they may be known as a job. The system identifies the successive requirements of the job according to its description in a job control language (JCL) and acts upon them.

13.4 Simple operating systems

Returning to section 13.2, as long as each task behaves itself, all will be well. However, there is an asymmetry present in the model. If task O carries out no output for some reason (nothing to output, or even program error), task C is never allowed any share of the processor's time. Similarly, if task C actually wants to perform some input or output of its own, under the arrangements presently given it will find it difficult. In a similar fashion, if task C fails to make the appropriate arrangements to interrogate the peripheral, control may never return to task O.

To get the best effects, the processor utilisation should be made as symmetric as possible for any or all users' tasks wanting its services. Because experience has shown that this will not be easy to enforce, tasks are divided into two kinds: trusted and not trusted. All users' tasks, unfortunately, fall into the second category. They are not expected (in general) to be concerned with the fine details of interrupt servicing. The trusted tasks, then, are left with the responsibility of dealing with interrupts and the processing of them. Because of this, it also falls to them to administer equitable sharing of the processor and peripherals among all other users. That, however, is the full extent of their duties. It is in the interests of all concerned that they be made as specialised, safe and efficient as possible. For this reason, they are supplied as an adjunct to the hardware in many general-purpose computer systems.

The group of trusted tasks is together known as an operating system or, perhaps more properly, as its kernel. In its simplest form, it makes use of the spare processor capacity which the user's program is unable to utilise to perform simple operations on its behalf. Also, in its simplest capacity it shares the computer system's store with the user's program. It has, indeed, been referred to in Chapter 12: it is the underlying software already talked about therein.

Its responsibilities are not usually onerous, but it does save the user's tasks from the details of many standard operations. Apart from dealing with interrupts in a disciplined fashion, it is also typically available to perform the following:

- load users' programs
- provide the current date
- provide the current time
- check disc or tape labels
- deal with abnormal program conditions
- synchronise input and output operations
- arrange for post-mortem program dumps

Such operating systems are provided with nearly every small computer system available today. They are for single users only and are of such a nature that they often reside in read-only memory (ROM). Very often they also have a high-level language system (for instance, BASIC or Forth) and simple file-handling routines included. Larger computer systems also have operating systems, but they are of a more complex nature, with other facilities included.

Nothing is without its disadvantages, however. The operating system necessarily takes up space in the computer system which might otherwise have been used for a user's program. Even though many of its operations are executed in time not otherwise available for users' programs, some still take a small fraction of useful time. This is estimated at about 2 per cent of the total, and while this may not appear very much, it can in certain circumstances become extremely important.

If the operations are not of a time-critical nature—for instance, simple input via a keyboard and output via a screen—the use of one second will matter very little. It will, of course, be noticeable, but as long as it doesn't occur too often, it will probably be ignored. If the computer is dedicated to a process control operation, though, a delay of one second might lead to a major catastrophe. If this appears extravagant, consider a computer-controlled steel mill. In such an application, steel may be processed at 30 metres per second and $700°C$. Control failure of even one-tenth of a second under such circumstances is not a welcome prospect!

The particular problems of process control are dealt with elsewhere in this book, while the remainder of this chapter concerns itself with processor management relating to general-purpose computer systems.

13.5 Multiprogramming considerations

If the computer system is presented with a 'typical' data-processing task, this is likely to consist of three phases, which may be repeated many times. In the first phase, some data will be read in. In the second, computations will be performed using the data. And in the last phase, the results will be output. During the first and third phases, the processor will have little work to do. It initiates the transfer and then waits for the peripheral controller to inform it that the transfer has been completed. Only during the second phase is the processor committed to the task, and that is seldom over-complex. In such circumstances, it is not particularly time-consuming.

It is quite feasible, then, that the processor is idle for up to 90 per cent of the time during which a typical user's task is being executed. The implications of this have already been discussed. Therefore, if the processor can be put to use on other tasks during the time which would otherwise be idle, more work could be done in total. As has also been remarked, one does not get anything for nothing. The cost in this case is an added complexity in the operating system which arises in part from the arrangements to be made for the sharing of storage between the different tasks; the sharing of the processor's time also imposes similar constraints.

This organisation makes a number of assumptions. First, that there are sufficient peripherals attached to the computer system to satisfy the needs of all of the tasks being obeyed. Secondly, that there is enough storage to hold all of the programs. However, there are also tacit requirements which must be satisfied. The operating system and the computer system between them should prevent any uncalled-for interference between any two programs concurrently resident. They should also ensure that all tasks proceed from initiation to completion in a reasonable time, with no one task attaining unwarranted pre-eminence over any other.

These requirements affect the operating system routines in a number of ways. More information is needed by the system to carry out its tasks efficiently. For each user's program in the system, it will need to know where its program counter is pointing, what its current status is, which peripherals it is using, and so on. This information will be used to arrange the share-out of processor utilisation among the various users' tasks. There will need to be a routine which takes all of the relevant data and decides which program is next to run and also, perhaps, for how long.

In addition to this, the computer system must be kept supplied with work. As each user's program terminates its execution, resources are returned for the system to use. The peripherals which the program used, along with the memory it occupied, are now free for use by another task. The amount of time for which it would otherwise have occupied the processor is also now available, but it is probable that in any well-run installation, at any time, more than one other program would be awaiting its turn to enter the computer system, there to commence its execution.

Another new component of the operating system will need to be aware of details of such incoming programs. This may include its requirements for peripherals, for memory occupancy, its expected duration of execution, its type of peripheral usage (for instance, 90 per cent of the time, or only 10 per cent), and so on. This part of the operating system must now decide which of the available users' tasks can be allowed entry into the computer system and arrange for that entry to be initiated.

Since multiprogramming operating systems have been in use for well over twenty years, the problems associated with them have all been very well described and investigated. This does not mean that all the problems have been solved—some of them are inherent in the structure of the system. Certain compromises have also been reached in some cases, some good, some not so good.

13.6 Processor scheduling

The sharing of the processor among the various tasks requiring its service is an important operation. It cannot, however, be allowed to become complicated. When that part of the operating system responsible for selecting the next task to be processed (the low-level scheduler) becomes active, it must not take too long over its deliberations. This is important, for as long as it is working, the users' tasks cannot be. It is therefore a good thing if its operations may be made as automatic (i.e. demanding of as little work) as possible. To begin with, it is helpful if the number of operations it has to consider are reduced to as few as possible.

Figure 13.4 shows an organisation covering the tasks resident within the

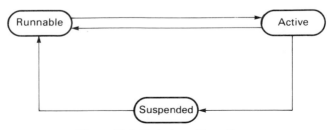

Figure 13.4 State transition diagram

system and their suitability to use the processor. If there is only one processor (the usual situation), at any time at most one task can be executing: the *active* state; others may be fit for execution, but not actually working: they are in the *runnable* state. The remainder are not ready or working for some reason: they are *suspended*. This may be because they have requested an input/output operation without which they cannot continue, but which is not yet complete. Or they may have become the victims of a programming error and cannot continue until special action has been taken. There are many reasons for being suspended, some of which are quite esoteric.

Before enlarging upon methods for low-level scheduling, a few further words about Figure 13.4. It is a state-transition diagram, with three states (already described) and four transitions (the arrows). An active task may become suspended, basically via an input/output request. It may become runnable, if another task is selected to become the active task. A suspended task may become runnable if the reason for its blocking ends (for instance, input/output completion). A runnable task may be selected to become the active task.

As soon as the low-level scheduler becomes active, the active task necessarily changes state to runnable. Hence the only tasks which need to be considered are those in the runnable state. This reduces the number of cases which the low-level scheduler has to consider. Even so, there may be a relatively large number of users' tasks in the runnable state at any one time. For this reason, other methods may be employed which reduce the options from which the choice must be made. Three of these will briefly be mentioned here.

13.6.1 Round-robin queue

The details of the tasks in the runnable state are formed into a queue. As tasks enter the runnable state, their details are attached to the tail of the queue. The information relating to the task which is to enter the active state is found at the head of the queue. In this way, every non-suspended task becomes ready in its turn; none is denied an opportunity to use the processor.

13.6.2 Priority list

This is not a queue. As tasks enter the runnable state, the relevant information is inserted into the list in a position corresponding to the task's importance. The greater the importance, the closer to the head of the list. The details of the task selected to enter the active state are found at the head of the list. This method allows important tasks to be recognised as such. Unfortunately, it can be subject to abuse.

13.6.3 Algorithmic priority

This is arguably the fairest, but also the most complex. Each task in the runnable state is subjected to an algorithmic evaluation of its worthiness for selection. This depends on its size, how long it has been in the runnable state but not working, what its peripheral needs are, and so on. The task with the highest score is selected to be the next active task. The algorithm must be carefully constructed: an exponential weighting of time-spent-waiting has been put to good use in this case.

13.7 Job scheduling

The other aspect of processor utilisation is in the selection of the tasks to enter the immediate system in the first place. This operation may seem somewhat distant from the direct problem of processor use, but is in fact very involved with in. Without being too precise, what would the effect of allowing two very large programs access to the system, when both were likely to be resident for some considerable time? No matter how many other programs required access, they would be unlikely to get it. Yet if only one of the large programs were admitted, the smaller, faster programs could be serviced 'in the gap', so to speak.

Similarly, it would be injudicious to allow too many (even two?) programs with heavy processor demand simultaneous access to the system. Unless the low-level scheduler were particularly astute, they might well produce a large imbalance in processor utilisation. It would be better to deny them admission to the system at the same time and, instead, replace one of them by programs making a greater demand on the peripherals.

The avoidance of such imbalance leads, in its turn, to a requirement for a high-level scheduling task to even out the load on the processor. Its operational parameters differ considerably from those of the low-level scheduler. It can afford to take quite a long time coming to a decision about which task to admit next, because that decision has to be made only once per user's task. The low-level scheduler, on the other hand, must make its decisions many times, as various users' tasks change their executability states during their residence within the immediate system. It is worth spending more time (which is effectively processor utilisation) at this stage, if the ultimate result is better overall system utilisation.

The information needed by such a high-level scheduler has already been discussed: the peripheral requirements, the amount of memory to be used, the length of time which the job will expect to require, and so on. To these might be added external items of information, such as the perceived urgency of the task, the time since the task was first presented to the system, or a time by which its processing must have taken place. The nature of the work might also be important: whether it was expected to be heavily processor-dependent or, more likely, to be peripheral-bound. These measures are often made only notionally and, as a result, the operation can sometimes be inaccurate.

As examples of high-level scheduling mechanisms operating on small amounts of information, the following have been used.

13.7.1 First-come-first-served (FCFS)

This is a very simple operation and consists merely of observing strict order in its presentation of incoming jobs to the system. This continues regardless of any other considerations. It does not imply that later applications are unable to complete their operations before earlier ones, but that they may not start before them. It is best implemented as a simple queue, with details of the incoming jobs being added at the tail. As job details reach the head, the corresponding jobs are allowed to enter the system when their resources become available.

13.7.2 Simple priority ordering (Figure 13.5)

This is similar to the FCFS operation, but it does allow later jobs to overtake earlier ones under certain circumstances. With every job submission is associated a notional priority, and incoming jobs are inserted in the presentation queue not at the tail but, rather, in a position dictated by their priority. As jobs reach the head of the queue, they are treated as in the FCFS method.

13.7.3 Variable priority scheduling

This is a further refinement of the preceding methods. From time to time, the queue of jobs waiting for entry to the system is inspected and reordered according to other criteria. If, for instance, a job is found able to have its

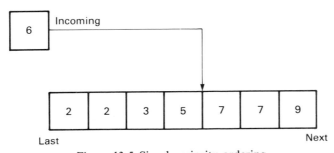

Figure 13.5 Simple priority ordering

requirement for execution satisfied, but is not at the head of the queue, it is promoted and allowed immediate entry.

Many such variations have been tried in working operating systems: the above are simple instances of them given as examples.

13.8 Multiprocessor operating systems

There is no reason why a computer should be limited to a single processor. When the cost of such electronics was high, the matter was economic. Since the remarkable fall in price of such components, that argument no longer has such relevance. Nevertheless, there is added complexity in the synchronisation of multiple processors, and a certain amount of computing power is used in that operation. Because of this, two processors do not do twice as much work as one: a factor of 1.8 is probably closer.

Processors being linked may be similar, or may differ radically. In the former case, one usually takes on the role of master, while the other one becomes its slave. This allows the controlling processor to attach the slave to various processes as it becomes available. The master will also allocate itself to processes if it has the opportunity. This approach was used by Burroughs during the 1960s. Their approach made the master/slave relationship permanent, although other implementations have allowed the first available processor to attach itself to the command process as it becomes necessary. This may apply to a system with many processors: multiprocessing is not confined to a dual operation.

The use of many identical (slave) processors has also been used in vector processors and discrete array processors (DAP). The former organisation is often used in so-called super computers, where there are advantages in carrying out many identical operations in parallel. The latter tend to have only limited facilities in each processor, but the overall effect can be of great power. The economic argument is particularly compelling in the DAP case: in large order lots, the cost of each processor is very small.

Even microcomputers use multiprocessing, but the option there often uses different processors. This is achieved by the inclusion of extra processor cards, usually to allow different operating systems to be activated. The original processor now becomes subordinate and may be relegated merely to managing the keyboard and display screen.

There are a number of ways in which multiple processors may be linked and organised internally. Some memory must of course be shared, but the processors may have no dedicated store of their own, exclusively sharing the same memory as the users' processes. Other examples allow processors to have private areas of memory to ease their organisation. These may need updating to reflect the operations of the other processors in the system from time to time, which is time-consuming. In the example of microcomputer processor cards given above, there is usually considerable on-card storage included with each new processor.

The effect of multiple processors is usually greatest on the low-level scheduler, as it must now pay attention not merely to multiple tasks wishing to share a single processor. It must also allow for alternative processor allocations according to possible task requirements, and this increases its complexity.

13.9 Exercises

1 Why cannot a suspended task become active?
2 Why cannot a runnable task become suspended under normal circumstances? What (exceptional) operation might lead to a runnable task becoming suspended?
3 The action of a round-robin queue for low-level scheduling may be simulated by specifying a number of tasks, each with a particular time to run (for this operation, known in advance!). The effect of different strategies for transfer between the states shown in Figure 13.4 should be included. These might involve running each task in turn, transferring to the next when an interrupt occurs. (Since the interrupts might include timer interrupts, this can allow imposed sharing.) How might a reasonable time quantum (the time between timer interrupts) be arrived at?
4 Repeat Exercise 3 for a priority list organisation. How do the two systems compare in complexity and in fairness?
5 Investigate (or invent) algorithms to assign priorities, as suggested in section 13.6.3. Is this method preferable to either of the previous systems?
6 Investigate the actions of high-level scheduling operations, as described in section 13.7. Use a similar technique to that suggested in Exercises 3, 4 and 5.

CHAPTER 14

The structure of an operating system

14.1 Overall organisation

The underlying software discussed in the previous chapter is one of the parts of the operating system of a computer. From its description, it can be seen to be the resident component of the supervisory system: the part that governs the running of all the other programs. There are other functions which such a system can perform, but the parts which carry these out are not necessarily always present in the main memory. Some operating systems, though, do consist solely of the resident underlying software described. Under such conditions, the program is given its own name, such as Director or Executive, because it is often referred to. It is sufficiently important in many cases that it has to be present before any other programs will run.

In those cases where the underlying software forms only part of the whole supervisor, the resident or most important component is referred to as the kernel. For the sake of simplicity, and for no other reason, it will be assumed that the underlying software discussed so far is indeed the kernel, regardless of its size or actual functions and organisation. But, however large the whole becomes, its organisation is straightforward. As with so many other seemingly complicated structures, once the idea behind its organisation is grasped, the whole organisation itself becomes much clearer. The supervisory software is entered via an interrupt, a servicing routine is selected to deal with the task to be performed, and the next process to be

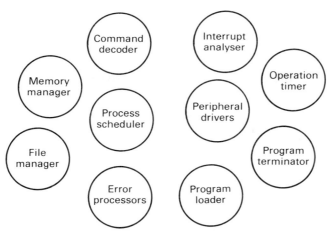

Figure 14.1 Elements of an operating system

activated is selected and entered. And that is all there is to it ... (Figure 14.1).

What makes the operation seemingly complex is the vast amount of detail which seems to intrude at this point. When the software available for this procedure occupies one or two million bytes of storage, it seems as if no-one could reasonably expect to comprehend all of it. This is very probably the case for a supervisor of such a size, but this does not mean that its overall approach should give any trouble. As with all well-structured software, it may be inspected at increasing levels of fineness. In such a way, only the immediate operation under consideration at any time is looked at in any detail. Other components are assumed to function following their definitions, and only their interfaces are of relevance.

To recapitulate: an interrupt is detected and acted upon, an interrupt service routine is selected and activated, and the next process is entered. It should be noted here that the interrupt service routine is not always the next active process. If it is one of those 'in residence', all well and good, and it is most likely to be activated thus. If, however, it is not presently in the main memory, it cannot be made active, and another task is chosen instead. In this way, the OCP is kept working at its greatest capacity, providing the greatest amount of service to the computer system and the programs it is running.

14.2 Analysing the interrupts

The interrupt analysis routine is not particularly complex: it has to decide which of a number of causes has led to its activation and select the next operation to be carried out as a consequence. It is not particularly worried if the chosen task is resident or not—that is the concern of some other part of the system. The aphorism 'Keep it Simple, Stupid' (KISS) applies here, as in so many other places. The interrupt analysis routine is the first part to be obeyed whenever the kernel is entered; and the kernel is as much a program as any other, with the same rules applying in its construction. Just because it possesses peculiar privileges is no reason that it be approached any more carefully than any other—all programs are important to careful implementors.

The way in which this selection is carried out has already been indicated. The category of interrupt has been previously determined and its relative importance assessed. This must be the case, of course: if the interrupt were not deemed of importance at this time, the bit settings in the interrupt flag register (IFR) and interrupt mask register (IMR) would not correspond, and no interrupt would have taken place—as far as the software were concerned, anyway. (Such an interrupt is kept 'pending' until the IMR is set to recognise it, or it is cleared on purpose. No interrupt can be totally ignored for ever.) It also suggests one of the first actions which must take place after an interrupt is recognised, and before the selection process can really commence. Any further interrupts must be suppressed until the system is once more able to deal with them, otherwise chaos will result.

The sequence of actions followed by the interrupt analysis routine must therefore consist of the following:

- save all registers needed for interrupt analysis
- disable all less important interrupts
- identify the current interrupt
- activate the interrupt service routine
- exit from the interrupt analysis sequence

The details of these operations vary from architecture to architecture, as does the help given by the hardware in each case. Some relatively unsophisticated processors have only one set of registers and no built-in data structures, such as a stack, to assist the routine. In such cases, each process liable to be interrupted must have associated with its storage the specialised area mentioned in Chapter 12 (the process descriptor record). This area must not be corrupted when a process has been interrupted, of course. This static approach makes the recursive calling of system routines quite cumbersome, and a stack of some nature has to be provided for such processes. If the architecture provides these as a matter of course, all is well (e.g. DEC PDP-11, VAX); if not, the approach may become quite complicated (e.g. IBM System 370).

Some systems allow an hierarchy of interrupts, automatically stratifying them into their relative priorities without the software needing to check them. In the same way, the disabling of interrupts may be made very simple in some architectures and relatively difficult in others. It may be that all interrupts are disabled until further notice, or for a number of instructions only. (They must be disabled for at least enough time to save the current IMR and replace it with a suitably set-up new value.) In certain systems, it is not possible to inhibit really important signals, such as 'Power off' or 'Store failure'. These are assumed to be of such overwhelming importance that nothing can ever get in their way.

In response to the frequency of use of the interrupt analyser, it must be made efficient. The more rapid the decision it makes regarding the next active routine, the better. If there are (say) twenty-two possible causes of interrupt, the easiest way of continuing is to number them 0 to 21. Once the correct index has been matched with the contents of the IFR, the process may be easily identified. This normally means that a table of routine addresses can be set up, and the index used in the selection. Sometimes the system hardware is very helpful—an interrupt weight (Figure 14.2) is also proffered at the same time as the interrupt flag—or a special shift instruction allows the contents of the IFR to yield such an index in a single instruction. However, there are systems which expect the use of iteration— shift, check and loop—to decide on the appropriate number to be used.

The final instructions in the interrupt analysis sequence are comparatively trivial: set everything up for the next routine (which will probably service the interrupt), and exit. But where to? This is not quite as obvious as one might expect, unless the situation has been met before! The next operation must be to select from among all of the runnable processes, taken in order of priority. This order must be maintained at all times and updated as necessary by a suitable routine. Therefore, it may well be to this process that entry is made directly. The two routines will always work together and be obeyed in this order: but to maintain a clarity of structure and organisation, it is better to think of them as distinct entities.

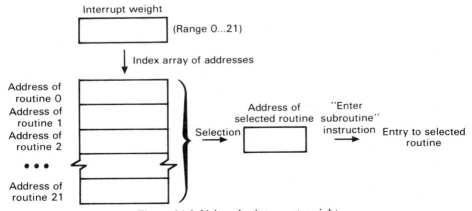

Figure 14.2 Using the interrupt weight

14.3 Parallel working for processes

The next step is, then, to scan the details of all of the runnable processes and to make one of them the active one. This may be quite a straightforward operation or it may need a touch of subtlety. The overall organisation first—if there are a number of different runnable processes, how is one to be chosen? It could be in some random fashion, but that does not accord too well with the way in which an orderly system should be seen to perform. Thus it follows that a reproducible system should be implemented to carry out the task. This corresponds exactly with the algorithmic concept of operation and is therefore ideally suited to computer operation.

It has already been pointed out that some processes are more important than others, and it should therefore be possible to rank all of them into order. This will continue to hold, even when some of them are runnable and some are suspended. (There will be no active ones at this time except the process performing the selection, of course.) Many, if not all, of the most important ones will belong to the supervisory part of the operating system and therefore will have well-understood characteristics. These can therefore be grouped into a preset order in a fixed part of the software and checked before any of the other processes, which have presumably been supplied by various users. The first runnable one found after checking the whole list in order is the one which will be next to be activated.

There is one set of exceptions to this simple rule, however: it cannot apply if the routine to be activated is not present in the main memory at the time. To see how this might come about, consider a computer system with 500 kilobytes of storage and three users' programs each occupying 120 kilobytes—the remainder (140 kilobytes) can therefore be put to use by the operating system. Unfortunately, this is some 220 kilobytes in total and therefore cannot all be present under those circumstances. It is therefore divided into a resident part, which is not actually too large, and an area for the other programs to use when they are actually in use. If a request is made for servicing from one of the parts which cannot be entered immediately because it is not currently available, some alternative action must be taken.

This consists, typically, of invoking a program-loading operation followed by entry of the appropriate routine. However, as this takes some considerable time (in computer terms), there is no reason why some program of otherwise lesser priority should not now take up the otherwise

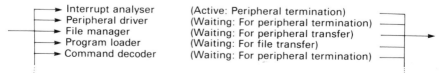

Figure 14.3 Parallel processes

unused time. Hence there may come to be chains of routines, the components of which are each waiting for the earlier links to be activated—and where the first operation is actually a loading operation! As soon as the loading is complete, the routines successively become active and thus are removed from the waiting list.

It should be obvious that the program-loading routine is a critical one and that under some circumstances many programs may be held up waiting for it to finish its previous request. The way in which it organises its operations is indeed important because, if it becomes confused, routines will not receive the servicing which they deserve. The data structures needed to make this operate correctly are not particularly complicated and can be described quite easily. As they are held in common with a number of other routines, the whole will be described together.

14.4 Data organisation and storage

It is one of the enduring principles of program design that to do the job properly—that is, efficiently and well—the structures for data should be designed at a very early stage. Trying to write a program without knowing what is to be manipulated and how it is put together is a much harder operation than it need be. There is some question whether it can be done at all, and anyone who thinks that it is possible is merely deluding him (or her) self. It is perhaps at somewhat of a late stage, then, that this is now approached, although it has been touched on in section 14.2 above. The tabular form of representation has the advantage of simplicity (remember 'KISS'?) and is adequate for the purpose. Such a table will need to be somewhat larger than the one holding merely routine addresses, but not at all difficult to set up and operate upon. Because of its nature, each entry will represent a single routine, which will be active (at most one only at any time, of course), suspended or runnable. As each of these may be said to be alive, a good name for it is the live routine table (Figure 14.4). First, its contents.

The addresses of the routines involved will certainly form part of each entry in the table, as already mentioned. These will be used in a similar way to the second mechanism discussed at the end of Chapter 12, that is to say, indirectly. Once the table entry corresponding to the routine to be activated has been selected, that entry address can be loaded into the program counter using an indirect or indexed branch. The routine will naturally be entered immediately this happens, so all of its registers must have been set up before this occurs. Working backwards from this, any registers needed for the process relinquishing control must be saved if they are going to be required again next time it becomes active. It is also a sensible precaution to save a

(Routine name)	Routine entry address	Return address	Saved registers	Other items
Interrupt analyser				
Peripheral driver				
File manager				
Program loader				
Command decoder				
⋮				

Figure 14.4 The live routine table

return address to be used after processing; although this may well be to a fixed location, as happens in some systems (Figure 14.5).

As long as there are not too many of those registers, and it is safe to say that routines in the interrupt processing path are notoriously mean in the way in which they use them, they may be stored in the live routine table entry corresponding to the routine in question. This in some measure replaces the process descriptor record for processes within the kernel, but may well be an adjunct to it for users' programs. Because, it must be realised, users' programs will also have their details stored in the table: they are processes just as much as any of the kernel or other supervisory routines. This really only applies in its full extent to multiprogramming systems, but is often extended to uniprogramming environments in the interests of simplicity (and where have you heard that before?).

Another value that is associated with each routine has already been given ample coverage: its status. That is to say, whether it is active, runnable or suspended. This need not occupy more than two bits, if the system feels that it is really in need of maximum economy of space; but a single byte entry seems adequate for many system designers. From this it leads, if a little indirectly, to the reasons for suspension for any routine in that state.

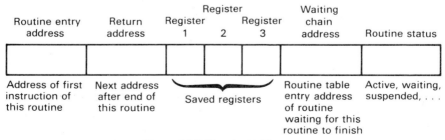

Routine entry address	Return address	Register 1	Register 2	Register 3	Waiting chain address	Routine status
Address of first instruction of this routine	Next address after end of this routine		Saved registers		Routine table entry address of routine waiting for this routine to finish	Active, waiting, suspended, . . .

Figure 14.5 Routine table entry

If a routine is held up for any purpose, there must be a way of revivifying it, and this will only come about through the intervention of another process. For instance, if there are three users' routines which have all requested the services of the disc drive management routine for reading a piece of information, at least two of them will be suspended. To start with, indeed, it is probable that all three will be, because of the speed at which external operations are executed (in this case, reading from the disc). The efficient way of managing this is to chain all of the participants together! The reading routine is chained to the first routine which put in the request, which is chained to the second, which is chained to the third. It is, of course, the free end of the chain (lucky it!).

Thus when the first request has been satisfied, the servicing routine follows the chain and alters the status of the first process from suspended to runnable, at the same time reattaching the chain to the second process and commencing to honour its request in its due turn; and so on. The chaining information can easily be held in the live routine table—the space for a single address or process number will suffice.

14.5 Routes within the supervisor

The categories of interrupt, which describe subsequent processes to be carried out within the supervisory programs of a computer system, have already been listed. Their varied importance has also been noted, but there remain one or two further points to be made. What, for instance, does it do when it runs out of other operations to perform? And what is the steady state of the system?

The answer to the first of the questions is quite an easy one to work out, because no system can ever be doing nothing unless it is switched off—there is always something happening. Also, as there is always the possibility that further work will be requested of the system (one would expect), it must always be listening (as it were) to determine if anybody wants anything to be done. From this, it can be seen that it should be ready for any interrupt which might come along and, as it has nothing better to do, then that is what it does. A simple 'Jump to current instruction' instruction is all that is needed, with interrupts enabled. This takes up very little room and otherwise meets the specifications (Figure 14.6).

There are some specialised systems which have a specific instruction to perform this function. Each time it is used, a report is issued to the outside world. In this way, the users know that nothing useful is happening and resolve to do better. Perhaps . . . However, it is a way of measuring the fraction of system time which is spent 'idling' and might well lead to better utilisation of the system after the reasons for its occurrence have been analysed. It may be used in the production of system usage statistics and

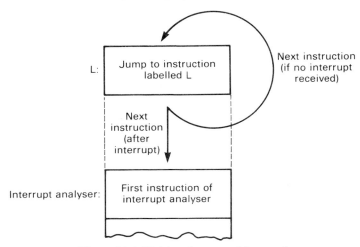

Figure 14.6 Waiting for something to do

to assist the system manager in optimising the mix of jobs which is admitted to the system.

The second question is a little more searching to answer, but not particularly difficult after its origins are understood. Let us imagine that the computer system has been switched on for the first time after a break and left to do whatever it thinks is a good thing. After some time (usually a second or two), it will settle down to do nothing, just as defined above; and do it extremely efficiently, of course. So what happens next?

Naturally, the only thing that can happen: an interrupt is sensed and acted upon. This can come from one of two sources only, because there are no non-supervisory processes in action: these sources are the timer and the operator's request. In the first case, of course, this is a regular occurrence and will lead to little further action, probably only the updating of the current time-of-day indications; but the second may lead to any one of a number of actions. These may include the loading of programs, checking of disc drives, or anything else which helps the setting up of the system's activities (Figure 14.7).

Once the system has swung into action, interrupts may come from a number of other sources. As input/output transfers terminate, the associated devices inform the system so that appropriate action may be taken. If there are no programs present, these are not absolutely ruled out, because the various devices may signal their presence in this way; or perhaps fault conditions develop and must therefore be dealt with. These are generally associated with the operations of users' programs, however, and have to be dealt with as they arise as a perfectly normal and acceptable part of the computer system's operations.

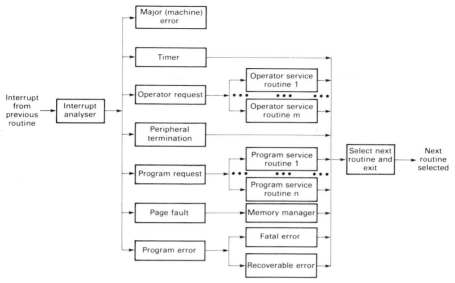

Figure 14.7 Major supervisor paths

Any other interrupts generally come about as a result of action by users' programs. These include the various calls that a program can make to obtain assistance from the operating system, such as input/output requests and other similar functions, or perhaps a program error. For the purposes of this analysis, these should be divided into the recoverable and the fatal categories. Suitable tidying up may take place after the former type, after which the program may be resumed; after the latter, no such resurrection can be undertaken. In addition, the possibility of an interrupt for the virtual memory management system (because of a page fault) cannot happen more than once at a time in the running of a program because corrective action must be taken. Somewhat akin to a no-fault fault, in fact!

Thus the action of the underlying software is to keep this flow moving round within the computer system. It has to ensure that there are no hiccups and that all interrupts are serviced within a reasonable time. This will also be achieved with the help of other routines which are called to assist, so that when there is room within the system for another program to be started, one is brought into use (if one is indeed waiting to be executed).

14.6 Areas of difficulty

This all sounds quite easy and, indeed, it is. As long as the whole is constructed along those well-defined lines of good practice and the architecture of such an operation is understood, what could go wrong? However, it is safer to be aware of the pitfalls which are still around to trap the unwary than to fall into them with that nasty sinking feeling that inevitably accompanies an avoidable error. One of them has only just been alluded to: that all interrupts are serviced with a reasonable time. As with so many others, it all depends on what is meant by 'reasonable'.

Consider, for instance, the case of the timer which is arranged to interrupt the system fifty times per second. This is quite a coarse measurement, but not too uncommon. It allows reasonable accuracy for elapsed program timings to be made, without incurring too much in the way of overheads by being invoked too often. The difficulty arises when one-fiftieth of a second has elapsed since the last timer interrupt and, for some reason, it has not been serviced. It may very well be the case that something particularly important has turned up, but that is no excuse. If this happens too often, the least thing that will go wrong is for all of the program timings to be inaccurate. Such measurements are usually cumulative and, if the errors are allowed to build up, it is not at all clear where this will ultimately lead.

The situation is somewhat more clear-cut in the case of embedded control systems. With each sensor and with each actuator is associated an obvious critical time within which its interrupt must be serviced, so that the information associated with it is not lost. In the case of the example given in Chapter 11, it is clearer that if something goes wrong there is the danger of a serious situation arising. Even if only critical cases may lead to serious happenings, it does not excuse the system designer from equal care in every other case as well, regardless of the perceived level of danger.

Because of this, there must be associated with every process within the servicing paths of the supervisory software a maximum time which it can take to operate; and with every interrupt requiring service a minimum critical time by which it must be attended to. If an interrupt then requires a service, but its critical time is exceeded by the time necessary to service it, something is potentially wrong and must be dealt with. This is not a difficult operation if the structure of the system has been built carefully, but is obviously of extreme importance. After all, if a house is to be built of different-sized bricks and blocks, they must fit together properly. Both the architect and the builder have a responsibility to the house-owners; and so do the system designers and system implementors to the users.

However, as in the case of building, there are certain obvious safeguards which are put into use. These typically come from the hardware designers in the case of computer systems, and a typical example is given from the way in which peripheral devices work. If such a device signals that it has terminated its operation and must now be attended to, it refuses to accept any other command until that termination has been duly acknowledged. It is a humbling experience as readers and printers, disc drives and terminals slowly grind to a halt because their terminating interrupts are successively ignored. It brings even the most trivial of coding errors into its correct perspective and leads to prompt corrective action, whatever the time of day or night!

14.7 Re-entering the world

The sequence of operations which has been described is all very well but, as far as the users are concerned, it has done no useful work whatsoever. The purpose of a computer system is not as a benefit for the system soft-ware, but for the applications programs that are going to run upon the ensemble. For the operation to be of any use, then, there must be a way of loading and entering those users' programs.

The actions are all implicit within the framework already given, so that it just remains to bring them out into the open. They are threefold: loading, executing and terminating. The executing phase will consist of many cycles into and out of the supervisory software by means of the interrupts des-cribed above, and so a single cycle only of each will be described.

14.7.1 Program loading

This will be undertaken following a request (via an interrupt, naturally) from the operator. The file holding the program will be read and the image of the program code formed in the main memory of the computer system. The tables containing the process information will be updated to contain the

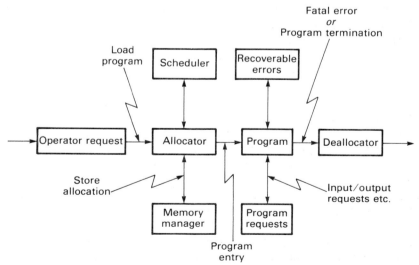

Figure 14.8 General system paths

details of the new arrival, which will be marked as a runnable process. After that, the situation is just the same as at any other time when the program finds that it is runnable.

14.7.2 Program resumption

When the program is runnable, at some point during the operation of the computer system it will be selected as the next process to be made active. Some of the criteria for this are discussed in the next chapter, but it will merely be assumed here that the operation has taken place. Its register images, saved from the loading operation (if this is immediately after it has been loaded) or from the previous time which it relinquished control, are replaced into the actual stores from the process descriptor record, and it is marked active. After this, it continues until another interrupt occurs, and entry is again made to the interrupt analysis routine.

14.7.3 Program interruption

When exit is made from the user's routine, it becomes runnable or suspended. In the former case, it may be the next one selected for activation, or may be overtaken in its priority. If it is suspended, then it will be awaiting some operation by the underlying software. In either situation, its working registers are stored away ready for its resurrection, as described above.

14.7.4 Program termination

This, too, is not a complicated operation. It may be voluntary, as occurs in the normal end of any calculation, or it may be involuntary after an error. The first of these is accomplished by a request to the supervisory system, the second by an error interrupt into it; and so in both cases an interrupt has been generated. As no continuation can take place, all open files are closed (one way or another) by one of the supervisory routines, all storage returned for other (subsequent) processes' operations, and all other resources similarly returned for others' use.

The overall cycle around the system is thus relatively simple in outline; the strategy which governs the whole is discussed in the following chapters.

14.8 Exercises

1 What weights would you assign to the interrupts described, assuming that the most important get the smallest values?
2 Suggest ways in which data might best be formatted for transfer between

the various routines within the supervisor. What data are likely to be used in the operations and what are their purposes in each case?

3 How should the discrete operations be organised into appropriate sizes to avoid missing interrupts?

4 How might the hardware of a computer system assist in organising the interrupts and ease the task of the problem referred to in Exercise 3?

5 What extra information might the operating system reasonably be expected to provide (on request) about a task? This may be during its running or at its termination; and may be from within the task or outside it.

Memory management

15.1 Levels of memory

When we talk of a computer's memory, this may be interpreted in a number of different ways. The generalised meaning is of somewhere to store data but, without any more clues, that isn't specific enough. Important parameters are volume, speed and volatility—how big, how fast and does it disappear when the power is turned off? Other points of interest might include cost and availability, but these are not the subject of this investigation.

In more immediately relevant terms, the distinction may be made between immediate access memory and backing storage. The former is often quoted as a figure for computer memory sizes, in terms of bytes. The latter relates to discs or tapes, and is discussed at greater length in Chapter 16. As a reminder, before any information may be manipulated, it must be present in the immediate access memory. For this reason, it is sometimes known as main memory, or merely as memory. The transfer operation may be arranged either explicitly or automatically, according to the available storage organisation, but must take place. (The detailed data manipulations are often performed in special areas, which are typically known as registers: these, however, are not usually explicitly mentioned in the overall size descriptions.)

The area of particular interest in this chapter is the immediate access memory, and it is with reference to its particular organisation that the discussion is concerned. Efficient memory utilisation is quite a complicated operation and also economically important. If storage of any kind can be used without waste, there is no need to provide an excess over requirements. This may sound trivial, but it must be carefully considered. The approach in some systems is to provide enough storage for any eventuality, but this is not always feasible and there is therefore a need to have a better appreciation of the actual necessities.

Any analysis is further complicated by changes in storage requirements during the execution of a program. Sometimes there may be a large number of intermediate results in storage; at other times the calculations may be complete and little extra storage required. By suitable rearrangement of the order of operations, the larger fluctuations in demand may be smoothed out. However, this should not be a concern of applications programmers: such storage matters are expected to be the concern of the system programmers.

The scope of their particular interests are quite wide-ranging. In the respect of memory management, there are many types of organisation to be considered. Even in a straightforward single-user system, there are a number of different possibilities available. When the extra complications of a multiple-user operating system are included, the possible combinations can increase dramatically. Naturally, if advantage is taken of virtual memory management techniques, there is consequent further added complexity, and this may apply to single- or multiple-user systems.

15.2 Single-user considerations

The single-user view of computer memory is the most straightforward. As far as she (or he) is concerned, all of the memory is available for use. This is indeed very much the case in some systems—if the user hasn't supplied it, it is not there. Such a situation might seem desirable, with no outside influences to worry about. There are no memory overheads at all. See Figure 15.1.

In practice, life is not quite so simple. As modern computer architectures all recognise the existence of interrupts, so must a go-it-alone user. This might not seem to be too difficult, but some operations (typically input and output) can only be managed by paying due attention to interrupts. Thus an independent user must be aware of these system programming aspects. This is satisfactory for some people, but not everybody reacts in that way.

A naive user might assume that a typical microcomputer is in this category. In this way, the memory size quoted (for example, 32 Kbytes) should be what is available for program and data storage. (This ignores backing storage operations, as will the remainder of the discussion.) Any

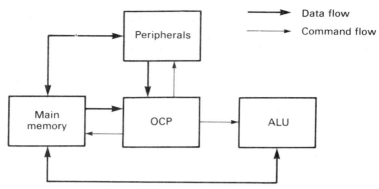

Figure 15.1 Computer organisation

user who has studied the problem, though, knows that this is not the case. There is a considerable overhead due to the control program, which is always resident within the computer system. Once again, it is no coincidence that this program is always present. Its mission is to perform all of the standard tasks needed so that typical application programs can be run without prohibitive difficulty. It handles all of the interrupt processing and, often, many other things besides.

For a typical application, then, in such a system, the memory usage appears similar to that in Figure 15.2. The control program occupies some fixed portion of the memory and the remainder is available to the user. In general, a user's program will not utilise all of the space allowed, so some will be unused. The relative proportions will, of course, vary, but the overall design is essentially true.

It will not have passed by unrecognised that there are several consequences of memory-sharing in this manner. One of these has to do with addressing within the user's program area. If the control program starts at address zero, the user's program cannot. Thus it follows that every user must be aware of the exact size of the control program. This makes any change of the control program size extremely inconvenient, unless some steps are taken to avoid the consequences. This problem is sidestepped if the control program is located so that its highest storage space coincides with the

Memory address

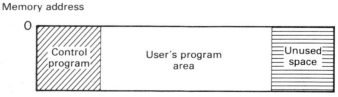

Figure 15.2 Simple memory sharing—I

highest addressable part of the memory. The situation then corresponds to Figure 15.3.

All is well as long as the user's program behaves itself but if, through some programming error, access is attempted outside the user's program area, there may be trouble. If the access is for reading, the only problem is the potential loss of privacy. This may not be pleasant, but it is not catastrophic. If part of the control program is overwritten, though, the effects are unpredictable. Some mechanism must therefore be implemented to avoid such corruption.

There are two essentially different ways in which this may be done: any attempt to use a 'forbidden address' may be stopped, or the actual attempt at access may be prohibited. The former requires less equipment and includes certain extra advantages, whereas the latter corresponds more closely to some of the microcomputer aspects.

If the first approach is chosen, an extra register (known, typically, as the base address register) has to be included in the computer's architecture. This is used to point to the lowest address available to the user's program. The addressing within the program can then be organised as if the control program were not present (i.e. as if the user's program started at location 0). The real address is formed automatically by the computer's hardware adding the contents of the base address register to the apparent program address. This mechanism becomes a fixed part of the architecture, and the control program arranges for the base address register always to be correctly loaded. For the control program, its contents would be zero and, in this case, it would appear to have no effect.

The second way of arranging addressing and protection places the onus for the former on the programmer. (The latter is still performed by the computer's architecture). The user's program is expected to be aware of its actual location within the memory and to arrange for its own addressing to be correct. Thus every program using the regime described in Figure 15.2 must make allowance for the size of the control program and, if that size is changed, every user's program has to be changed to match. The situation shown in Figure 15.3 poses no problems here, of course. The control program area may be realised as read-only memory: easy in modern microcomputer terms. More extensive systems have used mechanisms associating

Memory address

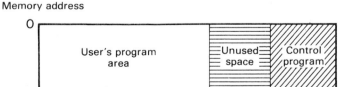

Figure 15.3 Simple memory sharing—II

a permission key with each part of the memory. The idea is similar and prevents overwriting of any area, but the details are more complex than the simple method just described.

15.3 Static memory allocation

Because of the great difference in speed between external devices and the order code processor in most computer systems (especially in interactive use), the latter is often doing no useful work. This time, spent waiting for input or output to finish, can be spent profitably if more computations can be undertaken. If more than one program can be accommodated in memory at once, the time unused by one program can be allocated to another. (The details of arranging for the order code processor to be shared are not discussed here.)

The simplest way to arrange for the memory to be shared follows directly from the discussion of section 15.2. Instead of there being two coexistent programs, however, there may be more. The arrangement which thus arises is pictured in Figure 15.5. It should be noted here that the different areas are not necessarily of the same size but that, once set up, they are fixed.

The computer's memory is divided beforehand into a number of separate areas, often called partitions. Into each of these, a user's program may be loaded to execute. All of the problems associated with multiple occupancy

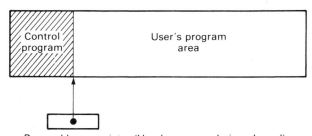

Base address register (User's program being obeyed)

Figure 15.4 Base register usage

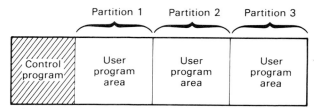

Figure 15.5 Memory partitioning

of a single memory already mentioned apply: the main ones being of addressability, and privacy and security. Fortunately, the solutions available remain largely the same as in the previous section.

Consider a typical user's program, as pictured in Figure 15.5. It will be loaded into its partition before its execution commences. It is unlikely that it will be of the precise size of the partition, but it must certainly be no larger. If the architecture is of the type that supports a base address register, that register must be loaded appropriately before the program commences execution. However, whereas in the previous analysis it was impossible to express any address liable to access the control program (see Figure 15.4), the situation is now a little more complex. It is now necessary to set an upper bound on the allowable addresses to avoid security violations. This may be done by a further register (often called a limit register), as in Figure 15.6.

In Figure 15.6, partition 2 holds the program currently being executed, while the programs in partitions 1 and 3 are awaiting their turns for use of the order code processor. As before, it is the responsibility of the control program to ensure that the registers are correctly loaded before a user's program commences execution.

The alternative addressing and protection strategy is still applicable, but needs further description. The simple process of storing the control program in read-only memory will no longer suffice. Instead, the series of permission keys is now necessary, as shown in Figure 15.7. These have to be set up by the control program as each user's program becomes active. In this case, it is the responsibility of each user's program to be aware of its location and to arrange its addressing appropriately.

This leads to the tailoring of programs to the fixed partitions provided,

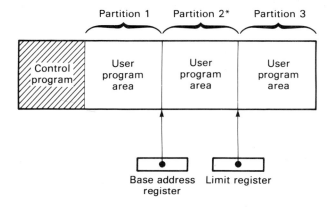

*Active program

Figure 15.6 Base addressing with limit register

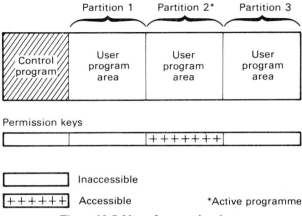

Figure 15.7 Use of protection key

so that a program may exist in different versions to take advantage of whichever partition happens to be free when it is loaded. This is somewhat restrictive, but is an accurate reflection of some operating systems.

15.4 Dynamic memory allocation

The preceding memory allocation method has the advantage of simplicity and consequent efficiency of implementation. Typically, though, it is wasteful of space when used. In the following example, the memory is divided into four partitions. The total size is 128 Kb and, for simplicity, each partition is of 32 Kb. One is allocated to the control program while the other three are available for users' programs. The users' programs do not all occupy their entire partition space (as might be expected), taking respectively 20 Kb, 24 Kb and 22 Kb. The system's memory appears as in Figure 15.8.

The unused space totals 30 Kb, almost certainly enough to accommodate another program. The space is not easy to use, though, because it is

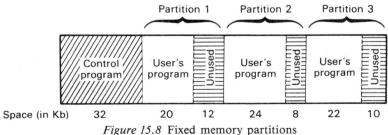

Figure 15.8 Fixed memory partitions

fragmented. Therefore, if the system could be made flexible so that fragmentation would be less of a problem, memory utilisation could be improved. What are the implications of making the memory allocation dynamic, instead of static? The partitions could then be allocated on demand, rather than fixed beforehand. No changes would need to be made in the use of base address/limit registers, or access keys (according to the mode in use), as long as they were set up correctly for the program being obeyed at any time. That part of the control program arranging the partitions would become more complex, but not prohibitively so. Dynamic memory allocation applied to the example described above would lead to the following situation, shown in Figure 15.9.

This method of dynamic allocation seems little different to the static allocation model. There are some added pieces of information needed within the operating system, however. With fixed partitions, the system could compute all of the relevant parameters once and for all at its initial entry. As that part would never be needed again, its storage could safely be overwritten, which would allow the control program's size to be kept to a minimum.

With dynamic allocation, the extra information would need to be calculated every time a new program entered the memory. This would require instructions resident in the control program, consequently increasing its size. The information needed would be the lower and upper bounds of the user's program area in each case, but extra instructions would be needed to allow adjacent unused areas to be recognised as such. They could then be combined and treated as a single, larger available area.

There are further considerations to take into account. With fixed partitioning, the programs may be prepared for loading as a store image. This implies that they appear in their *final* form when presented as loadable programs. There would be a separate version for each partition: not very neat, but easy to arrange. In this form, loading consists of no more than direct transfers from backing storage into main memory.

In the case of dynamic partitioning, this approach would not be practicable as there would have to be an inordinate number of versions, each corresponding to a possible loading position. Instead, a certain extra

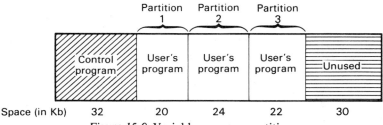

Figure 15.9 Variable memory partitions

amount of information is included with the loadable program, which allows an amended loader to insert a program anywhere into the memory.

15.5 Relocatable programs

The extra information to be included for full loading flexibility will differ according to the computer's addressing architecture. In the case of base address/limit organisation, all addresses will be given relative to the start of the program. All programs will, therefore, *appear* to start at address zero. The only further requirements to make the program loadable in different places will be an awareness by the control program of the position of the relevant partition. As it already has this information, it can hardly be classed as extra.

The situation for the permission key model is considerably different. Any program address which forms part of the data of the program must change its value according to the location of its partition. To clarify this, consider the address values in the two partitions in Figure 15.10.

The same program has been loaded into partition 1, based at address 10,000, and partition 2, based at address 30,000. The address data (which are usually called address constants) in locations A1 and A2 are actually two versions of the same item. A1 addresses data value D1, which is stored at location 15,000: A2 addresses data value D2, stored at location 35,000. In use, therefore, the value of location A1 will be 15,000 and of A2 will be 35,000. As they had the same form before they entered the memory, there must have been extra information to correct their final values. This relocation information, as it is known, is required by such systems.

The loadable program must contain the relocation information, so that each address constant can be corrected during the loading process. This relocation information will not be required after loading and will not therefore be preserved while the program is being executed. The operation may appear more complex, but it has been adopted by many architectures.

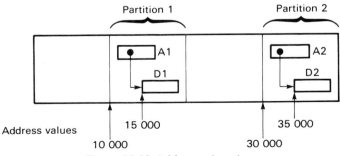

Figure 15.10 Address relocation

This discussion may appear to have exhausted the possibilities surrounding flexible memory utilisation: it allows best use of the available resources when programs are loaded and appears to ensure that wasted space is kept to a minimum. This would indeed be the case if, once loaded, programs executed indefinitely, but they terminate after their task is complete and the memory is thus freed for further use.

Because of this, the incomplete space utilisation which arose under static memory allocation could still arise, in a modified form. Memory fragmentation may occur as programs finish in their inevitable random order. This could be ignored if *all* programs were allowed to terminate before *any* new ones were loaded, but this would also lead to inefficient memory utilisation, as a proportion of the memory would be unused during some of the time. Hence memory fragmentation could still arise from any initial configuration. An example of this is shown in Figure 15.11.

In this case, programs have entered with sizes (in Kb) in order 20, 24, 22 and 26. The next programs requiring to be executed are respectively of size 24, 26 and 22. If one of the programs occupying partition 2 or 4 terminates first, the 24 Kb program may be duly entered. If, however, the program in partition 1 terminates first, no program can enter, even though the total memory available is 24 Kb (20 + 4). If partition 3's program is the first to terminate, the 22 Kb program may be executed.

Such a relatively haphazard arrangement is not particularly satisfactory. For best memory utilisation, all unused space should be found in one area. Unfortunately, programs do not always cooperate by terminating in the correct order. If programs could be moved within the memory, however, the unused parts could be made adjacent. They could then be compacted into a single unused area. Such compaction may be accomplished reasonably easily if the architecture is of the base address/limit type.

In moving the program in partition 2 so that the unused spaces are made adjacent, it may be placed at either end of the marked area: the result may be seen in Figure 15.12 on the upper or lower right. The effect is the same, so it does not really matter which is chosen. Once the decision has been taken, the appropriate store contents may be moved in their entirety. After the move has taken place, the program may be revivified, with its base

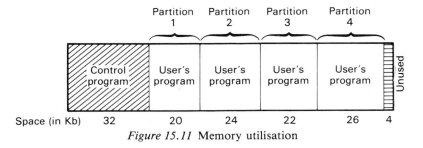

Figure 15.11 Memory utilisation

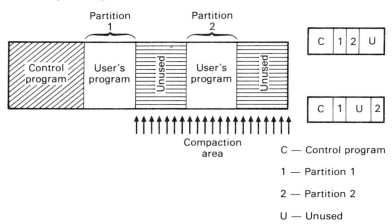

Figure 15.12 Alternative compaction tactics

address and limit registers suitably reset. After this, the previously inapplicable loading process may successfully be reinitiated.

If a peripheral transfer is in progress which references the program's area, there may be problems. Such transfers typically use direct memory access (DMA) methods, which employ absolute memory addresses. A program changing its position in memory during such a transfer could have disastrous effects. In such cases, the operating system would have to wait for the end of any such transfer before initiating any move and consolidation.

The architecture based on protection keys is not susceptible to this treatment. Any addresses originating in the original source text, or as the outcome of later computation, would need to be changed. This is not absolutely infeasible, but is unlikely to be easy to arrange. However, any registers or accumulators holding addresses would also have to be amended. Unless every address anywhere within the program's scope could be identified and updated suitably, trouble would ensue. For these reasons, programs using this type of architecture are not relocatable during execution.

15.6 Other addressing considerations

Attention has so far been concentrated on two of the most widely used addressing techniques. There are other strategies, however, and it is worthwhile discussing some of them. The emphasis in the base address/limit model is on transparency to the user. The properties of the protection bit model imply that the user must be aware of the responsibilities inherent in the situation. In implementations of high-level languages, the situation is somewhat modified. The protocols observed in address allocation are highly formalised and therefore allow relocation to be applied very selectively. Specific registers and particular areas of memory may exclusively be reserved for address usage. In this way, relocation can be effected more easily by the control program. Being based on a high-level language, such arrangements will be transparent to the users.

Such discipline may also be applied to low-level language programs, but the arrangements cannot then be hidden from the programmers. There is nothing inherently wrong with this approach and it has been put to good use in some systems but, once such mechanisms are allowed to become obvious to the programmers, other memory usage methods become available.

If the program organisation is further constrained, even the relocation of address constants may become a task for programmers, rather than being left to the operating system. This is a self-relocation operation. In general, one would expect low-level language programmers to be aware of precisely which items of data represent addresses. A small portion of the program would correct all of these values in an initialisation procedure.

The effect sought is the flexible use of memory, which is inhibited by store fragmentation. If programs were made up of self-contained segments, these could be placed independently. As the segments would be smaller, use could be made of fragments of memory not otherwise available. In this way, the overheads consequent upon memory compaction would be totally avoided. The discipline imposed upon programmers is not prohibitive: this scatter-loading technique (as it is known) is well-practised.

Self-relocation could, of course, equally apply if the program were fragmented, as long as a mechanism were provided identifying the locations of the various segments to each other. As the segments would be identified by the programmer, the program could be made aware of the implications. Not, perhaps, very elegant, but allowing programs to run at times which might not otherwise be feasible.

This suggests how a system such as that based on protection bits can still realistically be adopted. There are no operating system relocation overheads and, if a few formalities are acceptable (mostly to low-level language programmers), such a system remains adequately efficient in its memory utilisation. In fact, it may be able to provide other benefits.

It is not unreasonable to divide programs into their instruction and data components. These may then be separated and stored in different (though perhaps contiguous) areas of memory. This type of organisation provides natural ways of defining self-contained segments for scatter-loading techniques. Once such a program has been loaded into memory, its appearance may approximate that shown in Figure 15.13.

There is a difference between instruction segments and data segments of which advantage may be taken. It is not expected that instructions are to be altered (consider Read-Only Memory (ROM) in many microcomputers). Hence, an extension of the permission bit system will allow further protection. Memory may be designated as readable, writable, or both, or neither.

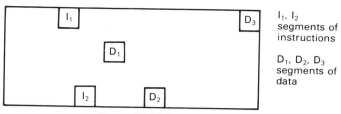

Figure 15.13 Storage paging

The blank areas shown in Figure 15.13 will be neither (other program areas should not be accessible). The areas I_1 and I_2 will be read-only; and the areas D_1, D_2, and D_3 will be both readable and writable. This allows the security of the computer system to be enhanced throughout. The cost is the provision of a two-bit protection key, one bit designating each of readability and writability.

The protection bit approach requires that each area of memory used by a program is appropriately keyed before the program is executed. It is not realistic to associate protection with individual words or bytes—the overhead is too great. It is usually arranged in blocks of memory, typically 1Kb or 2Kb at a time. A third bit is sometimes added to the protection key to designate executability: this allows further security, by prohibiting the execution of data.

A further modification avoids the continual loading and reloading of the protection bits as different programs are executed successively. Instead of each area having a single bit associated with it for (for instance) readability, protection is organised by a key. This is a number which is unique to each program in memory. When a program is loaded, its key is appropriately associated with each of its allocated areas of memory. On the program being executed, its key is loaded into a special permission register. Access is then only granted to areas whose keys correspond to the contents of that register.

15.7 Segmentation and paging

It is convenient to *equate* the logical address of any part of a program with a physical address in a computer's memory, but this need not necessarily be the case: the base address register (in an appropriate architecture) may dictate otherwise. As long as the logical to physical memory mapping is consistent, there is no reason for the two addresses to be equal. (For the mathematically minded, it is a one-to-one mapping.) Taking the situation to extremes, there is no reason why storage locations which are logically adjacent should ever be physically adjacent.

In practical terms, experience with scatter-loaded programs is useful here.

Once they have been loaded, such programs are never moved. It would be highly desirable if this feature, which involves no operating system overheads, could be allied with the user-transparency of the base address/ limit model. This implies that neither the user nor the program loader need worry about the relocation of the program on loading. The disadvantage (there always seem to be disadvantages!) would be the necessity of providing sufficient base address/limit register pairs. Every address would then be made up of two parts: a base register reference and an offset within the appropriate segment. Such segmented programs are maintained under some operating system regimes, which testifies to the efficacy of the method.

A more popular and widespread mechanism occurs when all of the segments are of the same size. In the organisation to be described, they are then known as pages. It should be noted that this is not difficult to arrange. The logical address space provided is continuous, regardless of the physical addresses involved. In this case, the limit register is no longer required, and to the programmer the situation appears as in Figure 15.14(b), although the physical arrangement is as shown in Figure 15.14(a).

A closer inspection of the addressing arrangements will be useful. Each address within the program, as seen by the programmer (the logical address), consists of two parts. Conventionally, the upper (more significant) part specifies the register holding the page's base address; the lower (less significant) part gives the offset within the page. To retrieve the physical address, the contents of the base register are combined with the offset. This is carried out by the hardware of the computer system. In most systems, the page is specified to be a convenient size: for instance, 1 Kb or 2 Kb. The combination operation need not then be an addition (and is therefore faster to execute), because all of the pages can be arranged to start at a physical address whose lower part is zero. The retrieval operation is described diagrammatically in Figure 15.15. (By convention, the pages are numbered to correspond to their base register numbers.)

With these approaches, many programs can conveniently be loaded into a computer's memory. As each is executed, the page base registers can be loaded with the appropriate values. The size of each program's memory space is limited by the number of base address registers, but that is no more

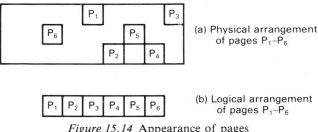

(a) Physical arrangement of pages P_1–P_6

(b) Logical arrangement of pages P_1–P_6

Figure 15.14 Appearance of pages

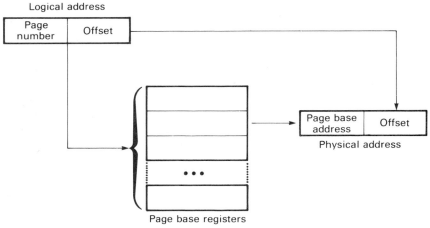

Figure 15.15 Addressing of pages

than the limitations imposed by any finite memory size. If the computer's memory is of, for instance, 128 pages of 1 Kb, 128 registers would allow all of the memory to be addressed in any case. Using modern technology, that is not a particularly expensive or complicated option to provide.

15.8 Virtual memory management

In the course of the execution of a program, during any particular small time span, the number of locations referenced is small. One location will contain the current instruction and the others will be its operands. In most programs, successive instructions are stored close to each other; in many the items of data are also contained in a small range of addresses. Advantage may be taken of this locality of reference (as it is known) in conjunction with paged memory addressing.

Even in large programs, it is generally true that most activity is confined to a small area at any one time. In terms of paged organisation, this means that only a few pages are generally in use (active), which implies, in turn, that most pages are not active. Nevertheless, they take up memory space. If active pages could take their place, there would be an overall increase in computer utilisation. The information could not be thrown away, because it might be needed at another time. Therefore it would have to be stored in a suitable place, and this is typically on magnetic disc.

As each active page is referenced, the normal execution proceeds, but if an attempt is made to use (part of) a page which is currently located on the backing storage (and therefore presumably not in the main memory), a difficulty arises. Before it can be used, it must be loaded into the memory. The problem which is most pressing, though, is the identification of the situation. Attempts to access an area of memory may now have alternative outcomes: success, which merely delivers the desired item; or failure, which signals that the relevant page is not immediately available. The overall arrangement is outlined in Figure 15.16.

If reference is made to an inactive page, the process making the request cannot immediately proceed. Another process may be initiated or resumed and arrangements set in motion to load the page required. Once the page is available, the first process may be resumed, as necessary.

One side-effect of this organisation is that processes may be executed which would expect to occupy considerably more memory than that provided by the immediate access storage. The size difference between the *real* memory and the *virtual* memory may be considerable. The critical size is no longer that of the immediate access store, but that of the backing store.

The precise mechanism is not the subject of this discussion, but it should be noted that the overheads of virtual memory systems are incompatible (in general) with the requirements of process control applications. Their utility is in the flexible provision of computing facilities for applications which are not so critical of response. With careful organisation, conversational usage may coexist with virtual memory management but, in general, it has its best effects in areas which are not otherwise time-constrained in the short term.

There are many other books dealing with this aspect of run-time computer support. As a good example, which includes further reading, the text by Deitel cited in the bibliography offers many useful examples.

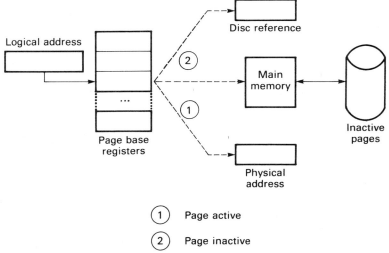

Figure 15.16 Active and inactive pages

15.9 Exercises

1 How should parts of a computer's memory with special functions be treated? (In some computer systems, particular fixed memory locations have reserved powers: for instance, as a clock, special indexing or memory-mapped input and output.)

2 What would the base address register contain if the memory organisation is that described in Figure 15.2:

   (a) for the user's program;
   (b) for the control program?

3 Devise suitable data structures to store a loadable program and its relocation information. Develop an algorithm to effect the correct loading of such a program, given the address of its partition.

4 Under what circumstances may virtual memory systems become incompatible with conversational usage?

CHAPTER 16

Peripheral management

16.1 Peripheral characteristics

What happens 'inside' a computer may be realised in many ways. The storage and the calculation functions, the instruction representation and execution, and even the specific interpretation of some forms of data, have all received different treatment in different circumstances. These factors have not always been achieved electronically, either. From the various gear-driven Babbage engines to more modern hydraulic logic control circuits, not excluding at least one rather bizarre ball-bearing driven device, however, the overall intention is broadly the same. The fact remains that, as long as it satisfies the computational requirements, it does not really matter *how* it does it; and, because it is internal to the computer, it is most often the case that it is totally invisible to the outside world.

What is far more obvious to the user of a computer system, though, is its interface with that world outside it. This may be considered on two levels. The first of these is one of physical environment—is the printer, for instance, one with a daisy-wheel, or does it use a dot-matrix? The second has little, if any, reference to the manufacturing technology involved. It is concerned with the human interaction more directly—does the keyboard have a 'qwerty' layout, or is it set out in some different way? This latter aspect, that of the human–computer interface (HCI), is not addressed here; the computer-related aspects of the physical situation are the concern of this chapter (Figure 16.1).

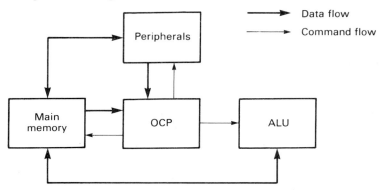

Figure 16.1 Computer organisation

The example given above, relating to printer technology, is on a small scale only. Nevertheless, it represents typical alternatives to be considered within a computer system. However, where choices do exist for peripheral configurations, they may often be more radical than that. Considerations for output may include character printers with a maximum transfer rate of 10 characters per second at one end of the scale, and laser-based printers working at up to one page per second at the other.

That may appear an extreme range of speeds of operation. If the page printed is one of 60 lines, with 160 characters making up each line, that latter case represents 'only' 9,600 characters per second. The ratio is thus of the order of 1,000:1 between the fast output peripheral and its slow counterpart. The important fact to remember is that there is another similar order of magnitude difference between the fast printer and the speeds typical of the internal operations. Internal character movement times are measured in microseconds in many cases, corresponding to transfer rates of one million characters every second. More advanced computers measure their character timings in nanoseconds, with tens (or in some special cases, hundreds) of millions being transferred each second.

The discussion of peripherals will be governed by physical devices which are necessarily significantly slower than the purely electronic items with which they are interfaced. When looked at from another aspect, this is inevitable anyway. The moving parts within circuits are electrons and move at fractions of the speed of light ('speed of electro-magnetic propagation', if one wishes to be really formal!). This is about 300 million metres per second: but because the electrons are forced to move within conductors and semiconductors, their speeds are typically only one-third to one-tenth of this. A mere thirty thousand kilometres per second!

Captain Grace Hopper, USN, has a most vivid demonstration of the timings involved. One nanosecond is one thousand-millionth of a second or, more succinctly, $1 \text{ ns} = 10^{-9}$ second. In this time, light travels one foot— and to show this, she produces a piece of wire a foot (sorry, 30 cm) long.

The difference in mass between electrons, which are very small indeed, and the relatively large items making up standard peripherals is enormous. The consequent difference in inertia between the two kinds of moving parts, which determines the rates at which they can be persuaded to move, explains the necessary great difference in operating speeds. The lesson carries through: that if one wishes to make peripheral reactions rapid, one must make the relevant parts light. Whether this is related to input or to output peripherals is unimportant. This does not stop the machines themselves being quite large overall. It is the critical parts which have to be made as small and light as possible, as long as they can stand up to the appropriate stresses. In either case, too, it is the *changes* in motion which are important. If the motion is continuous, and the structures involved are rigid, then relatively high peripheral speeds are possible.

Peripherals can be grouped into two broad classes, according to their speeds, regardless of whether they are for input, output or both. One class includes the so-called slow peripherals, which interface exclusively with the world outside the computer. The other class comprises the file-transfer peripherals, which are generally used for bulk data storage, although they are sometimes used for physical data transmission.

16.2 Peripheral interfaces

As suggested in Chapter 14, it is often convenient to add a secondary processor to a peripheral so that the order code processor (OCP) is not held up unduly awaiting the peripheral's availability. This is more usually adopted in larger and more powerful systems, but some microcomputers have similar arrangements. In such cases, when a second processor is added, either it (or the original) diverts all or part of its capabilities to peripheral management (Figure 16.2).

Because of the great difference in the speeds of processors and peripherals, there is still ample capacity for even a slow processor to control several of the latter (if necessary). It happens quite frequently, therefore, that a number of peripherals are controlled by a single peripheral processor. This processor has the task of interpreting all of the signals from all of its 'slave' peripherals, and arranging that the data required or made available by them are properly routed. It synchronises with its order code processor, and presents its data in a uniform aspect, even when the actual peripheral devices are not particularly uniform in nature.

This is carried out as a hardware or firmware function, and is not the subject of programmer control at any level. There are a number of obvious advantages to this arrangement, even though it may seem a little inflexible.

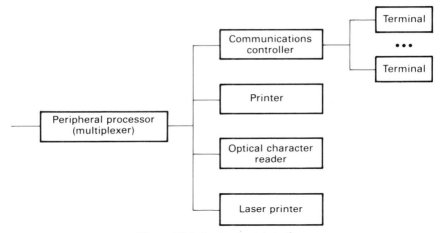

Figure 16.2 A standard interface

The connection between the peripheral processor and its corresponding peripheral must be made in an extremely precise fashion, exactly to suit the peripheral in question. Because of this, any matching that takes place within the combined construction may take place so as to present the required standard face to everywhere else requiring its services. Thus there need be no apparent difference, as far as the programmer is concerned, between a floppy disc drive, a visual display unit and a line printer. All differences will occur on the 'other side' of the corresponding peripheral processor.

This adoption of extra processors to provide uniformity and ease of use is of some importance. All input peripherals may be made to appear (more or less) alike. The same is true of output peripherals. True, some may have extra commands available: it is standard practice to rewind a magnetic tape, but not a typewriter keyboard. But those which they have in common can now be made to appear identical. From the programmers' point of view, it does not matter so much which peripheral is in use at any time, because all peripherals capable of working in the way needed at that point appear just the same.

There are other consequences of such a scheme. The power of the peripheral processor is usually such that it can perform a significant amount of work as well as the direct control of its peripherals. Because of this, it can be given instructions in the way any other processor can be given them. Thus a complete set of output formatting commands might be presented to the peripheral (as it now appears to the programmer) as well as the characters to be printed. This might cause it to start a new form, print a complete line, insert three blank lines, and so on: all included in a single command issued by the OCP. The peripheral processor would then access the appropriate data at the correct time quite independently of the OCP.

Its retrieval of information would therefore be direct and asynchronous. Such treatment is known as Direct Memory Access (DMA). It frees the OCP from detailed consideration of such transfers and allows it to continue solely with the actual computation.

The treatment of peripherals by their processors may vary somewhat according to their transfer rates and complexities. Many 'slow' devices may be serviced by a single multiplexor, while only a few disc drive units are managed by a single disc controller. In some architectures, the faster processors are known specifically as channels. Such channels may have a considerable repertoire of commands which they can execute on behalf of a program. Indeed, in specialised cases, a large number of communication peripherals are handled by what is effectively a computer in its own right. From the programmers' point of view, there are a large number of separate devices, and that is as it should be: the repetitive work is done by the system, while the programmers can concentrate on the more creative aspects.

16.3 Slow peripheral devices

The peripherals truly working with the outside world cover an extremely large range of capabilities. In some cases, the use of the word 'slow' is questionable. As already noted, very high-speed printers operate in the region of 10 Kcps (1 Kcps = 1000 characters per second). The principle adopted in this section will be to consider those devices which will not perform both input and output. While this is perhaps a little unfair, it corresponds to common usage. Those discussed will be the reasonably popular ones. Complex units, such as speech synthesisers or recognisers, are sufficiently specialised as to require separate treatment.

16.3.1 Input devices

Among these are included those which have been in use as computer peripherals for a considerable time. Card readers and paper-tape readers are still available and operate by sensing holes made in a strip of paper or card. Early models used this as a binary switching mechanism, with one and zero bits corresponding respectively to the presence or absence of a hole. They are no longer used as primary input media capture devices, but are often made available for the purposes of computer maintenance engineers. They are rugged and well-behaved. For general-purpose use, they are convenient devices to accept small-to-medium volumes of data being transferred from other computers (Figure 16.3).

Variants of card or paper-tape readers are useful when data are captured from non-computer-related applications. Optical mark readers (OMR) can be used for processing simple documents easily and cheaply prepared away

Peripheral type	Typical transfer speed
Card reader	1000 cards/minute
Paper-tape reader	100 characters/second
Typewriter keyboard	10 characters/second
Optical character reader	3 pages/minute
Optical mark reader	10 pages/minute
Magnetic ink character reader	1000 lines/minute

Figure 16.3 Input peripheral characteristics

from main computer installations. They sense marks (or the absence of them) on standard documents, and behave similarly to punched card readers, although they tend to be slower in operation. Optical character readers (OCR) are finding increasing favour in smaller computer systems, although they usually include quite complex dedicated processors of their own; they are capable of reading typescript in a number of different fonts. Magnetic ink character readers (MICR) are used by banking systems to allow rapid processing of cheques. Methods similar to OCR are employed but, with a smaller 'vocabulary', they operate significantly more rapidly.

Specialist reading devices are available for particular types of commercial data capture. Among these are readers for bar codes employed in retail merchandising. 'Kimball Tags', regarded as simple turnaround documents, are similarly employed, although these are becoming less popular. In the case of bar code reading, a certain amount of so-called intelligence allows for immediate code checking. In this way, only validated data are transmitted to the main computer system for processing. This utilisation of otherwise spare capacity in the peripheral processor is in general operation. It may appear as simple as parity checking in some cases, or as complex as reconciliation between interacting fields in others.

Perhaps the most widespread input device in current use is the basic keyboard. It may, however, have sophisticated additions in some cases. Definitely a slow device, it is limited by the speed of a human operator. There may also be some local storage incorporated, so that the peripheral processor may capture a line of data and allow, for instance, for its verification before onward transmission. In some larger systems, the unit of verification may be of several lines, if required.

16.3.2 Output devices

Corresponding to the less frequently used card and paper-tape readers are the card punch and the paper-tape punch. These have also been available for much of the life-span of computers in general. They are less used than their input counterparts, and may now well be regarded as obsolete (Figure 16.4).

For human-readable output, much is provided by various types of

Peripheral type	Typical transfer speed
Card punch	100 cards/minute
Paper-tape punch	300 charcters/second
Visual display unit	2000 characters/second
Daisywheel printer	30 characters/second
Dot-matrix printer	60 characters/second
Chain printer	300 lines/minute
Drum printer	1500 lines/minute
Laser printer	2 pages/second

Figure 16.4 Output peripheral characteristics

printer. The slowest of these are the simpler typewriter mechanisms, presenting one fixed format character at a time. The technology may correspond to the traditional moving-carriage machine, or may use a golf-ball, daisywheel or similar mechanism. It may be based on a dot-matrix scheme and, in that case, may also offer limited medium-quality graphics capabilities. Some versions of this variety also allow presentation in colour, although the printing speeds in this case are quite slow. Printing speeds may be increased by use of ink-jet techniques, but the cost is higher.

Higher printing rates and capacities are offered by line and page printers of various kinds. These usually accept, as their name suggests, either a complete line or a complete page before commencing the physical printing operation. The presentation may be buffered by the corresponding peripheral processor so that characters are accepted one at a time. The actual printing takes place when sufficient characters have been introduced or when a specific 'print now' command is received. The technology involved is highly varied: drum and chain printers present a line of information at a time, while laser and magnetic printers work in terms of pages. Bulky output may be minimised, at no loss of information, using microfilm or microfiche. These require specialised readers, but need much less storage space. Being realised photographically, these are more akin to page printers than any others, since they perform a frame at a time.

For graphical output, various types of graph plotters are available, depending on the quality required. These, too, may produce multiple-coloured diagrams to high resolution, but are slow. One type is based on a flat bed, where the paper is static and the pen in use moves along two axes. Another operates with the paper moving on a cylindrical drum to provide one axis of the mechanism, the pen's movement giving the other axis.

It is likely that screen output is currently the most widely used method. It may use a matrix representation, with a large static array of dots suitably illuminated to transmit the information. Alternatively, it may be raster-driven, more after the style of a television set. (Television pictures are formed by a continuously moving electron beam scanning across the screen at a constant rate. The entire picture surface is covered for every picture displayed, whether or not there are many bright parts within it. The brighter areas are produced by making the beam more powerful as it scans across them.)

It, too, may be monochromatic, or may provide different colours. These may be chosen from a very wide range for specialised graphic applications, or may have as few as four shades. This method of output is very useful for transient information which need not be preserved.

16.4 Bulk storage

The other types of peripheral are those less fully 'on the outside'. They are definitely not part of the electronics-only internal network, but they do occupy a more sheltered portion of the organisation than do the peripherals of the previous section. Their realisation is largely by use of magnetic media, although there are other storage methods available in certain restricted circumstances.

The main usage of such peripherals is as backing store: an adjunct to the immediate access store. Any data not currently taking part in computation may conveniently be passed to backing storage, so that the main memory may be used for the immediate purposes of the current task. This may be done explicitly, or on an automatic basis not under the conscious control of the programmer. Examples of this latter type of use of backing storage occur in virtual memory systems or in archiving activities.

The two main categories of magnetic media used for these purposes are magnetic discs and magnetic tapes. These are reusable in that during some of their operations they may be used for writing, and during others for reading. They vary widely in their speeds, capacities and capabilities within each general type as well as between types. Consequently they have different employments according to their particular characteristics in each case.

16.4.1 Magnetic tape storage

This is a serial medium and typically allows large volumes of data to be stored at a relatively low cost. The tape may be stored on compact cassettes similar to those used in domestic sound recording, or on larger reels requiring specialised writing and reading mechanisms. The least expensive units are also unidirectional and extremely slow, with transfer rates less than 100 characters per second. Those devices specifically designed for computer use, however, have peak transfer rates in excess of 60 Kcps (Figure 16.5).

Because of their serial nature, they tend to be much used for sequential processing. It is possible, with suitable software support, to attempt indexed or direct manipulation. This is very limited in its application, however, and is seldom practised since the advent of relatively inexpensive random access

Description of tape	Tape length (metres)	Volume of data (bytes)	Transfer rate (bytes/second)
Compact cassette	40	9 K	50 K
3/4-in. reel-to-reel	100	200 K	30 K
1/2-in. reel-to-reel	1000	12 M	60 K
Tape cartridge	90	2.5 M	6 K
Streamer tape	120	40 M	90 K

(The above figures are intended to be examples only, as a general guide)

Figure 16.5 Magnetic tape characteristics

magnetic media. However, in cases where sequential operations are desirable, so are magnetic tapes.

It might appear that larger computer systems have little use for magnetic tapes, relying instead upon magnetic disc units of various kinds. This may sometimes be true for general applications programs, but does not follow for system usage. As examples of the latter, microcoded firmware is stored on compact tape cassettes for some machines, and streamer tapes are used for high-speed archival in others. As a medium for bulk transfer of data between different computer systems, magnetic tape forms a robust and convenient system, where a single 10-inch reel of ½-inch wide tape can easily hold in excess of 10 Mbytes.

16.4.2 Magnetic disc storage

This is a so-called direct access medium. The implication is that it is possible directly to retrieve any item of data stored on a magnetic disc without passing any intervening items. While this is not entirely true, it is certainly *not* of the serial organisation imposed on magnetic tape. As with magnetic tape, the data stored on it may be erased and replaced by new information. It may be read from and written to many times; and, except in the case of 'floppy' disc storage, has an effectively wear-free environment (Figure 16.6).

The different characteristics exhibited by the type of disc described are largely due to their physical attributes. As all discs rotate on their axes during use, the rate of information transmission at a given storage density is

Decription of disc	Access time (milliseconds)	Volume of data (bytes)	Transfer rate (bytes/second)
8 inch flexible	200	240 K	50 K
5-1/4 in. flexible	300	360 K	50 K
3-1/2 in. flexible	200	700 K	100 K
Winchester disc	25	20 M	500 K
Replaceable disc pack	50	200 M	500 K
Fixed-head disc pack	25	500 M	1 M

(The above figures are intended to be examples only, as a general guide)

Figure 16.6 Magnetic disc characteristics

a direct function of the speed of that rotation. The more rigid the disc, the greater the rate of rotation it is possible to attain. Hence flexible discs are less able to transfer information at high rates than are rigid discs.

There is also a different physical mechanism employed for reading and writing in the two cases. The magnetic medium used is the same in each, but the flexible discs are in actual contact with their corresponding recording heads. Because of this, the speeds of rotation available are further reduced. The rigid discs employ 'floating' heads, avoiding direct contact between the moving parts with a very thin cushion of air, only a few micrometres thick. The manufacturing tolerances involved are thus very small indeed: on this scale, a particle of smoke is many times larger than the airgap. It is, of course, for reasons similar to this that a clean environment is essential for modern computers.

A $5\frac{1}{4}$-inch floppy disc will store between 100 Kb and 4 Mb, according to the method used. This will be read or written at up to 30 Kb/second peak rate, although the average is very much less than that for various physical reasons. A large fixed-head disc will carry up to 1 Gb, with a peak transfer rate of towards 1 Mb/second. Such devices are physically large and quite expensive, and are rapidly being superseded by 'Winchester' technology. (Winchester technology is based on the use of self-contained disc units. This differs from those disc packs which can be changed as necessary, but which each use the same reading mechanisms. They also differ from floppy discs, which are approximately the same size, in that they are rigid. This allows rapid access and transfer rates in a small space. Capacities of up to 60 Mb are not uncommon with such units.)

It is interesting to note that some computers are limited in the disc storage which they can put to use because the peak transfer rate is too great for the immediate access memory to accommodate!

16.5 File organisations

The file storage devices have been selected or made available. It is now necessary to decide how the information they contain should be organised, so as to make best use of them. Alternatively, once the best information organisation has been selected for the given application, it has now to be mapped on to the devices which are available. In either case, the ways in which the files of information are to be stored and accessed must be decided and implemented suitably.

These are dependent on the devices to a greater or a lesser extent. As an example of this, it would be better to allocate files to a magnetic medium if their contents might need to be changed. While the information held by a piece of paper tape can be altered, it is a tedious business and quite time-consuming. This is hardly dependent on its organisation at all, but is connected with the basic way in which information is held. For the sake of simplicity, the remainder of the discussion will assume that magnetic media are used. This is the most generally applicable case, and may easily be extended if necessary.

Even when a magnetic medium has been chosen, however, its characteristics must still match the application. If information held on a magnetic tape is to be changed in a non-predictable way (in that it is not easily possible to predict which record is *next* to be altered), this can take an inordinate amount of time. If the record holding the information is at the 'wrong' end of a 3600-feet-long tape, it may take up to four minutes to access, change and replace that information: not very desirable.

For such an operation, magnetic disc storage is far better. Why, then, are magnetic discs not used throughout? The answer is twofold: not only are they generally more expensive, but they are usually more delicate. It is possible to damage a non-flexible magnetic disc irretrievably by dropping it even a small distance: a fall of merely two centimetres can do great harm to such a storage medium.

The way in which information is organised will in any case aim to achieve a balance between a number of factors. If access speed is one of these, and another is cost, the question which will have to be faced is one of relative importance. In general, the faster the access to information, the greater the cost. Other factors which arise are storage volume (not *usually* physical size, but amount of information to be stored) and volatility. However, supposing that the correct devices are always available for use—an interesting aspect of Utopia—there remains yet one more question to be answered.

Some applications possess a natural order, and all operations relating to them can then be carried out in that particular order. An example of such a situation is the printing of quarterly telephone accounts. These always take place in the same sequence and so can usefully be stored on a medium which is naturally organised in this way. Such sequential operations are often associated with the use of magnetic tape. The accounts themselves, of course, are printed on continuous stationery; this is another example of sequential organisation.

This book is a further example of sequential organisation, but it has an added aspect. If it had been produced on microfilm, it would have appeared as a serial file and its sequence would have been defined in two ways: the page numbers, and the chapter and section numbers. The paper copy which you now hold demonstrates the other kinds of characteristics. It has sequential organisation, but exists on other than a strictly serial medium—after all, you can turn from one page to any other page. Suppose, however, that you wished to turn from Chapter 16, section 5 to Chapter 8, section 3. While the latter precedes the former, it is not obvious *precisely* where it is to be found. You could make a rough guess, and perhaps find Chapter 7, section 2. A better way, though, would be to turn to the chapter and section index at the front of the book, and find the appropriate page number. This would allow more accurate (and therefore more rapid) access to the item required. Such organisation is often reflected in computer terms.

In the same way, some computer files are organised to include an index. To retrieve a succession of items, the file is accessed sequentially. If a new start is to be made 'at random' in the file, the index is consulted, and the correct position for the next item is found in that way. This mixture of sequential and indexing is known as indexed sequential organisation and is nearly always associated with magnetic discs. There is a storage overhead incurred for the index and also for the instructions to use it. It is, however, generally held to be worth the extra cost (in time and storage) because of its flexibility in many applications.

There is sometimes a need for files with no sequential component at all. In these, there is no intrinsic logical connection between any piece of information and those physically adjacent to it. All access must, therefore, be performed via an index. At this point, one of the strengths of computer systems may be invoked: that of rapid calculation. The index may be organised in such a way that there is a simple algorithm leading from the item to be found to its physical position. The algorithm is so arranged that, given some key part(s) of the information sought, its address (in a suitable form) is immediately forthcoming. Such direct access to information has great relevance in time-critical operations. However, careful planning is necessary beforehand if best use is to be made of the facility.

In many computer systems the actual medium and associated mechanisms used may be hidden from the user. There are a number of reasons for this, usually relating to flexibility of use. More and more aspects of operations are being taken within operating systems to aid such flexibility. System users, therefore, need to make fewer decisions during the implementation of applications programs. This allows them to concentrate more carefully upon the important individual aspects of each application and, in this way, the chance of making errors is decreased. Typical examples of this are found in CP/M and MSDOS operating systems for microcomputers, and in any mainframe operating system.

While this is adequate, and even desirable, for many applications, it may be too general for some. Process control demands rapid response, even when files are used. For this reason, the access to filed information may even be made less flexible to allow it to be made faster. Apparently indivisible operations, such as 'read a record', may be broken down into a number of steps, so that other parts of the system may be interrogated between those steps. An example of such a breakdown is given in Figure 16.7, as it might be applied to access made to a flexible disc.

The application of peripheral processors in such a circumstance now becomes more obvious. The information may be retrieved asynchronously, so that no processing power is diverted from high-priority tasks. There may

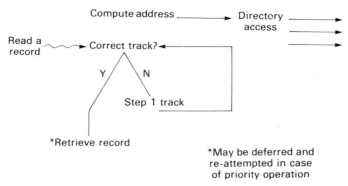

Figure 16.7 Divisible operations

be some problems in particularly critical situations involving the technique known as cycle-stealing, under direct memory access. In general, though, the situation is generally much improved under such circumstances.

16.6 Peripheral allocation

If programs are working in mono-programming environments, there is no ambiguity about peripheral availability. If the computer system contains a particular peripheral, it is available: if not, then it isn't. The difficulty arises in cases when the computer is shared by several programs in any way. Such a multiprogramming environment may be one of a number of types: multi-access, multi-tasking, roll-in-roll-out, and so on. The *precise* form does not matter in this discussion.

In such a multiprogramming environment, the peripherals may be allocated dynamically, upon request, during the running of a program. This will be accomplished by a call to the operating system. In many programming languages such a request has the keyword OPEN associated with it. It allows the requested peripheral to be allocated to the program until it is released. Appropriate information is then returned to the program by the operating system, in the form of a file or route value. This is used for all subsequent transfers and allows device-independent operation— particularly valuable when a choice of peripherals of a given type is available. Peripherals may be released subsequently by a specific program request, often with the associated keyword CLOSE. Alternatively, it may occur at the end of the program's execution, by default.

Difficulties arise, of course, if the device requested is unavailable, either because the operating system does not support the device or because it has been claimed previously by another program. In such cases, the value returned by the OPEN call will reflect the difficulty. A program may act accordingly: to try later, to request an alternative, or merely to abandon processing if the peripheral is crucial to continuing operations.

It is possible, though, for other difficulties to occur at this time. If two programs (called A and B, somewhat prosaically) each need peripherals P and Q, often all will be well. If A requests and releases both P and Q before B requests either, the situation will be as described in the previous paragraph. But if A requests P and B requests Q (both requests being satisfied), danger may arise with subsequent requests. The precise condition, known as deadlock or, more picturesquely, as a deadly embrace, occurs when each holds one peripheral and requests the other, and neither will relinquish the one it holds. This is shown diagrammatically in Figure 16.8.

In the figure, program A's execution path proceeds from left to right, and that of program B from above downwards. (The execution of A can never go from right to left, nor can that of B go from below upwards. One cannot 'undo' execution!) In the example, paths are given to represent various possibilities of execution ordering. Entry into the shaded area implies that deadlock will be reached.

To avoid such difficulties, the operating system may request that any peripherals to be used by a program must be specified before it commences execution. If any *potential* for deadlock occurs, the operating system may then deny an otherwise acceptable request. This corresponds, in Figure 16.8, to denying the combined operation path any entry into the shaded area. Of course, a request for a device not prespecified will automatically be denied.

Other operating systems may request prespecification and may then attach peripherals gradually, as they become available. This operation will alter the program's job description in the queue of jobs awaiting execution. It is very easy to administer, but leads to less efficient system utilisation. Other systems even ignore the problem of deadlock. In such cases, it may even be left to the computer operator to take suitable action! This is less satisfactory: if such problems *can* be avoided, it is obviously better that they be so.

For such peripheral allocation to be accomplished, the operating system must keep a series of tables relating to each program and to each peripheral. The table of program details will announce, among other things, which peripherals a particular program is using, or may wish to use in the future. It will be suitably amended at each peripheral allocation and deallocation for that program. The table of peripheral details will record the programs which are using, or wish to use, a given peripheral in a similar fashion. These tables will be used to allow detection of difficulties of the types described above. In most cases they will enable this to take place *before* the trouble becomes real and while it is only a possibility. In this way, of course, the computer system will be able to work to its best potential.

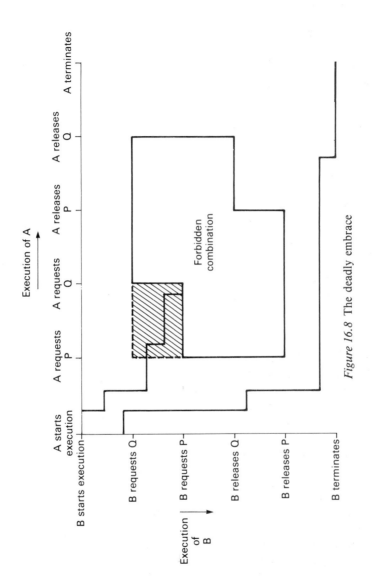

Figure 16.8 The deadly embrace

16.7 Virtual peripherals

Another aspect of the argument of peripheral allocation is that of economic usage. It is all very well allowing a program to use one of the peripherals in a computer system. What is the consequence, though, if the program is poorly written (from a resource-using viewpoint) and holds up the running of other programs? These might otherwise, if the program under consideration were better written, have been able to execute at the same time. This would naturally have made better use of the whole system.

This is often the case with primary output peripherals and, to a lesser extent, with corresponding inputs. In some solutions to this problem, this has led to the substitution of a less heavily used peripheral for another more popular one. However, who would want to use a slow typewriter terminal if a line printer were nominally available? The answer often used to be: somebody who would prefer an inconvenient output medium *without waiting*. The problem of printing the results is then transferred from on-line to off-line working. Slower, perhaps, in action, but faster overall. Of course, this only works as long as the slow terminal does not then become too popular in its substituted role . . .

It was also remarked that, within multiprogramming systems, the popular output device (perhaps the line printer) was not actually active all of the time. Why not, then, arrange for its 'free' time to be put to use in some way? The reason is that the program wishing to use it was not necessarily ready at the same time. The difficulty remains of *how* to arrange the free times to coincide. The program attempting the output operation has to be put into suspended animation in some way, until the printer is free to carry out the transfer, or vice versa. The problem may now be seen to consist of two components. The information to be output must be received as it is produced; it must then be saved until the output operation is actually ready to take place, when the corresponding device has become available.

What does a computer system have that might allow this to be done? The requirements are straightforward. There must be a storage medium which can hold a significant quantity of data. It can, fortunately, be re-used when its job is done. Therefore the choice is quite plain: magnetic tapes or magnetic discs have just these characteristics. There merely remains the organisation of it all.

Therefore, when the program requests an output peripheral, it is to be dissuaded from explicitly specifying a popular one. It must, instead, use a magnetic tape or disc, and output is made to this. When the program terminates, and *all* of the output is available, the tape or disc may be assigned to a (very small) program. Its only task is to print the data previously stored in this manner.

So, where's the advantage? Instead of the line printer, say, being available to the programs which really want it, *none* of them can use it

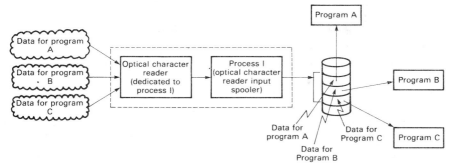

Figure 16.9 Realisation of spooling

directly. Also, there is a small portion of the system which uses the line printer continuously as long as there is any printing to be done. There is, overall, a slight slowing down, but for any one program there is a guarantee of a fair share.

There is some tidying up to be done. What has been suggested above appears to apply only to output operations, but it is simple to adapt the method for input. The small program in this case claims exclusive use of, say, the bulk card reader. It transfers the data for each program to a magnetic disc or tape, which may subsequently be associated with the appropriate programs, and now, because these small programs could always be expected to be associated with a particular device, they could be incorporated into the operating system software. This is shown diagrammatically in Figure 16.9.

Such small service routines allow the peripherals to be simulated within any program, and this leads to the term spooling (see section 9.6). Since the *real* device is not made available for general program use, the aspect shown is that of a *virtual* or a *pseudo* device, and the latter terms are also used in describing such operations.

It would appear that a disc or tape unit has been substituted for a slower device. In economic terms, this makes little sense, because the former devices tend to be more costly. If the effective cost could be spread among a number of programs simultaneously, it would be reduced overall. This

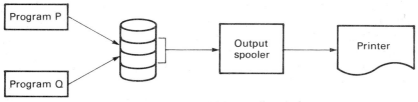

Figure 16.10 Disk spooling

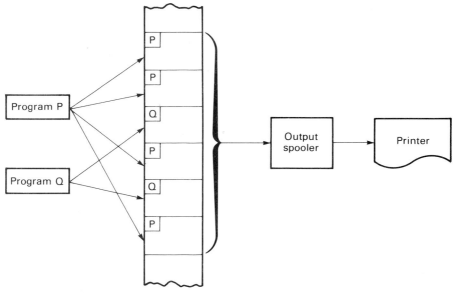

Figure 16.11 Tape spooling

can be attained, in the case of magnetic disc storage, by allocating separate areas of the disc to each participating program, rather than using the whole of the disc. The operating system routine can then check these areas as each program terminates, and print the appropriate information (Figure 16.10).

The same applies to magnetic tape although, because of the serial nature of this storage medium, it is a little more complex. Each block of information written must have an appropriate identification tag attached to it. The printing routine must then await all programs outputting to the tape to finish, before attempting any information transcription. The tape has to be read as many times as there are participating programs to achieve all the transfers in the correct order. This is illustrated in Figure 16.11.

16.8 Peripheral sharing

It must by now be obvious that some peripheral devices, such as magnetic discs, may be used, apparently simultaneously, by a number of programs. At least, the same physical device, if not the same precise area of it, may be shared. This will not work for other devices at all. As a very simple example of this, what would be the effect of two programs sharing the same visual display unit (VDU)? Parts of messages from each would be intermingled, effectively at random, and the overall effect would be nonsensical.

It follows, then, that even though sharing can take place, it must be carefully regulated. Each transfer order *must* be mediated by the operating system to avoid corruption of areas not assigned to the program under consideration. In most operating systems, transfer requests from different programs are placed on to a queue and processed in order. Each consists of a specification of position and direction of transfer (i.e. read or write). Such a disc address contains three parts—which disc surface is to be used, which is the track on that surface (which may involve a physical recording head motion to access), and whereabouts on the track the information is located.

This represents a very different aspect to that discussed at the end of section 16.5. The splitting up of the reading of the record described in Figure 16.7 cannot take place in this queuing operation. All transfers must be accounted as indivisible: once embarked upon, though, such splitting could take place. Hence there may possibly be a higher-level and a lower-level disc transfer controller. The higher-level one is to deal with the queuing described, the lower-level one is for any separate simpler operations.

There will typically be a considerable amount of traffic associated with a shared disc storage unit. Because the requests are essentially random, some systems do not operate on a fixed queue basis, but sort the requests into some kind of order. As long as any program is not allowed to 'overtake' itself, all movements of the recording mechanism are arranged to be in one direction only. This continues until the inner or outer edge of the disc is reached, and the motion is then reversed. In this way, the randomness is somewhat smoothed and better performance times are claimed for such systems. This is illustrated in Figure 16.12.

The checking which takes place is usually straightforward. Any disc file may be private to a single program, or it may be shareable among several programs. In either case, all those programs which are allowed access will specify their intentions when the file is opened for use. An overall check

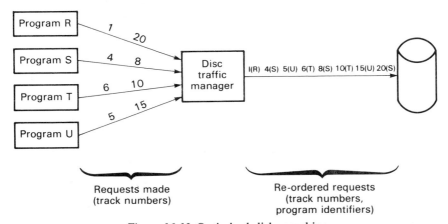

Figure 16.12 Optimised disk searching

may be applied at this time to determine whether any access whatsoever is to be granted. Assuming that this is allowable, each transfer thereafter is checked to conform to the limits of the file's storage area—files are always logically contiguous, although not necessarily so physically—and any illegal operations may be inhibited.

If more than one program may be allowed concurrent access to a shared file, a further test must also be applied. If the file is being written to, its contents are so liable to volatility that no other program will be allowed access while this is occurring. If the file is in a stable state, more than one program should be able to read its contents. The details of this process are beyond the scope of this work, but are well documented elsewhere for the interested reader.

16.9 Exercises

1 Investigate the peripherals of the computer systems which you use. What are their transfer speeds, access speeds, capacities and organisations, and what interfaces do they present to the system?

2 How might a file organised in an indexed sequential fashion best be implemented using a direct access device? What would be the full implications of using a serial access device?

3 In a multiprogramming operating system, what peripheral allocation policy would you recommend in order to allow the scheduling algorithms to work most efficiently?

4 When peripherals are shared between two or more processes, critical situations may arise (for instance, deadlock or race conditions). Investigate the necessary and sufficient reasons for these to happen, and suggest ways in which they might therefore be avoided.

5 What alterations must be made to the operating system tables to allow for the provision of virtual peripherals? What are the implications for the system interfaces to the peripherals and for the device driver routines in such a system?

CHAPTER 17

Software maintenance

17.1 The position of maintenance □ 17.2 Types of maintenance □ 17.3 Planning for software maintenance □ 17.4 Alterations to software □ 17.5 Documentation considerations □ 17.6 Measurements of maintainability □ 17.7 Maintenance costs □ 17.8 Exercises

17.1 The position of maintenance

The operations *known* as maintenance are possibly misnamed. Strictly, a product should only require maintenance if errors are detected in its performance. Too often, though, software specifications are changed for some reason. Because of this, the software itself has then to be altered to meet the change. It is not unknown, also, for changes to take place in the operating system which supports the software. In extreme cases, even the hardware may be changed. In all of these situations, the software product has to be amended accordingly.

Hence the operations historically referred to as maintenance really describe modifications, for whatever reasons. Partly because of this misuse of the language, the area defined has grown even larger. Additions to the facilities provided by a piece of software are also described as maintenance. As a result of this, the proportion of programmers' time spent in so-called maintenance typically exceeds, by a considerable margin, the time spent on original production and testing. Figures quoted suggest that the ratio of 3 : 1 is not surprising.

Nevertheless, the requirements in any software system are the same for each aspect if the operation is to be carried out with a minimum of discomfort. After all, each requires a nominally finished product to be changed in some way. It is, therefore, important that the *current* status of any piece of software be carefully described. Using that description, any alterations can then be made much more easily and safely. The prospect of changing any system with insufficient information to do it is unpleasant, at the very least.

In all cases of such changes, two things stand out. The process of change is made feasible by good design carried out initially, and the documentation of the system must be equally well designed and executed. Every experienced implementor has met the results of shortcomings in either area. A poorly designed procedure is difficult to modify because side-effects 'pop up' in unexpected places. A poorly documented operation is difficult to understand in the first place. In extreme circumstances, it may render any attempt at modification almost fatal.

In the descriptions given here, the term 'maintenance' will be used impartially: it will cover any changes to be made for whatever reason. A glossary would include 'modification', 'change', 'adaptation' and various other synonyms. It is not the present intention to reform the language in current use: far be it from us any such intention. In fact, it is most unlikely that this could now be accomplished. While one is usually entitled to expect careful use of terms within descriptions of computing operations, this is one area to bow out of as gracefully as possible.

A number of actions contribute to the costs of maintenance and the estimation of the total is difficult to undertake with accuracy. The factors themselves are not too hard to deal with, however. They relate to the sources of maintenance already mentioned in obvious ways, but the figures themselves are more elusive.

In summary, costs can be incurred from, among others:

- changes in computer system hardware
- changes in operating system software
- changes in the external environment
- changes in specifications
- changes in support staff
- increased program lifetimes

17.2 Types of maintenance

While allowing that the word is misused, maintenance falls overall into three broad classes. Some must be carried out because of errors, found after the program has been delivered to its customers. (Errors found before delivery are corrected, naturally! . . . all part of the validation operations.) Some maintenance is carried out as an improvement, included to enhance the performance of the program in some way, following user or implementor requirements. Finally, some takes place due to changing requirements being introduced by the program's environment. These are named, following Somerville (see the bibliography):

- *corrective* maintenance
- *perfective* maintenance, and
- *adaptive* maintenance

respectively (Figure 17.1).

17.2.1 Corrective maintenance

This contributes between 15 and 20 per cent of the total maintenance activity. It represents shortcomings on the part of the implementors, and the identification and correction of such errors. The effort involved in such 'debugging' activities is usually concentrated in the former activity. It is often far more difficult to ascertain precisely what gives rise to an error than subsequently to correct it. (It is not *altogether* a joke that debugging has been defined, anonymously, as 'The process of replacing one error by another'.)

The key to minimising the effects of corrective maintenance, rather than the other categories, lies in the careful application of correct validation procedures. This, in its turn, relies on adequate testing and on quality control. The provision of test data and results which exercise all of the program may be extremely extensive, but its lack will lead ultimately to more labour in the form of corrective maintenance, when it will have to be supplied anyway.

17.2.2 Perfective maintenance

Interestingly enough, this has been found to account for upwards of two-thirds of the maintenance operations. It has two alternative sources: the customer or original specifier, and the implementor.

The corrector   The perfector   The adapter

Figure 17.1 Maintenance operators

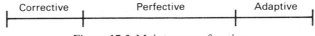

Figure 17.2 Maintenance fractions

In the early days of computing, much perfective maintenance was due to the implementors attempting to reduce storage requirements or to minimise execution times. This attitude is less prevalent now, when storage is relatively cheap and easy to expand, and when the power of processing units is much enhanced. It is more often the case that the application user makes 'small' alterations in the specifications, leading to a need to amend the program to correspond to the change.

As this is such a common source of maintenance requirements, it is worthwhile noticing that approximately half of all maintenance in commercial applications arises from the user—who may well be found in a different department in the same overall organisation. As in many cases up to three-quarters of the overall application cost arises from maintenance, it would appear to follow that nearly 40 per cent of programming costs arise because the originators of an application changed their minds for some reason. (From the same source as before, enhancement was defined as 'A means of introducing errors into a working program'.)

17.2.3 Adaptive maintenance

The contribution to maintenance arising from changes to a program's mutable theoretical background—for instance, changes in pay rates for a payroll application—is similar to that for corrective maintenance. Perhaps in many instances it is possible to *foresee* which factors of this nature are liable to change. It is thus feasible to design and implement systems in such a way that these changes, when they have to be made, are relatively easy to effect (Figure 17.2).

17.3 Planning for software maintenance

This is quite serious. The best way to be least affected by trouble is to prepare for it. Just as ocean-going vessels hardly expect to hit an obstacle, but still include life-boats, so should professional implementors plan ahead to minimise adverse effects when they arise. Experience is quite plain on the matter—the effects *will* occur. Hence careful planning is essential.

When a bicycle malfunctions, it is seldom replaced in its entirety. If one of its tyres is punctured, the approach adopted by a professional is to replace just the affected part, usually an inner tube. (The damaged tube may be repaired later, but that's another story.) From such a commonplace operation, there are a number of lessons which are easy to learn.

First, there are a number of components making up a bicycle. This may seem elementary, but that makes it no less important. A bicycle is *not* made as a single unit. Secondly, each component does its own job without encroaching on those allotted to others; and, thirdly, those components are made to fit together accurately, with neither an excess of material nor a deficit.

How can these apparently irrelevant lessons usefully be transferred to the problems relating to program maintenance? Quite directly, in fact. The first lesson is that, for programs to be easily maintained, they should be made up of a number of smaller parts. Then, when anything goes wrong, any changes which have to be made will be local ones only. This has the added advantage that the units of translation (often known as modules) will be kept small and, therefore, the time taken to amend and retranslate them will not be too great. This is in contrast with the same operations if the program is a single larger structure. It is unlikely that, if the design work has been properly carried out, there will be much repercussion elsewhere, either.

This arises after considering the other ideas suggested; the second lesson of which was that those components which make up the program do not overlap in function. This is sensible in terms of total work undertaken, because there is a minimum duplication of effort.

Put as baldly as this, it is surprising that it should ever be contemplated, but it sometimes *appears* expedient. Perhaps an output file might be closed in a number of places for various differing reasons. This may seem reasonable in each individual case but, viewed together, the situation may be quite different and may even suggest weaknesses in overall structure. In any case, such an approach makes maintenance more difficult. It is a generator of unnecessary work, because the whole has then to be kept in step throughout. Instead of the single execution of any alteration being necessary, it must be undertaken in each instance.

The third lesson is that modules must not communicate in a poorly disciplined fashion. All shared information should be easy to identify and no unauthorised tampering with any other items is allowed. This latter operation is unfortunately widespread in poorly structured programs and is known as a 'side-effect'. Each time a side-effect is used, it may appear reasonable and expedient. Taken in total, however, they can make maintenance of programs quite difficult.

As an example, consider a program designed to print paginated text. It allows for 60 lines per page and, whenever these have been printed, a new page is begun. A line counter has to be used in at least three places: to be initialised, to be incremented as each line is printed, and to be interrogated to determine when a new page is to be commenced. The side-effect usually occurs, of course, in the latter. The line counter will be reset for each new page. If anything affects the line counter elsewhere, there will be unexpected extra effects.

The planning, then, is relatively straightforward. It will save considerable time overall if maintenance is made easier, even if that planning itself actually consumes considerable resources. After all, planning only has to be done once, but maintenance is a recurring burden. Further thoughts on this important topic may be found in the reference by Myers cited in the bibliography.

17.4 Alterations to software

The basis of software maintenance is that of changing the software concerned to suit the appropriate requirements. There are two different viewpoints concerning this: that of the implementor and that of the computer system. While the operations may well be initiated by the implementation team, if they do not meet the approval of the computer and its operating system, the whole maintenance procedure is a waste of time and effort.

From the human point of view, before the software can be altered, it must first be understood. It may be possible to change source text without its operation being fully comprehended, but such an operation is very likely to be a major source of error. Hence, the best approach to achieving trouble-reduced maintenance is to make the software's operations as clear as possible.

The rules for such preparation are well laid down. The names by which the objects in the program are referred to should be meaningful and not too long. The purposes of each major procedure and data structure should be described carefully in the documentation and also, where possible, in the source text commentary. The structure of the program should be clear and well-founded, and the text should be clearly laid out.

After the situation is comprehended properly, the text can be amended. This will probably involve a text editor; and this should be as friendly a tool as is available. There is no gain in using a blunt chisel, and poor software tools are equally undesirable. Thus the software development cycle already discussed in Chapter 2 is particularly relevant here. The maintenance function is applied to human-readable software. From this point it has to pass through the successive translation, verification and testing phases used before. It would be as unfortunate to avoid such actions at this point as it was during the original software production.

Indeed, one of the difficulties arising from changing the software is in the quality control of the changes. It is suggested that there is a substantial chance—up to 50 per cent—of introducing further errors while in the process of correcting earlier faults. This is because, even though well-designed and constructed, the parts of the program cannot always be as independent as they should. To avoid this kind of knock-on effect, not only must the structure be very carefully realised, but its attendant documentation must detail the possibility of such happenings.

The only way in which such trouble can be avoided, then, is by *meticulous* testing and validation practices. Unfortunately, this is time-consuming and, therefore, more costly. There is thus a temptation ever present to assume that good design will obviate the need for more than local testing of software alterations. Sooner or later, as modifications are made to changes, the integrity breaks down. The resulting confusion is far worse than the original trouble. There is *no* substitute for doing the job properly.

17.5 Documentation considerations

There is a lesson to be learnt from the preceding discussion, which parallels the message of Humpty Dumpty: 'When I use a word . . . it means just what I choose it to mean—neither more nor less.' That is all very well, but if its meaning is not the same to subsequent readers, it has failed in its mission. The task of words is to establish communication and to convey meaning; particularly true in technical descriptions, of course. Therefore, in this, as in all other documentation, careful identification of the true meaning is *essential* in any possibly ambiguous area. It is rather painful so to emphasise this trite subject, but in maintenance documentation, a mistake in meaning can lead to an inordinate amount of extra labour.

As discussed in the previous section, maintenance is virtually impossible without the documentation. What, then, should that documentation contain? First, it is not all in words; and, secondly, not all in documentation folders or books. Some concepts are better dealt with pictorially or diagrammatically, as is the case with structure diagrams; and self-contained documentation, kept within and local to a program, is very valuable— program comments. However, throughout it all, some guidelines should be followed quite carefully.

For any program, three components of documentation must be supported: these are for the users, for the maintenance team and for the program validation team. Activity in the maintenance team may lead to modifications in any, or all, of these categories, but they must above all be in step with each other and with the product which they describe. Inaccurate documentation is, in some instances, worse than none at all.

The documentation in each area should therefore be accurate and concise. It must, overall, be exhaustive; and there should be only as much overlap as is unavoidable within each context. After all, the validation and maintenance teams each expect access to the user's documentation. The maintenance team, in its turn, will expect access to the validation documents. The converse, however, is not necessary in each case. It is the maintenance team which needs the totality of information, at a technical level.

Technical writing is a peculiar area of work and not generally well understood. It is, though, most important, as the preceding discussion demonstrates. A technical report is not an English essay, neither is it the description of an experiment in chemistry, although it is closer to the latter than the former. There are a number of simple rules which make the whole easier to follow and which may well apply in other areas. Nevertheless, they are offered here as particularly relevant to an important topic.

● Use *short* sentences within *short* paragraphs.
● Be careful about grammar and spelling. Annoying irregularities are a distraction from the important parts.
● Use headings and subheadings to concentrate attention.
● When the subject is complex, don't be afraid to explain it from different viewpoints, if it is necessary. Nevertheless, don't use five words where three will do.
● Itemise points and topics.
● Do be *precise* and *accurate*: define any terms which may be ambiguous.
● Make sure it is all well structured and well indexed.

17.6 Measurements of maintainability

Maintainability relates to the cost of maintenance. If the cost is high, whether measured in terms of money or time, the maintainability is low. If the cost is low, the maintainability is high. However, that does not really give a proper feeling for *how* high or *how* low such a factor is in any particular case.

Perhaps the provision of a precise metric is not at issue. It is unnecessary, and very probably impossible, to process two software systems and to produce the answer 'System A is 42 per cent more maintainable than system B'. However, to give an answer, with reasons, that 'System Y is significantly easier (or cheaper) to maintain than system Z' is an important step towards proper quality control. See Figure 17.3.

To achieve a high maintainability, the guidelines to follow are well understood. Not only that, most of them have been discussed in the preceding sections. Programs should not be made complicated, but simplicity should be sought. The aphorism 'Keep it Simple, Stupid' (and its acronym, KISS) is a very desirable goal. Hence the conceptual basis for any single item should be made as small as is conveniently feasible. A well-conceived hierarchy of procedures is fitted together carefully and exactly. Each procedure is given data on a basis of need-to-know: no procedure is given access to any more information than it needs to carry out its tasks.

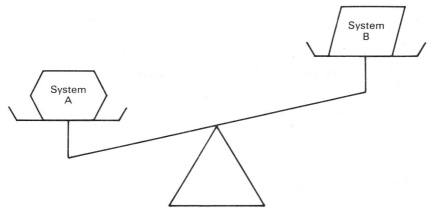

Figure 17.3 Scales for system measurement

This is the principle of 'data hiding'. In this way, individual procedures possess great internal integrity.

Together with this, those individual procedures are bound together as loosely as possible. No links, then, are forged unless they are absolutely necessary. This increases maintainability, because changes within a procedure will not affect its environment, except on the previously well-defined bases.

Given a program, how might one assess its maintainability? Following the principles given, it has to be easily understandable. Its structure should be such, then, that it is easy to decompose into its conceptual pieces, and each piece's operation should in turn be easily understandable. And finally, the connections between those pieces should be understandable. This recursive operation terminates when the individual statement level is reached: the statements must themselves be easy to follow, at that level.

From understandable units and couplings come ease of testing and of modification. It is quite in order that the more understandable the structure and its components are, the easier they are to test, both singly and collectively. A similar argument applies to their modification; and as modification, otherwise known as maintenance, is the subject of this discussion, the applicability of maintenance measurements follows.

This leads to an hierarchy of maintainability measurements. Each organisational level has to be maintained, and therefore any one level should be easy to maintain, in its own terms, if its maintainability is to be high. A little analysis suggests that the overall maintainability would be related to the product of the individual measurements, which accords quite well with theories of complexity. For further information on this aspect, the reader is directed to the text by Myers.

17.7 Maintenance costs

As already mentioned, costs come from a number of sources and accurate forecasting of them is impossible in the general case. Careful design will, however, allow some costs to be minimised, although others are not so cooperative. Some of the technical factors are unfortunately unpredictable.

Whatever the sources may be, evidence from live systems suggests very strongly that the greatest costs are attributable to maintenance. Estimates for systems of reasonable size (perhaps one man-year upwards) vary from a minimum of 50 per cent of the total to over 90 per cent in some of the more extreme cases. This should not necessarily be interpreted as weakness in the system design or implementation. They arise because of the nature of computer systems and the people who use them. The following categories are given as contributory to the maintenance costs, following the summary given in section 17.1.

17.7.1 Changes in computer system hardware

This is not necessarily a major source of maintenance costs. At first sight, the replacement of some (or, in extreme cases, all) of the system hardware might presage a major software upheaval. While this may have been true in previous decades, the effect is much less marked following successive standardisation exercises in the software environments. Of course, if the programming techniques in force do not follow a sensible approach and make use of 'clever tricks', this is not the case. Such systems may incur large maintenance costs if their hardware is changed.

17.7.2 Changes in operating system software

Ideally, this should have similarly little effect, thereby making only small contributions to the maintenance costs. It is, after all, the function of the parts of an operating system to insulate the user from the real computer environment. This has become a more powerful argument since the introduction of standard operating systems, such as UNIX or CP/M. Even so, these are not always as standard as they ought to be. In the worst cases, changes in operating systems (often called upgrades or enhancements) necessitate considerable changes to applications software. Fortunately, such happenings are mercifully rare.

Good programming practice suggests that all interfaces to the environment are to be most carefully designed and documented. In this way, even if any part of that environment—hardware or software—changes, alterations will be localised, and any adverse effects minimised in their scope. Such practice also allows easier transportation to other computer systems.

Benefits of this nature highlight the worth of planning ahead, besides the cost-saving effects.

17.7.3 Changes in the external environment

As well as the software and hardware surroundings in which programs execute, there are other environmental considerations. These are the ones imposed by the applications which programs are devised to implement. Not all programs are equally prone to such effects: for instance, the value of π used in a mathematical program cannot be changed under any circumstances.

Those which depend on human-devised values, however, incur maintenance costs if these values are changed for any reason. Typical instances are those of an hourly pay rate or a taxation rate. Stock levels or reorder quantities may be changed in a stock control program, and so on. The method for minimising such maintenance costs resembles those already discussed. All such values are best handled symbolically within a program, by making an explicit symbolic constant of the correct value. Any changes necessary may thus be localised.

17.7.4 Changes in specifications

This is a situation which is unfortunately familiar, and is impossible to guard against. If the specifications of the program are changed at any time, maintenance will inevitably be required to meet the new requirements. Such adaptive maintenance may be difficult to handle with a view to minimising costs. If the changes are sufficiently far-reaching, it may even be better to rewrite the entire program than to attempt to adapt it. Nevertheless, thorough documentation will alleviate the problems to whatever extent such a desirable condition may be achieved.

17.7.5 Changes in support staff

Even with the best descriptions and the most accurate documentation, a new implementor will find it harder comprehending a new application, and its corresponding program will be harder for a new implementor than one who has been associated with them from their inception. There are, therefore, maintenance costs associated with turnover in the personnel responsible for software. These arise largely from familiarisation and training operations, rather than directly from corrective actions. Because of this, they may be reduced by careful assignments of staff to appropriate tasks. It would be extremely unwise to attempt to remove such costs: they are implicit in the nature of such work.

17.7.6 Increased program lifetimes

The longer a program has a use, the more likely it is to encounter one of the changes suggested above. As a secondary effect, then, maintenance costs accrue if a program is used for a long time. It also follows, as a further outcome, that the more a program is altered, the less its original integrity can be effective. It is instructive to investigate program lifetimes as they were originally envisaged, compared to the actuality. Generally, the latter are somewhat greater than the former.

As a postscript, the following rather pessimistic (but quite realistic) offering is made:

'Hofstadter's Law

It always takes longer than you expect, even when you take into account Hofstadter's Law.'

17.8 Exercises

1 Investigate the differences in operating systems provided by different manufacturers, with a view to the alterations necessary in transporting programs between any two. (Different versions of the same operating system (e.g. UNIX, CP/M) are best for this exercise.) What kinds of trivial differences are there? Which differences are more fundamental?
2 In systems which you have developed, what proportion of the time was spent in design, implementation and maintenance? Why is this (possibly) not a realistic model of what happens in production computer systems programs?
3 With which area of maintenance (see section 17.2) are you most familiar? How should initial design and implementation be carried out to make subsequent maintenance in this area as easy as possible?
4 With reference to any previous documentation with which you have been associated, how well has it been produced according to the checklist given in section 17.5? What recommendations would you make for improvements (if any)?

PART V

Summary

CHAPTER 18
Summary

18.1 The components □ 18.2 The system □ 18.3 Envoi

18.1 The components

Once more, the elements of correct and efficient production of different types of software are threefold: the design, the implementation and the maintenance. It is now most opportune to consolidate each of those components, starting with their individual parts, in the context of the other two.

Of course, each of them is equally important and there is no sense whatsoever in skimping on any of them. It might be said at this point, for instance, that extra attention to design, which is the first component of the software provision system, can save considerable grief during the later stages. However, that suggests little more than that the design operation is the one most likely to be poorly addressed. This may well correspond to experience and the way in which this has taken place in the past, but better appreciation of the total system should lead to a better balance being struck.

Nevertheless, our perceptions of the system may be a good guide to the correct proportion of effort to invest in each part, and experience is also a most valuable (could it be 'the only'?) teacher here. Our perceptions, then, should be tempered by our experience. Not necessarily only our own experience, but all that can be gathered. Further, it is also proper, now that all of the individual components have been investigated in detail, to consider the total amounts of each that should be used. Those components are shown in Figure 18.1, and will be discussed in due order.

18.1.1 The planning operations

The approach here is necessarily forward-looking. When the operations

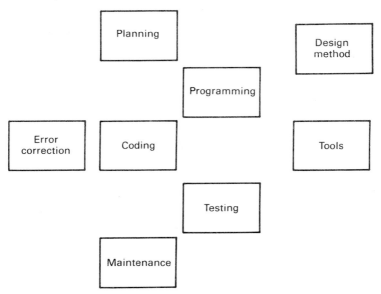

Figure 18.1 The implementation components

commence, no part of the system exists. (It has to be noted that this book starts at a point already part of the way along within the total implementation cycle: it has been tacitly assumed in a number of places that the system to be implemented has already been subjected to what is traditionally but incorrectly known as systems analysis.)

The design method has to be chosen or may, perhaps, be achieved by a synthesis of a number of individual methods. It will reflect the requirements of the area within which the implementation is found; there are specialised aspects which must be considered in chemical plant design which do not always occur in a payroll application! The result in either case is a tested implementation strategy, which takes into account all that is known about the system to be realised. After it has taken place, not only does the implementation plan exist, but also the means by which the final system is to be tested and maintained. This may explain why design is sometimes skimped: it starts from nothing (or so it may seem), and has to invent the whole master-plan before anything else can take place; but the worry is definitely worth the effort in the long run.

18.1.2 The implementation operations

This is the part so often assumed by the uninitiated to be the sum total of computing: the programming. This is, as we all know, by no means the case. Neither would it be fair to confuse this operation with the coding phase, because there is much more to it than that. It is possibly the easiest part to carry out—as long as the planning has been done properly, and the tools to carry the job out are there.

The implementation operations have their own planning aspects, but these are internal rather than global in nature. They depend heavily on the design operations which have preceded them and have some influence on the maintenance operations which follow. It is not proper to put any more emphasis on the relationship of implementation to maintenance than that, because the real driving force is found in the design stage. Perhaps the dependence of maintenance on implementation is tactical, then, rather than strategic.

What is most important here is the availability of the correct tools for the implementors' use. These are also likely to be used during maintenance, anyway, and so correct provision at this stage will be doubly useful during the lifetime of a typical piece of software.

18.1.3 The maintenance operations

These will always be with us, in even the most carefully regulated of implementations. If human beings were as unimaginative as are computer systems, that might not be the case. However, people change their minds, and software has to follow suit. There is also a thread running through the maintenance operations, the appreciation of which allows them to be carried out efficiently and correctly: this is a thorough understanding of the construction of the computer system which hosts the implementation.

We have perhaps ignored the effects of error, because everyone who has followed the precepts in this book . . . (Well, just in case . . .) There are also the problems associated with human error, in whichever way these choose to manifest themselves. These affect the maintenance in a number of ways and, therefore, the way in which maintenance is carried out. Errors in implementation are aggravating, perhaps, but can be approached in a well-understood and structured fashion, having regard to the established testing procedures. What are more difficult to deal with are design errors, which necessitate significant work outside the scope of 'maintenance'. Once again, the temptation to patch a software system or to make do with a quick fix must be avoided.

18.2 The system

A system is not just the parts which make it up, but the way in which they fit together. A human body is a good example of this. Even if we suspect that we can emulate Dr Frankenstein, an anatomy exercise could never be

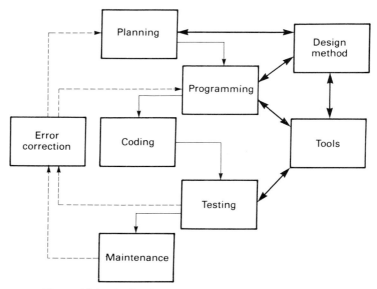

Figure 18.2 The implementation components connected

any more than the equivalent of a jigsaw puzzle (you could still see the joins ...). So it is with the provision of software: if the ways in which the parts fit together are not used properly, there will be no progress.

Whenever there is a temptation to regard the parts of programming (in its widest sense) as separate, this must be avoided. In every case, the effects of any changes to one part of a system cannot be confined to just that single part. So, as in any diagram, the connections between the parts of the system, shown in Figure 18.2, are equally important as the components. This is transparently clear in programming design operations and has exactly the same weight in this discussion.

18.3 Envoi

The authors have attempted to set out those rules of thumb which have served them well during their software operations with the same approach which has been used for their presentations which have taken place during a number of years. It has been noticeable that the subject covered has been a shifting target, even during the relatively short time which the formal preparation of this book has occupied. So their last message of all must remind us of the Red Queen's advice to Alice, given over one hundred years ago:

'Now, here, you see, it takes all the running you can do, to keep in the same place. If you want to get somewhere else, you must run at least twice as fast as that!'

However, it must be tempered with optimism, because you are not alone and many people are in the same situation—and they have survived and prospered by being professional in their approach.

Bibliography

The following texts have been used as technical reference sources in a number of places within this book. They are by no means the only books which deal with such matters, but represent those more used by the authors than others.

Barnes, J. G. P. (1982). *Programming in Ada*, Addison-Wesley. ISBN 0–201–13792–5.

Bornat, Richard (1979). *Understanding and Writing Compilers*, Macmillan. ISBN 0–333–21732–2.

Brooks, Frederick P. Jr. (1979). *The Mythical Man-Month: Essays on Software Engineering*, Addison-Wesley. ISBN 0–201–00650–2.

Brown, P. J. (1979). *Writing Interactive Compilers and Interpreters*, John Wiley. ISBN 0–471–10072–2.

Clare, Chris and Loucopoulos, Peri (1987). *Business Information Systems*, Paradigm. ISBN 0–948825–55–3.

Deitel, Harvey M. (1984). *An Introduction to Operating Systems*, Addison-Wesley. ISBN 0–201–14502–2.

Exception Handling, Language Structure and Operating Systems. Proceedings of E.W.I.C.S., Oldenbourg, Munich, 1983. ISBN 3–486–28111–9R.

Findlay, W. and Watt, D. A. (1985) *Pascal: An Introduction to Methodical Programming*, Pitman. ISBN 0–273–02188–5.

Holmes, B. J. (1984). *Structured Programming in COBOL*, D.P. Productions. ISBN 0–905435–41–9.

Howe, D. R. (1983). *Data Analysis for Data Base Design*, Edward Arnold. ISBN 0–7131–3481–X.

Ibbett, Roland N. (1982). *The Architecture of High Performance Computers*, Macmillan. ISBN 0–333–33229–6.

Kelly-Bootle, Stan (1985). *The Devil's DP Dictionary*, McGraw-Hill. ISBN 0–7–034022–6.

Kernighan, Brian W. and Plauger, P. J. (1981). *Software Tools in Pascal*, Addison-Wesley. ISBN 0–201–10342–7.

Kernighan, Brian W. and Ritchie, Dennis M. (1978). *The C Programming Language*, Prentice-Hall. ISBN 0–13–110163–3.

Knepley, Ed and Platt, Robert (1985). *Modula-2 Programming*, Reston. ISBN 0–8359–4602–9.

Levine, Ronald D. (1982). Supercomputers, *Scientific American*, Vol. 246, No. 1 (Jan.). ISSN 0–0036–8733.

Manna, Zohar (1974). *Mathematical Theory of Computation*, McGraw-Hill. ISBN 0–7–039910–7.

Martin, James *et al.* (1985). *Fourth Generation Languages—Volume ii Survey of Representative 4GLs*, 2nd edn, Savant. ISBN 0–906774–26–8.

Myers, Glenford J. (1975). *Reliable Software through Composite Design*, Van Nostrand Reinhold. ISBN 0–442–25620–5.

Naylor, Jeffrey (1987). *Introduction to Programming*, Paradigm. ISBN 0–948825–45–6.

IT Review, Price Waterhouse, 32 London Bridge Street, London SE1 9SY.

Sommerville, I. (1982). *Software Engineering*, Addison-Wesley. ISBN 0–201–13795–X.

Theaker, C. J. and Brookes, G. R. (1983). *A Practical Course in Operating Systems*, Macmillan. ISBN 0–333–34679–3.

Tsichritzis and Bernstein (1974). *Operating Systems*, Academic Press. ISBN 0–12–701750–X.

Willis, Neil (1986). *Computer Architecture*, Paradigm. ISBN 0–948825–40–5.

Zaks, Rodney (1978). *Programming the 6502*, Sybex. ISBN 0–89588–009–1.

Index